Purchasing

Second Edition

PEARSON

Boston   Columbus   Indianapolis   New York   San Francisco   Upper Saddle River
Amsterdam   Cape Town   Dubai   London   Madrid   Milan   Munich   Paris   Montréal   Toronto
Delhi   Mexico City   São Paulo   Sydney   Hong Kong   Seoul   Singapore   Taipei   Tokyo

Pearson

Editorial Director: Vernon R. Anthony
Executive Acquisitions Editor: Alli Gentile
NRA Product Development: Randall Towns and
   Todd Schlender
Senior Managing Editor: JoEllen Gohr
Associate Managing Editor: Alexandrina B. Wolf
Senior Operations Supervisor: Pat Tonneman
Senior Operations Specialist: Deidra Skahill
Cover photo: Hemera/Thinkstock

Cover design: Karen Steinberg, Element LLC
Director of Marketing: David Gesell
Marketing Coordinator: Les Roberts
Full-Service Project Management: Barbara Hawk and
   Kevin J. Gray, Element LLC
Text and Cover Printer/Binder: LSC Communications
Text Font: Minion Pro, Myriad Pro Semicondensed

Photography Credits

Front matter: i Hemera/Thinkstock; vii (left) Suhendri Utet/Dreamstime; (right) Meryll/Dreamstime;
viii (top) Mtr/Dreamstime; (bottom) Stratum/Dreamstime; ix (bottom left) Aprescindere/Dreamstime;
xv (bottom left) Petar Neychev/Dreamstime; 24, 56, 114, 170, 191, 221, 222 Nikada/iStockPhoto

All other photographs owned or acquired by the National Restaurant Association Educational Foundation, NRAEF

10   18

ISBN-10:   0-13-218164-9
ISBN-13: 978-0-13-218164-8

ISBN-10:   0-13-272489-8
ISBN-13: 978-0-13-272489-0

Contents in Brief

Contents

About the National Restaurant Association and the National Restaurant Association Educational Foundation

Founded in 1919, the National Restaurant Association (NRA) is the leading business association for the restaurant and foodservice industry, which comprises 960,000 restaurant and foodservice outlets and a workforce of nearly 13 million employees. We represent the industry in Washington, DC, and advocate on its behalf. We operate the industry's largest trade show (NRA Show, restaurant.org/show); leading food safety training and certification program (ServSafe, servsafe.com); unique career-building high school program (the NRAEF's *ProStart*, prostart.restaurant.org); as well as the *Kids LiveWell* program (restaurant.org/kidslivewell) promoting healthful kids' menu options. For more information, visit www.restaurant.org and find us on Twitter *@WeRRestaurants*, *Facebook*, and *YouTube*.

With the first job experience of one in four U.S. adults occurring in a restaurant or foodservice operation, the industry is uniquely attractive among American industries for entry-level jobs, personal development and growth, employee and manager career paths, and ownership and wealth creation. That is why the National Restaurant Association Educational Foundation (nraef.org), the philanthropic foundation of the NRA, furthers the education of tomorrow's restaurant and foodservice industry professionals and plays a key role in promoting job and career opportunities in the industry by allocating millions of dollars a year toward industry scholarships and educational programs. The NRA works to ensure the most qualified and passionate people enter the industry so that we can better meet the needs of our members and the patrons and clients they serve.

What Is the ManageFirst Program?

The ManageFirst Program is a management training certificate program that exemplifies our commitment to developing materials by the industry, for the industry. The program's

EXAM TOPICS

ManageFirst Core Credential Topics

Hospitality and Restaurant Management
Controlling Foodservice Costs
Hospitality Human Resources Management and Supervision
ServSafe® Food Safety

ManageFirst Foundation Topics

Customer Service
Principles of Food and Beverage Management
Purchasing
Hospitality Accounting
Bar and Beverage Management
Nutrition
Hospitality and Restaurant Marketing
ServSafe Alcohol® Responsible Alcohol Service

most powerful strength is that it is based on a set of competencies defined by the restaurant and foodservice industry as critical for success. The program teaches the skills truly valued by industry professionals.

ManageFirst Program Components

The ManageFirst Program includes a set of books, exams, instructor resources, certificates, a new credential, and support activities and services. By participating in the program, you are demonstrating your commitment to becoming a highly qualified professional either preparing to begin or to advance your career in the restaurant, hospitality, and foodservice industry.

These books cover the range of topics listed in the chart above. You will find the essential content for the topic as defined by industry, as well as learning activities, assessments, case studies, suggested field projects, professional profiles, and testimonials. The exam can be administered either online or in a paper-and-pencil format (see inside front cover for a listing of ISBNs), and it will be proctored. Upon successfully passing the exam, you will be furnished with a customized certificate by the National Restaurant Association. The certificate is a lasting recognition of your accomplishment and a signal to the industry that you have mastered the competencies covered within the particular topic.

To earn this credential, you will be required to pass four core exams and one foundation exam (to be chosen from the remaining program topics) and to document your work experience in the restaurant and foodservice industry. Earning the ManageFirst credential is a significant accomplishment.

We applaud you as you either begin or advance your career in the restaurant, hospitality, and foodservice industry. Visit www.nraef.org to learn about additional career-building resources offered by the NRAEF, including scholarships for college students enrolled in relevant industry programs.

MANAGEFIRST PROGRAM ORDERING INFORMATION

Review copies or support materials

FACULTY FIELD SERVICES
Tel: 800.526.0485

Domestic orders and inquiries

PEARSON CUSTOMER SERVICE
Tel: 800.922.0579
http://www.pearsonhighered.com/

International orders and inquiries

U.S. EXPORT SALES OFFICE
Pearson Education International Customer Service Group
200 Old Tappan Road
Old Tappan, NJ 07675 USA
Tel: 201.767.5021
Fax: 201.767.5625

For corporate, government, and special sales (consultants, corporations, training centers, VARs, and corporate resellers) orders and inquiries

PEARSON CORPORATE SALES
Tel: 317.428.3411
Fax: 317.428.3343
Email: managefirst@prenhall.com

For additional information regarding other Pearson publications, instructor and student support materials, locating your sales representative, and much more, please visit *www.pearsonhighered.com/managefirst*.

Acknowledgements

The National Restaurant Association is grateful for the significant contributions made to this book by the following individuals.

Mike Amos
Perkins & Marie Callender's Inc.

Steve Belt
Monical's Pizza

Heather Kane Haberer
Carrols Restaurant Group

Erika Hoover
Monical's Pizza Corp.

Jared Kulka
Red Robin Gourmet Burgers

Tony C. Merritt
Carrols Restaurant Group

H. George Neil
Buffalo Wild Wings

Marci Noguiera
Sodexo—Education Division

Ryan Nowicki
Dave & Busters

Penny Ann Lord Prichard
Wake Tech/NC Community College

Michael Santos
Micatrotto Restaurant Group

Heather Thitoff
Cameron Mitchell Restaurants

Features of the ManageFirst books

We have designed the ManageFirst books to enhance your ability to learn and retain important information that is critical to this restaurant and foodservice industry function. Here are the key features you will find within this book.

BEGINNING EACH BOOK

Real Manager

This is your opportunity to meet a professional who is currently working in the field associated with the book's topic. This person's story will help you gain insight into the responsibilities related to his or her position, as well as the training and educational history linked to it. You will also see the daily and cumulative impact this position has on an operation, and receive advice from a person who has successfully met the challenges of being a manager.

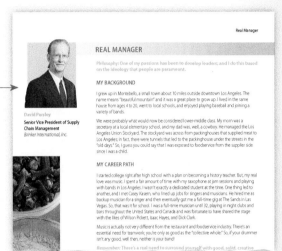

BEGINNING EACH CHAPTER

Inside This Chapter

Chapter content is organized under these major headings.

Learning Objectives

Learning objectives identify what you should be able to do after completing each chapter. These objectives are linked to the required tasks a manager must be able to perform in relation to the function discussed in the book.

Case Study

Each chapter begins with a brief story about the kind of situations that a manager may encounter in the course of his or her work. The story is followed by one or two questions to prompt student discussions about the topics contained within the chapter.

Key Terms

These terms are important for thorough understanding of the chapter's content. They are highlighted throughout the chapter, where they are explicitly defined or their meaning is made clear within the paragraphs in which they appear.

THROUGHOUT EACH CHAPTER

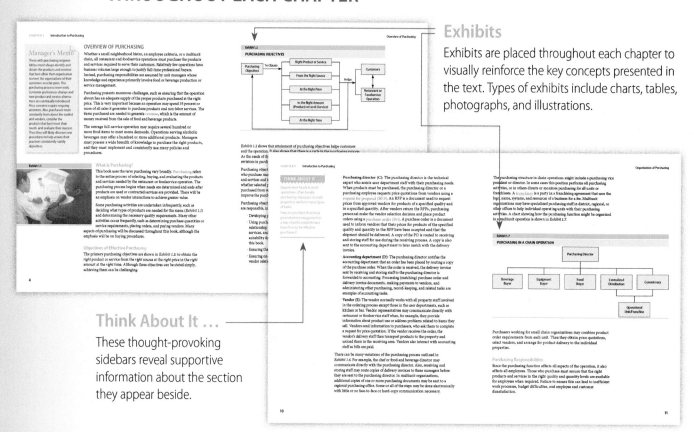

Exhibits

Exhibits are placed throughout each chapter to visually reinforce the key concepts presented in the text. Types of exhibits include charts, tables, photographs, and illustrations.

Think About It ...

These thought-provoking sidebars reveal supportive information about the section they appear beside.

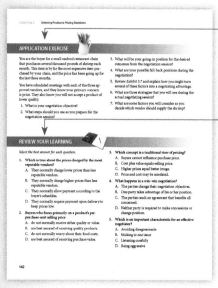

AT THE END OF EACH CHAPTER

Application Exercises and Review Your Learning

These multiple-choice or open- or close-ended questions or problems are designed to test your knowledge of the concepts presented in the chapter. These questions have been aligned with the objectives and should provide you with an opportunity to practice or apply the content that supports these objectives. If you have difficulty answering the Review Your Learning questions, you should review the content further.

AT THE END OF THE BOOK

Field Project

This real-world project gives you the valuable opportunity to apply many of the concepts you will learn in a competency guide. You will interact with industry practitioners, enhance your knowledge, and research, apply, analyze, evaluate, and report on your findings. It will provide you with an in-depth "reality check" of the policies and practices of this management function.

David Parsley
**Senior Vice President of Supply
Chain Management**
Brinker International, Inc.

REAL MANAGER

Philosophy: One of my passions has been to develop leaders; and I do this based on the ideology that people are paramount.

MY BACKGROUND

I grew up in Montebello, a small town about 10 miles outside downtown Los Angeles. The name means "beautiful mountain" and it was a great place to grow up. I lived in the same house from ages 4 to 20, went to local schools, and enjoyed playing baseball and joining a variety of bands.

We were probably what would now be considered lower-middle class. My mom was a secretary at a local elementary school, and my dad was, well, a cowboy. He managed the Los Angeles Union Stockyard. The stockyard was across from packinghouses that supplied meat to Los Angeles; in fact, there were tunnels that led to the packinghouse under the streets in the "old days." So, I guess you could say that I was exposed to foodservice from the supplier side since I was a child.

MY CAREER PATH

I started college right after high school with a plan on becoming a history teacher. But, my real love was music. I spent a fair amount of time with my saxophone at jam sessions and playing with bands in Los Angeles. I wasn't exactly a dedicated student at the time. One thing led to another, and I met Casey Kasem, who lined up jobs for singers and musicians. He hired me as backup musician for a singer and then eventually got me a full-time gig at The Sands in Las Vegas. So, that was it for school. I was a full-time musician until 32, playing in night clubs and bars throughout the United States and Canada and was fortunate to have shared the stage with the likes of Wilson Pickett, Isaac Hayes, and Dick Clark.

Music is actually not very different from the restaurant and foodservice industry. There's an essential need for teamwork; you're only as good as the "collective whole." So, if your drummer isn't any good, well then, neither is your band!

Remember: There's a real need to surround yourself with good, solid, creative people—and realize that you won't be the only one with good ideas.

At this point in my life, I realized I couldn't spend all of my time on the road. So, I sold all of my instruments and asked a friend for help. He got me a job as a junior buyer at an industrial gasket company. That's how I really got involved in purchasing.

I went back to school—as a more serious student this time—and received my bachelor's degree, and later my MBA. At the same time, I started moving up the ladder into other purchasing positions, working my way up to supervisor of the purchasing department for a division of Baxter Healthcare.

At that time, Denny's corporate facilities were nearby. Most of the people in leadership positions there came from the aerospace or pharmaceutical industries. Vern Curtis, the CEO at that time, recognized the company generally didn't have a lot of sophistication at the support level. Most of the purchasing people had come from other administrative positions, and were not specifically trained for strategic purchasing. So, Vern began to reach back to the aerospace and health care companies for people who might be able to take purchasing to a new level.

I was recently married to someone who also worked at Baxter, and at that time, we could not both remain working for the company. So, when I got a call from a recruiter about a purchasing manager position at Denny's, the timing was perfect! It was an interesting transition moving from a science-based, stiff, corporate environment to a situation focused on providing a great dining experience for our guests. There was a lot of opportunity to make a difference, so I stayed.

You should understand that there are a lot of career options in the restaurant and foodservice industry, other than service. It's an industry in which you can work hard, add value, make a good income, and have financial stability. I've focused on attaining a position in the supply chain field to be able to influence the guidelines and rules, rather than just implement them. And you can, too!

You can really make a difference here. But you need to thrive on change and interaction; you need to be committed; and you need to get your priorities straight. You know, at one company, I was making changes and collaborating with the head of the quality assurance team. At 5:05 p.m. one day he came in and said, "With all the work you're generating, my team is having a hard time keeping up. I need more people." Of course, all of his team had left at 5:01 p.m. He didn't need more people; he needed his team to put in the work hours to make the business a success!

Something I always think about: You always have to be willing to learn. To be successful, you have to become a student of the industry. Always seek more knowledge; always continue to elevate the industry you're in. Be introspective, be reflective, and remember if you can't see the need, you'll never make the necessary changes.

WHAT DOES THE FUTURE HOLD?

I believe supply chain management, of which purchasing is a critical part, will be an increasingly important factor in the restaurant and foodservice industry in the years ahead. Profitability cannot always be driven by increased sales and adding stores; you need to manage costs. Managing costs can enhance shareholder value as well as maintain and improve the guests' experience.

So, this role will grow in importance for the organization. But I think that this position will not be a simple, finite role; rather it will be more of a "renaissance man" approach. In the past, purchasing was just about "buying stuff cheaply" (*Wall Street Journal*, March 10, 2008). In the future, you'll have to be good at a variety of things such as knowledge of procurement and logistics, relationship management, process thinking, and technology management just to name a few!

MY ADVICE TO YOU

You must be ready to work smart and work hard. Focus on identifying problems and presenting solutions to those problems. Your success will be dependent on your ability to come up with solutions to problems, and then implement and execute the solutions.

I remember when I was hired by Carl Karcher Enterprises to take their supply chain to a new level. I had asked my previous manager for advice, and he said, "When you go into an organization, as important as the people are, you first have to assess the overall organization and look at their goals, what they're doing, what they want to accomplish, and where they need to be. Then you can structure it the way it needs to be, and you'll see where people fit into that structure."

Remember: Surround yourself with great people who challenge you and push you to see other ways of doing things. If you're consistently good, you can tend toward greatness.

1

Introduction to Purchasing

CHAPTER LEARNING OBJECTIVES

After completing this chapter, you should be able to:

- Describe purchasing objectives and the impacts of effective purchasing.

- Explain how the purchasing function is organized in small- and large-volume operations.

- Describe the basic steps in the purchasing process.

- Identify internal and external factors that impact the purchasing process.

- List common restaurant and foodservice purchases.

- Discuss the evolution of purchasing systems.

KEY TERMS

benchmarking, p. 18

centralized purchasing system, p. 9

competitive advantage, p. 7

convenience food, p. 12

decentralized purchasing system, p. 8

delivery invoice, p. 9

distribution channel, p. 17

franchisee, p. 11

green purchasing, p. 18

issuing, p. 9

job description, p. 14

job specification, p. 12

point-of-sale (POS) system, p. 6

purchase order (PO), p. 10

purchasing, p. 4

quality, p. 5

request for proposal (RFP), p. 10

revenue, p. 4

value, p. 5

CASE STUDY

"The problem is getting worse and worse!" said Tyler.

"Which problem?" replied Yasmine. "We have so many at the Café."

"I'm talking about how we purchase. We're a small operation and everything has to be approved by the owner. He stops in only two or three times a week. If products aren't delivered, we have to contact him for permission to order from somebody else. Other times, he says we should wait to order and then we run out!"

"I agree," said Yasmine. "I think we should set up a system in which the cook, the dining-room manager, and the head bartender all order what they need. That would work so much better."

1. What are the advantages and disadvantages of the decentralized system that Yasmine is describing for a small-volume operation?

2. What things will the owner need to consider if Tyler and Yasmine approach him with their idea?

Manager's Memo

Those with purchasing responsibilities must always identify and obtain the products and services that best allow their organization to meet the expectations of their customers at a fair price. The purchasing process never ends. Customer preferences change and new product and service alternatives are continually introduced. Price concerns require ongoing attention. Also, purchasers must constantly learn about the market and vendors, consider the products that best meet their needs, and evaluate their success. Then they will likely discover new procedures to help ensure their practices consistently satisfy objectives.

OVERVIEW OF PURCHASING

Whether a small neighborhood bistro, an employee cafeteria, or a multiunit chain, all restaurant and foodservice operations must purchase the products and services required to serve their customers. Relatively few operations have business volumes large enough to justify full-time professional buyers. Instead, purchasing responsibilities are assumed by unit managers whose knowledge and experience primarily involve food or beverage production or service management.

Purchasing presents numerous challenges, such as ensuring that the operation always has an adequate supply of the proper products purchased at the right price. This is very important because an operation may spend 35 percent or more of all sales it generates to purchase products and non-labor services. The items purchased are needed to generate **revenue**, which is the amount of money received from the sale of food and beverage products.

The average full-service operation may require several hundred or more food items to meet menu demands. Operations serving alcoholic beverages may offer a hundred or more additional products. Managers must possess a wide breadth of knowledge to purchase the right products, and they must implement and consistently use many policies and procedures.

Exhibit 1.1

What Is Purchasing?

This book uses the term purchasing very broadly. **Purchasing** refers to the entire process of selecting, buying, and evaluating the products and services needed by the restaurant or foodservice operation. The purchasing process begins when needs are determined and ends after products are used or contracted services are provided. There will be an emphasis on vendor interactions to achieve greater value.

Some purchasing activities are undertaken infrequently, such as deciding what types of products are needed for the menu (*Exhibit 1.1*) and determining the necessary quality requirements. Many other activities occur frequently, such as determining purchase quantities or service requirements, placing orders, and paying vendors. Many aspects of purchasing will be discussed throughout this book, although the emphasis will be on buying procedures.

Objectives of Effective Purchasing

The primary purchasing objectives are shown in *Exhibit 1.2*: to obtain the *right* product or service from the *right* source at the *right* price in the *right* amount at the *right* time. Although these objectives can be stated simply, achieving them can be challenging.

Exhibit 1.2

PURCHASING OBJECTIVES

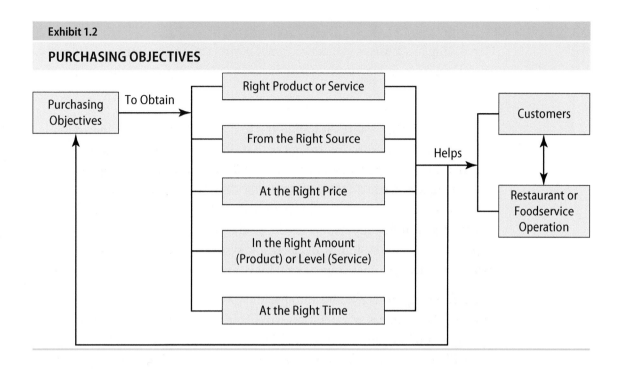

Exhibit 1.2 shows that attainment of purchasing objectives helps customers and the operation. It also shows that there is a cycle in the purchasing process. As the needs of the customers and operation change, this may lead to revisions in purchasing objectives, and the process continues.

Purchasing objectives drive what purchasers should do. For example, those who purchase must help determine the operation's specific needs for products and services and identify the best sources. Purchasers can assist in deciding whether selected products and services should be provided by employees or purchased from vendors. They can also help assess how technology can improve the purchasing process.

Purchasing objectives also drive the day-to-day activities for which purchasers are responsible, including:

- Developing purchasing policies and procedures.
- Using purchasing practices that yield the best value, defined as the relationship between the price paid and the quality of the products, services, and information received. The concept of quality, or suitability for intended use, will be discussed many times throughout this book.
- Ensuring that products and services are available when needed.
- Ensuring on-time vendor payments, and maintaining appropriate vendor relationships.

Impacts of Effective Purchasing

Purchasing has a direct impact on many aspects of a restaurant or foodservice operation. This section discusses some of the most important impacts.

MAINTAINING ADEQUATE QUANTITIES

There are few things more disappointing to customers than ordering an item only to be told, "I'm sorry. We're out of that right now." It is important to ensure that an adequate supply of all necessary products is available to prepare every menu item. Managers do this in numerous ways. For example, they analyze point-of-sale (POS) system information, including sales histories, so they can forecast the number of portions needed and determine the quantity of products to purchase. A POS system is an electronic system that collects information about revenue, customer counts, item sales, and other operating data.

The forecasting process looks into past historical data to help suggest the number of customers an operation will likely serve in the future. For example, the number of customers served in March last year may suggest the number that will visit this March. This information can be made even more accurate if managers also consider factors such as weather forecasts, current economic conditions, and estimated community visitors to conventions and festivals, as they make customer count forecasts.

MAINTAINING QUALITY STANDARDS

Each item produced by an operation must meet quality standards that have been developed for it. Ensuring consistent quality begins when purchasers develop reasonable quality standards. It continues when these quality standards are clearly communicated to vendors and correctly checked during the receiving process.

Quality standards for food products may be set by the chef, manager, or owner in an independent operation. In a multiunit operation, they are usually established by persons at company headquarters. Quality is relatively easy to establish and verify when brand-name products such as canned or frozen food items, alcoholic beverages, and condiments are purchased. The task is more difficult for unbranded items such as fresh produce, meat, and seafood. Determining how to define freshness and other quality features for these items can create challenges.

MINIMIZING COSTS

No purchaser has unlimited funds to buy unlimited amounts of products at any given time. Costs and available cash are always important, and purchasers must make purchasing decisions with these concerns in mind. Bills must be paid when due, and cash is needed to do so. Tying up large amounts of money for stored products that will produce revenue at a later time can cripple an establishment's ability to operate. Buying too many products can be as harmful as purchasing too few.

Purchasers can use several strategies to minimize unnecessary investment in storage:

- Purchase according to an accurate customer forecast.
- Anticipate cash needs for a given period.
- Consider the amount of available storage. Most operations have limited storage space. Although additional storage might be purchased, this alternative should be carefully considered to ensure it is cost-effective.
- Think about future costs. Prices for many food items rise and fall depending on the season and weather conditions, among other factors. It is sometimes cost-effective to buy larger quantities of certain items in season, while prices are lower, if the greater quantities can be effectively used. Likewise, smaller quantities might be purchased in times when prices are falling, which allows the buyer to have adequate supplies for the near term while also taking advantage of lower prices for future purchases (*Exhibit 1.3*).

MAINTAINING A COMPETITIVE ADVANTAGE

Purchasers compete for the best prices to obtain a competitive advantage, which is a benefit an operation has that allows it to generate greater revenues or retain more customers than its competition. For example, if Operation A can obtain better pricing or services than Operation B for similar items, then Operation A has a competitive advantage.

Although simple in concept, achieving this advantage in practice is difficult. Competitors rarely disclose their costs, and vendors often apply pricing levels unevenly among establishments by giving their higher-volume customers an advantage in pricing and added services.

To obtain a competitive advantage, managers can use several purchasing practices:

- Select vendors who provide the best combination of price and services for the property's operational needs. Vendors sell more than products. They also sell services including frequency of delivery, emergency and odd-hour deliveries, flexible payment terms, low minimum orders, and consistency and dependability. Some larger vendors also include added services such as menu printing and consulting services. The criteria for selecting vendors will be discussed more fully in chapter 4.
- Ensure that every dollar spent for products is wisely spent. Purchases should be based on the concept of intended use. In other words, do not waste money buying a product that is of a higher quality than necessary. Use chopped olives, not super colossal olives, on salad bars. Use canned tomato pieces, not canned whole tomatoes, for soups and stews. Use alternate garnishes when prices for the usual garnishes increase.
- Use effective receiving practices to be sure that incoming products meet the operation's quality requirements.

Exhibit 1.3

Manager's Memo

Failure to consider any of the purchasing objectives when making purchasing decisions can create situations that negatively impact an operation. Failure to maintain adequate inventories can create product shortages. Failure to maintain quality standards can result in purchasing products and services that do not meet customer expectations. Although customers might forgive the occasional inconsistency, "consistent inconsistency" will lead to a loss of business.

Purchasing too much product or "overpurchasing" can tie up an excessive amount of cash, and paying too much for products and services affects cash available for other purposes. Just as important, it reduces profits that are required to remain in business.

Exhibit 1.4

RECOGNIZING USAGE COSTS OF PURCHASED PRODUCTS

Purchasers must know the true cost of using a product. For example, a gallon of Floor Cleaner A may be more expensive than a gallon of Floor Cleaner B. However, because of its concentration, the cost to clean one square foot of flooring may be much less than with the "less expensive" Floor Cleaner B (*Exhibit 1.4*). Pre-cleaned lettuce may be more expensive to purchase than heads of lettuce that must be cleaned and trimmed. Wise purchasers consider all costs, and the pre-cleaned lettuce may actually be less expensive when labor costs are considered.

Preparation loss and labor costs must be controlled, and this begins when purchasing decisions are made. This topic will be discussed in detail in chapter 2.

ORGANIZATION OF PURCHASING

Regardless of an operation's business volume, someone must perform all of the activities necessary for effective purchasing. Many purchasing activities impact all aspects of the operation, either directly or indirectly. As a result, it is important that those involved in purchasing establish and maintain close working relationships with the employees. Then the needs of the operation and, ultimately, those of the customers will be better met.

Decentralized Purchasing

In independent or single-unit operations, the person responsible for purchasing is often the owner-manager. In some medium-sized independent operations, responsibilities for purchasing are divided among the owner or general manager and other managers. For instance, the owner might be responsible for purchasing expensive equipment. The chef might purchase food items, the bar manager might be responsible for beverage purchasing, and the dining-room manager might purchase dining supplies. A typical purchasing system for small- to medium-sized independent operations is shown in *Exhibit 1.5*.

Exhibit 1.5

PURCHASING IN SMALL- TO MEDIUM-SIZED INDEPENDENT OPERATIONS

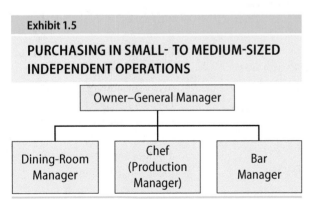

The system shown in *Exhibit 1.5* is called a decentralized purchasing system, wherein all or most purchases are made by department heads or a designated employee in the department. In some operations, the general manager must approve purchases, especially those that involve significant costs or large quantities.

Properties with all but the smallest volumes employ or retain one or more accounting professionals. These persons assist with the bill payment activities of purchasing.

Centralized Purchasing

Large-volume operations including those in hotels may have a full-time purchasing director, buyers, and clerical employees for the purchasing function. Large operations typically use a centralized purchasing system in which most or all purchases are made by a purchasing director for the entire organization. Purchasing requests are routed to those with specialized responsibilities, who then assist property staff with their purchasing needs.

Exhibit 1.6 shows an overview of a possible purchasing process in a large operation. It identifies the various departments and staff that may be involved.

Exhibit 1.6

PURCHASING IN LARGE OPERATIONS

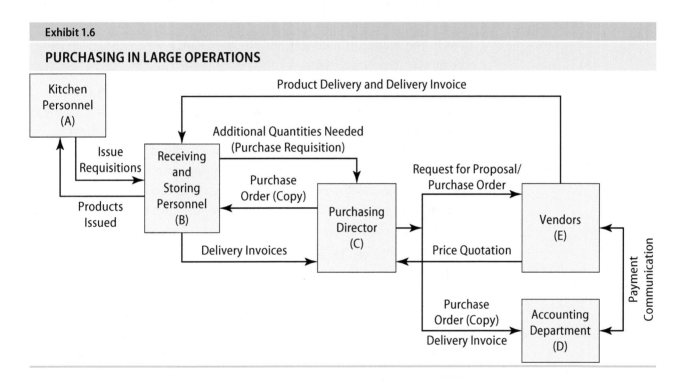

Consider these parties in *Exhibit 1.6*:

- **Kitchen personnel (A):** Kitchen staff request required food products from receiving and storing staff, who issue the products from the central storage area. The task of issuing involves transferring products from storage areas to user departments so user staff can meet production needs.

- **Receiving and storing personnel (B):** These employees inform the purchasing director (C) when additional product quantities are required to maintain inventory levels. They also receive incoming product deliveries from vendors and route applicable delivery invoices to the purchasing director. Delivery invoices are documents signed by a representative of the operation to transfer product ownership to the property.

THINK ABOUT IT . . .

Department heads in small operations often handle purchasing. Managers in small properties perform many types of tasks.

How do you think that those promoted to management in a low-volume establishment learn how to be effective purchasers?

- **Purchasing director (C):** The purchasing director is the technical expert who assists user department staff with their purchasing needs. When products must be purchased, the purchasing director or a purchasing employee requests price quotations from vendors using a **request for proposal (RFP)**. An RFP is a document used to request prices from approved vendors for products of a specified quality and in a specified quantity. After vendors return the RFPs, purchasing personnel make the vendor selection decision and place product orders using a **purchase order (PO)**. A purchase order is a document used to inform vendors that their prices for products of the specified quality and quantity in the RFP have been accepted and that the shipment should be delivered. A copy of the PO is routed to receiving and storing staff for use during the receiving process. A copy is also sent to the accounting department to later match with the delivery invoice.

- **Accounting department (D):** The purchasing director notifies the accounting department that an order has been placed by routing a copy of the purchase order. When the order is received, the delivery invoice sent by receiving and storing staff to the purchasing director is forwarded to accounting. Processing (matching) purchase order and delivery invoice documents, making payments to vendors, and administering other purchasing, record-keeping, and related tasks are examples of accounting tasks.

- **Vendor (E):** The vendor normally works with all property staff involved in the ordering process except those in the user departments, such as kitchen or bar. Vendor representatives may communicate directly with restaurant or foodservice staff when, for example, they provide information about product use or address problems related to items they sell. Vendors send information to purchasers, who ask them to complete a request for price quotation. If the vendor receives the order, the vendor's delivery staff then transport products to the property and unload them in the receiving area. Vendors also interact with accounting staff as bills are paid.

There can be many variations of the purchasing process outlined in *Exhibit 1.6.* For example, the chef or food and beverage director may communicate directly with the purchasing director. Also, receiving and storing staff may route copies of delivery invoices to these managers before they are sent to the purchasing director. In multiunit organizations, additional copies of one or more purchasing documents may be sent to a regional purchasing office. Some or all of the steps may be done electronically with little or no face-to-face or hard-copy communication necessary.

The purchasing structure in chain operations might include a purchasing vice president or director. In some cases this position performs all purchasing activities, or in others directs or monitors purchasing for all units or franchisees. A **franchisee** is a party in a franchising agreement that uses the logo, name, systems, and resources of a business for a fee. Multiunit organizations may have specialized purchasing staff in district, regional, or other offices to help individual operating units with their purchasing activities. A chart showing how the purchasing function might be organized in a multiunit operation is shown in *Exhibit 1.7*.

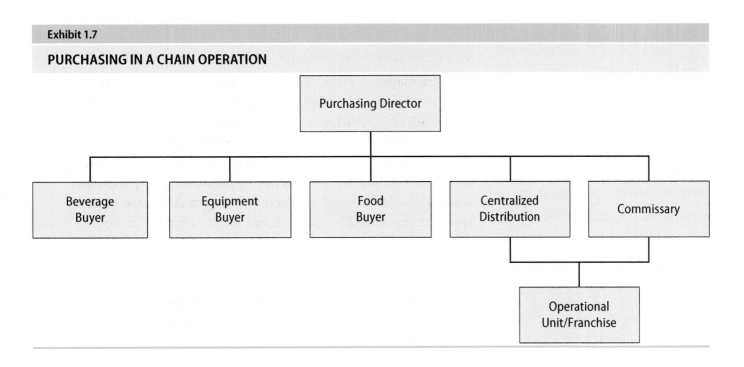

Exhibit 1.7

PURCHASING IN A CHAIN OPERATION

Purchasers working for small chain organizations may combine product order requirements from each unit. Then they obtain price quotations, select vendors, and arrange for product delivery to the individual properties.

Purchasing Responsibilities

Since the purchasing function affects all aspects of the operation, it also affects all employees. Those who purchase must ensure that the right products and services in the right quality and quantity levels are available for employees when required. Failure to ensure this can lead to inefficient work processes, budget difficulties, and employee and customer dissatisfaction.

The effectiveness of purchasing activities affects these members of the operation's team:

- **General manager:** Purchasing has a significant impact on the budget in terms of revenue if dissatisfied customers do not come back, and expenses as the wrong purchases can increase costs. The general manager, who is responsible for the success of the business, must carefully study revenue and costs to keep them in line with the budget. Problems can often be traced to ineffective purchasing. For this reason, an ongoing review of purchasing practices and the products and services purchased is always in order. The general manager also expects those who purchase to be professional representatives of the operation when dealing with vendors. Purchasers must avoid all unethical, illegal, and unprofessional interactions with those from whom they buy.

- **Other managers:** Purchasers must cooperate with other managers, many of whom will probably not have buying authority. For example, in decentralized purchasing, a chef or production manager who purchases garnishes for the entire operation must provide what the bar manager needs. Likewise, the bar manager might purchase beer, wines, and spirits used in food production. In centralized purchasing, the purchasing manager might help food-production managers determine whether specific items should be prepared on-site "from scratch" or if a convenience food alternative should be purchased. A **convenience food** is one in which some or all of the labor required to prepare the item is "built in." example, should ground beef be purchased in bulk with employees making the patties, or should pre-portioned patties be purchased? Purchasers also provide a service to other managers by identifying potential vendors and products that have recently come on the market.

- **Hourly employees:** Purchasers must ensure that employees have the tools and products needed to do their jobs. This includes everything from uniforms, scales, and dining-room supplies to bar glasses.

- **Other departments or teams:** Purchasers in centralized operations work with most, if not all, departments. This poses a number of challenges and opportunities. In many operations, employees see the organization from the perspective of their department. In contrast, purchasers must have a big-picture view. While these relationships have the potential for friction, they also offer an opportunity for better understanding of the needs and goals of the entire operation.

Purchaser Qualifications and Job Duties

Every job in a restaurant or foodservice operation requires specific knowledge and skills, and this information can be stated in a job specification. For example, a job specification for a department manager in an establishment with decentralized purchasing might include product knowledge to purchase items needed by the department. This task would represent the purchasing responsibility that is part of the job. In an operation with centralized purchasing, most of the purchaser's job specification would relate to purchasing knowledge and skills.

Regardless of whether purchasing is done by a manager with many duties or a purchaser whose primary responsibilities relate to that activity, the same basic knowledge and skills are needed. A close look at these abilities is important for understanding what is required to be an effective purchaser.

THE PURCHASER'S JOB SPECIFICATION

An effective purchaser must have different types of abilities:

- **Technical skills:** Purchasers must understand the detailed requirements for the products and services they buy and how employees will use them. In addition, purchasers require other skills including the ability to negotiate with vendors, to determine the quantities of products to purchase, to prepare RFPs, and to implement new technologies that improve purchasing efficiency and inventory management.

- **Conceptual skills:** Purchasers must understand how the job affects the establishment's overall success, taking a big-picture view of the operation. Examples of conceptual skills include determining ways to reduce costs without reducing quality, organizing the purchasing function, and helping managers identify the types of products needed.

Exhibit 1.8

- **Interpersonal skills:** Purchasers must be able to work well with other managers, employees, and vendors, among others. Examples of interpersonal skills may include training receiving staff (*Exhibit 1.8*), dealing with vendors' delivery staff, and cooperating with other managers.

- **Other skills:** Effective purchasers, like those successful in other positions, must also possess other important general qualities such as appropriate education and work experience. Also, purchasers must exhibit ethical character (integrity, honesty), an interest in the success of their organization, and a strong concern for customers.

THINK ABOUT IT . . .

Purchasers must have a wide variety of knowledge, skills, and abilities to effectively perform their job.

What are some examples of technical, conceptual, and interpersonal skills that help purchasers succeed?

THE PURCHASER'S JOB DESCRIPTION

Exhibit 1.9 shows an extensive list of tasks that might be included in a job description for a purchasing director. A job description indicates the tasks that a person working in a specific position must perform. The specifics of each task will be covered in later chapters. Recall that someone in decentralized purchasing operations will need to do most, if not all, of these tasks.

Exhibit 1.9

SAMPLE JOB DESCRIPTION TASKS FOR PURCHASING DIRECTOR

- Identifies potential vendors, selects vendors; negotiates prices and contract terms.
- Coordinates the purchase of products, services, equipment, and supplies.
- Communicates with vendors to obtain product or service information including price, availability, and delivery schedules.
- Selects products for purchase after testing, observing or tasting, and examining items.
- Determines purchase method such as direct purchase or bid.
- Prepares purchase orders or bid requests.
- Reviews vendors' price proposals and negotiates contracts within scope of authority.
- Approves invoices for payment.
- Expedites delivery of products to users.
- Recommends improvements in overall purchasing procedures.
- Determines correct purchase quantities.
- Keeps current with vendors to forecast costs and availability of required products.
- Stays informed about new product developments.
- Develops and monitors purchasing department's budget.
- Manages purchasing files, policies and procedures, systems, best practices, and goals for the purchasing department.
- Reviews, revises, and maintains product purchase specifications.
- Maintains vendor handbook and vendor information.
- Establishes and maintains proper vendor relationships.

Manager's Memo

Wise purchasers ask for, require, use, and are willing to pay for information they receive from vendors. They want to deal with vendors who are experts in the products and services they sell, and they know the cost of information is an element in the price they pay.

For example, if a wine vendor informs the buyer that the price of several wines will be increasing, there is an advantage to purchasing in larger-than-usual quantities. The purchaser can then inform the appropriate manager about the pending price increases so the manager can make a decision about purchases.

BASIC STEPS IN THE PURCHASING PROCESS

Effective purchasers use a series of steps to ensure that all concerns are addressed when they plan and implement a purchasing system. *Exhibit 1.10* reviews these steps.

Consider these details of the purchasing steps outlined in *Exhibit 1.10*:

Step 1: Identify product need.

Need is driven by what customers want. Their needs should be addressed in the menu, which determines the food products that must be purchased. This step also applies to services. For example, if the operation has landscaping needs, this service must be purchased unless employees can perform these tasks at the required level of quality and an acceptable cost.

Step 2: Determine quality requirements.

Quality considers how suitable a product or service is for its intended purpose. Ground beef can be purchased with different percentages of fat content, and it can be purchased fresh or frozen. Olives can be purchased chopped for a pasta salad or super colossal for a salad garnish.

Step 3: Determine quantity to purchase.

Products can be purchased in large or small volumes, and services can be purchased for short or longer time periods. Factors affecting product quantity purchase decisions include available storage space, the possibility of theft, and concerns about loss of quality while products are in storage. The purchase of quantities above normal purchase levels may need approval from the manager because of the higher costs that will be incurred.

Step 4: Identify vendor sources.

Purchasers often have several vendors who can provide products and services. Their experience, vendor references, and trial orders with potential vendors can help determine a "short list" of vendors who will be used.

Step 5: Select vendor for order.

Which potential vendor should provide products or services? The answer depends, in part, on the type of purchasing system used. Vendor selection decisions may be based on best prices determined through purchase order exchanges for each specific order. Alternatively, pricing may be established in long-term contracts that enable a vendor to provide products or services for several months (or longer) at a price agreed on before the first delivery is made.

Step 6: Order product.

Products can be ordered after the proper quality and quantity are known (steps 2 and 3) and the vendor has been selected (step 5).

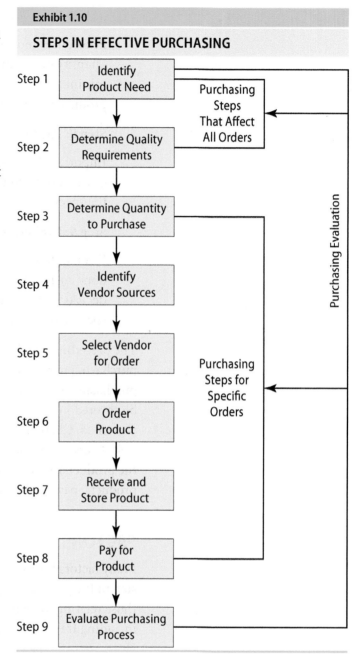

Exhibit 1.10

STEPS IN EFFECTIVE PURCHASING

Step 1 — Identify Product Need
Step 2 — Determine Quality Requirements
Step 3 — Determine Quantity to Purchase
Step 4 — Identify Vendor Sources
Step 5 — Select Vendor for Order
Step 6 — Order Product
Step 7 — Receive and Store Product
Step 8 — Pay for Product
Step 9 — Evaluate Purchasing Process

Purchasing Steps That Affect All Orders

Purchasing Steps for Specific Orders

Purchasing Evaluation

Step 7: Receive and store product.

Procedures must be in place to ensure that the proper quality and quantity of products are delivered. Products must be properly stored to minimize quality or theft problems. Record-keeping tasks applicable to product storage are also needed.

Step 8: Pay for product.

Important factors include the timing of payments, concerns about fraud during processing, and basic accounting concerns for assigning costs to the specific operating departments that incur them.

Step 9: Evaluate purchasing process.

Evaluation is useful to ensure that each step in the purchasing process is done correctly. This concern applies to the way basic purchasing process decisions are made (steps 1 and 2) and to activities undertaken for specific orders (steps 3–8).

The preceding purchasing overview provides a basis for the discussion of purchasing management in this book. Specifically, the first two steps of purchasing, identify product need and determine quality requirements, will be covered in chapter 2. In chapter 3, purchase quantity issues (step 3) will be presented. Chapter 4 will explain step 4 (identify vendor sources) and step 5 (select vendor for the order). Chapters 5, 6, and 7 will address step 6 (ordering the products). Chapter 8 will conclude by explaining steps 7, 8, and 9 (receive products, pay for them, and evaluate the purchasing process).

FACTORS THAT AFFECT PURCHASING

Many factors impact the specific policies and procedures used to manage each step in the purchasing process. Some have been already identified, such as those relating to ownership, involvement with a multiunit organization including franchise arrangements, and the specific customer market served. However, other factors can influence the purchasing process used by a specific establishment.

Internal Factors

Purchasers must consider the skills and abilities of their staff members as buying decisions are made. The decision referred to earlier about making specific menu items or buying convenience food products is an example. Forecasted business volume, available storage space for products, and timing requirements for service deliveries are important. The operation's ability to pay for the products and services it purchases on a timely basis and the quality standards that drive many aspects of purchasing are additional factors.

The use of decentralized or centralized purchasing systems affects the decision-making process. The reporting relationships of purchasers and the flow of hard-copy or electronic documents throughout the operation also impact the purchasing process. Increasingly, the extent to which technology is used for purchasing activities is an important internal influence. Each of these factors should be considered as a purchasing system is planned, implemented, and evaluated in a specific operation.

External Factors

Several factors outside the establishment also impact purchase decisions. Some of these are identified in *Exhibit 1.11*.

Exhibit 1.11 shows that customers are an external influence on the purchasing process used by an operation. Concerns about consistently meeting customers' expectations apply to all aspects of the operation. Should the services of a band be purchased for the lounge? Do customers want fresh bread baked on-site? Will customers select fresh seafood (*Exhibit 1.12*) or unique desserts flown in from a distant city? Each of these is an example of a customer-related demand that may be a priority in a purchase decision.

Vendors, manufacturers, and others in distribution channels also influence purchasing decisions. A **distribution channel** includes the organizations and individuals involved in the process of making a product or service available to an organization. Each adds value as products move from the manufacturer, processor, or grower to the purchaser's property. Many organizations in distribution channels become larger by merging with or buying other related businesses, and they can then offer one-stop shopping alternatives. This allows purchasers to buy a wide range of products or services from a single vendor, reducing the number of necessary supply sources. This, in turn, makes it possible to reduce the labor costs required to determine order quantities, assess vendor prices, place orders, receive products, and make payments.

Exhibit 1.11

EXTERNAL FACTORS IMPACTING PURCHASING DECISIONS

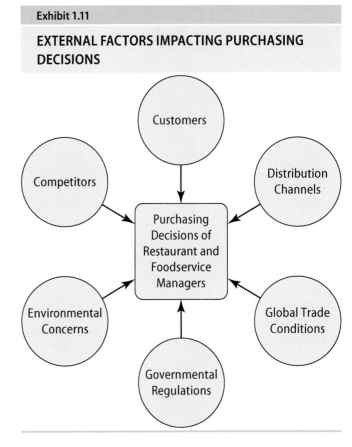

Exhibit 1.12

WHAT'S THE FOOTPRINT?

The farm-to-fork movement merges two external factors that can impact purchasing. The term *farm-to-fork* refers to the path food follows from those who grow or raise it to those who prepare and serve it. Ideally, this path is short in order to maximize freshness, minimize health risks, and be environmentally friendly.

Increasingly, purchasers are aware that buying locally produced food is good for business, for customers, and for their local economy. Customers are increasingly knowledgeable and concerned about the source of food items they buy. Consumer issues of food safety, sustainability, freshness, and quality are powerful drivers of the farm-to-fork movement.

There are several advantages to buying locally grown food products:

- They are often fresher and may be of better quality than products processed and shipped from far away.
- They can often be purchased cost-effectively.
- Many customers appreciate them.
- Buying locally supports family farming.
- Buying locally strengthens local economies.

The other external factors identified in *Exhibit 1.11* are as follows:

- **Global trade conditions:** Today's increasingly global society conducts business across international borders. Many manufacturers are becoming global organizations, and improved transportation systems make products from almost anywhere available at almost any time. The global economy impacts product availability and prices paid by all organizations, including those in the restaurant and foodservice industry.

- **Governmental regulations:** Federal laws in the United States regulate the interstate (between-state) transportation of some products, and they control the inspection of many food items. State laws directly affect how alcoholic beverages may be purchased and sold. Other laws impose taxes on the purchase of products and services. Laws also impact the purchase, storage, and handling of many items including cleaning chemicals and pesticides.

- **Environmental concerns:** Consumer demands and the interest of establishments in being good community citizens impact many green purchasing decisions. Green purchasing procedures place a priority on a product's environmental impact. Examples are recycling of packaging materials, purchasing of environmentally friendly cleaning supplies and other chemicals, and giving consideration to the disposal of non-reusable items.

- **Competitors:** Many managers study how competitors do things in efforts to improve their own processes, including those related to purchasing. Benchmarking is the search for best practices and an understanding of how they are achieved. It is used to determine how well an organization is doing and to learn ways to become even better. Also, efforts to improve on the products and services offered by competitors impact the actual products and services to be purchased.

COMMON RESTAURANT AND FOODSERVICE PURCHASES

Restaurant and foodservice operations are unusual in the business world because they both manufacture (produce) and sell products and services to customers. This requires them to purchase a wide variety of products and services that can generally be divided into categories. *Exhibit 1.13* provides an overview of product categories and examples of items included in each category. Duplications occur in several categories because the item can be purchased outright or contracted as a service. For example, a manager can purchase table linens and launder them on-site or contract with a linen service to provide them.

Exhibit 1.13

PRODUCT AND SERVICE CATEGORIES

Food and Beverage Products: These are the items operations prepare for customers. Examples include the following:

Food Items

- Meat
- Poultry
- Eggs
- Processed food products
- Fish and other seafood
- Dairy
- Produce
- Dry, frozen, and canned products

Alcoholic Beverages

- Spirits
- Beer
- Wine

Nonalcoholic Beverages

- Soft drinks
- Coffee and tea
- Juices
- Bottled waters

Nonfood Items: These items are directly related to the sale of food and beverages. For example, linens, candles, and flowers are used for tabletops, and paper bags are used for takeout orders. Other examples include the following:

- Uniforms
- China and glassware
- Silverware
- Bar supplies
- Paper products
- Cleaning supplies
- Menus and beverage lists
- Music
- Kitchen utensils and supplies

Furniture, Fixtures, and Equipment (FF&E): Items in this category may be purchased or leased. Examples include dishwashing machines, dining-room tables and booths, and beverage dispensing equipment. These relatively expensive items typically require maintenance and repair. Other examples of FF&E:

- Chairs and barstools
- Lighting fixtures
- Bars
- Cooking equipment
- Refrigeration
- Plumbing fixtures

Business Supplies and Services: These services and supplies are required for the management or marketing of the operation:

- Office supplies and equipment
- Point-of-sale (POS) systems
- Computers
- Cell phones
- Credit card processing equipment
- Financial and legal services
- Insurance
- Marketing and advertising

Support Services: These services are tied to the actual operation of the business:

- Linen and uniform rental
- Waste removal
- Flower services
- Music services
- Pest control services
- Parking and valet services

Maintenance Services: Maintenance services are required for the upkeep of the facility. These may include the following:

- Cleaning services
- Plumbing and heating
- Groundskeeping
- Painting and carpentry
- Equipment repair and maintenance

Utilities: This category includes charges for utilities required to operate the business:

- Gas
- Oil heating
- Electricity
- Water and sewage
- Telephone service
- Internet access

THINK ABOUT IT . . .

A typical operation requires a wide range of products and services.

What are additional items that might be included in each category of *Exhibit 1.13*? What departments (production, service, beverage, or general operations) need the items you identify?

EVOLUTION OF PURCHASING SYSTEMS

Managers in many establishments have rethought the goals of their purchasing activities to determine how to best use their resources to gain a competitive advantage and achieve financial success. Executives in large, multiunit chains are also reconsidering the role of purchasing and every other aspect of management and marketing to help ensure that they can realize maximum benefits.

Exhibit 1.14 reviews how the purchasing function is changing in restaurant and foodservice operations. Three phases are evident.

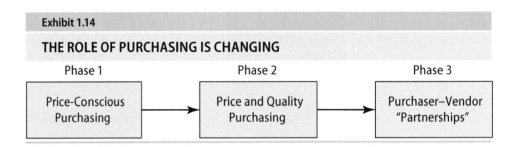

Exhibit 1.14

THE ROLE OF PURCHASING IS CHANGING

Phase 1	Phase 2	Phase 3
Price-Conscious Purchasing	Price and Quality Purchasing	Purchaser–Vendor "Partnerships"

Price-Conscious Purchasing

In this traditional approach to purchasing, the operation wants to implement strategies to purchase products at the lowest price. While perhaps somewhat overstated, the preferred relationship with vendors is one of "I win; you lose." This relationship is often much more adversarial than mutually beneficial.

When price-conscious purchasing is the goal, most of the purchaser's time and efforts are spent ordering products and determining how to reduce costs. The purchasing function is evaluated on the basis of lowest cost per unit and efficiency. There is little recognition of how the purchasing function can impact nonsupply aspects of the organization. The primary purchasing goal is to "get the products here on time, at the very lowest cost."

Price and Quality Purchasing

Operations with this purchasing philosophy are still concerned about the cost of products and services, but the quality of what is being purchased is also of concern. Purchasers are driven by value from the customer's perspective, and they recognize that the best product is not necessarily the least expensive.

Organizations in this purchasing phase also recognize the importance of information provided by their vendors. They know that there are several important components of purchase prices including product, information, and service, and they are willing to pay for each of them. Those with purchasing responsibilities interact with others in the organization to determine quality requirements. Top-level managers recognize that those with purchasing responsibilities can help the organization be profitable in ways beyond reducing purchase costs to the lowest possible levels.

Purchaser–Vendor "Partnerships"

Operations in this phase recognize a broader role for purchasing, and they see how it can become a competitive advantage. Vendors are considered a resource, and expertise is an important consideration as vendor decisions are made. Products and vendors are continuously monitored, and those with purchasing responsibilities help others in the establishment address and resolve their problems.

SUMMARY

1. **Describe purchasing objectives and the impacts of effective purchasing.**

    Purchasing is the process of selecting, buying, and evaluating products and services needed by the operation to generate revenue. Its objectives are to obtain the right product or service, at the right price, from the right source, in the right amount, and at the right time.

    Purchasing impacts many aspects of the operation. Adequate products must be available when needed, and quality standards must be met. Also, costs must be minimized to maintain a competitive advantage. Wise purchasers know that the actual usage cost of a product, accounting for all factors such as labor, is most important.

2. **Explain how the purchasing function is organized in small- and large-volume operations.**

    Small-volume operations use decentralized purchasing. All or most purchases are made by department heads or someone in their department. Large purchases are often subject to approval of the manager. Large-volume operations may use centralized purchasing. All or most purchases are made by a purchasing agent. Communication among department staff, receiving and storing employees, the purchasing director, vendors, and accounting staff is very important. Documents such as purchasing requisitions, purchase orders, and delivery invoices must be carefully routed.

    Purchasing affects every team member of the operation. Purchasers must have the technical skills to understand requirements for products and services. They must have conceptual skills to recognize the operation's needs and interpersonal skills to interact with employees and vendors. Purchasers must perform a wide range of tasks related to making quality and quantity decisions, ensuring that the best prices are received, and interacting with vendors.

3. **Describe the basic steps in the purchasing process.**

   The basic purchasing steps include identifying product needs, determining quality and quantity requirements, and identifying and selecting vendors. Then products must be ordered, received, and paid for, and the purchasing process should be continually evaluated.

4. **Identify internal and external factors that impact the purchasing process.**

   Purchasers must consider the skills and abilities of employees when buying decisions are made. They must ensure the operation can pay for products and services on a timely basis and that quality standards will be met. The use of decentralized or centralized purchasing affects the flow of information throughout the operation, and use of technology impacts the process as well.

   External factors that impact purchasing decisions relate to customers, distribution channels, global trade conditions, governmental regulations, environmental concerns, and competitors.

5. **List common restaurant and foodservice purchases.**

   Purchasers buy a wide range of products and services in several categories: food items; alcoholic and nonalcoholic beverages; nonfood items; furniture, fixtures, and equipment (FF&E); business supplies and services; support services; maintenance services; and utilities.

6. **Discuss the evolution of purchasing systems.**

   The role of purchasing is changing as primary concerns evolve. Concerns range from price only, to price and quality, to ways that purchasers and vendors can form partnerships so the relationship benefits both parties.

APPLICATION EXERCISE

It is often a challenge to evaluate purchasing because it is difficult to determine the cause of problems that might or might not be caused by the purchasing process. Assume you were the manager of a restaurant or foodservice operation with the following problems. How might you determine their cause?

1. The food cost is high when compared to the operating budget. Is the problem caused by the high cost of food or by the lack of control procedure?

2. The cooks complain about the quality of some food products. Is the problem due to the wrong quality of food being purchased or to improper inventory and other quality control procedures?

3. The operation runs out of some food products frequently. Is the problem that the purchaser buys the incorrect amount or are there production or control problems creating the problem?

REVIEW YOUR LEARNING

Select the best answer for each question.

1. **When does the purchasing process begin?**
   A. When orders are placed
   B. When vendors are selected
   C. When needs are determined
   D. When inventories are assessed

2. **What is the definition of value?**
   A. The relationship of purchase price and product quality
   B. The least expensive product available from the vendor
   C. The right product obtained from the right source
   D. The suitability of a product for its intended use

3. **Quality is most difficult to establish for what type of products?**
   A. Fresh produce
   B. Canned goods
   C. Condiments
   D. Alcoholic beverages

4. **The concept of "competitive advantage" relates to benefits that the organization has over its**
   A. competitors.
   B. employees.
   C. customers.
   D. vendors.

5. **A decentralized purchasing system is most often used by which type of establishment?**
   A. Large-volume operation
   B. Single-unit operation
   C. Chain operation
   D. Franchise

6. **The document used by purchasers to accept a vendor's price is called a**
   A. product issue.
   B. purchase order.
   C. delivery invoice.
   D. purchase specification.

7. **What type of skill does a purchaser use most when determining how to reduce costs without reducing quality?**
   A. Interpersonal
   B. Conceptual
   C. Technical
   D. General

8. **What does a job description describe about a purchaser's position?**
   A. Tasks that are performed
   B. Personal qualities that are needed
   C. Product knowledge that is required
   D. Technical skills that must be possessed

9. **With what type of purchasing system are vendors considered a resource?**
   A. Price-conscious
   B. Price and quality
   C. Purchaser–vendor partnership
   D. Purchaser information–communication

10. **Who should receive a copy of the purchase order when the purchaser authorizes shipment from a vendor?**
    A. The operation's auditor
    B. The operation's manager
    C. The applicable department head
    D. The operation's receiving personnel

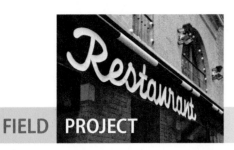

FIELD PROJECT

Select an independently owned (not a chain-affiliated) restaurant or foodservice operation that you would like to learn about. Ask permission to interview the owner, manager, or food-production manager. Ask him or her the questions on the Restaurant or Foodservice Operation Field Project Questionnaire.

In addition, identify a relatively large-volume local vendor to interview. Ask the vendor the questions on the Vendor Field Project Questionnaire that follows the previously mentioned form.

If time permits, your instructor may ask you to share some of the responses with your classmates.

Note that the question responses will be used to complete the purchasing field project exercises in other chapters and at the end of the book, so please save both forms.

Restaurant or Foodservice Operation Field Project Questionnaire

Name of establishment: _____

Name/position of interviewee: _____   **Date of interview:** _____

For Chapter 2: Make-or-Buy Analysis

1. How do you consider whether to make or buy a menu item such as a salad dressing or fresh-baked dessert?

2. Who is involved in make-or-buy decisions?

3. How, if at all, do you obtain your customers' input about a make-or-buy decision?

For Chapter 4: Vendor Selection

4. What factors are most important when determining to which vendors you send requests for proposals (RFPs)?

For Chapter 6: Ordering Products: Use Effective Decisions

5. How do you order food and beverage products? What works well? What challenges does your operation face?

6. Can each department head (cook, dining room, bar) order products separately? Who orders other items? If so, is there a dollar limit above which management approval is needed?

7. What process is used to obtain price quotations and to award purchase orders?

8. Who (what position) receives products and what procedures are used to receive them?

For Chapter 7: Purchasing Ethics and Vendor Relations

9. What are some things you do to help maintain a good relationship with your restaurant or foodservice vendors?

10. What are some things that vendors do that make you less interested in buying from them?

For Chapter 8: Purchasing Follow-Up

11. Who approves delivery invoices for payment?

12. What are your suggestions for the most effective procedures to use when delivery invoices or vendor statements are processed for payment?

Vendor Field Project Questionnaire

Name of vendor's business: _____

Name/position of interviewee: _____ **Date of interview:** _____

For Chapter 2: Make-or-Buy Analysis

1. What assistance can you give to buyers who want to conduct a make-or-buy analysis for alternative products?

2. What are the most frequent errors that buyers make when they do a make-or-buy analysis?

3. What is the cost per case for your best blue cheese dressing?
   $ _____ per case   Case size (Example: 4 1-gallon bottles): _____

For Chapter 4: Vendor Selection

4. What factors should be most important to buyers when they determine to which vendors their requests for proposals (RFPs) should be sent?

For Chapter 7: Purchasing Ethics and Vendor Relations

5. What are some things that you do to help maintain a good relationship with your restaurant or foodservice buyers?

6. What are some things buyers do that, from your viewpoint, make you less interested in continuing a professional relationship with them?

For Chapter 8: Purchasing Follow-Up

7. What are your suggestions for the most effective procedures that restaurant and foodservice managers should use as they process and pay a vendor's delivery invoices or statements?

2 Quality Requirements

CHAPTER LEARNING OBJECTIVES

After completing this chapter, you should be able to:

- Explain the importance of consistently purchasing products of the proper quality, and describe how the establishment of quality standards is an important first step in defining quality needs.

- Explain the role of properly constructed product specifications in communicating product quality needs to vendors, and tell how product specifications are developed and implemented.

- State the importance of make-or-buy analysis, and describe how the process should be done.

KEY TERMS

CASE STUDY

"I think I know why we are going to check out the cost differences from making some products in the kitchen compared to buying them already made," said Yoko to another cook at Shining Stars Restaurant.

"Really?" replied Jules. "Please explain."

Yoko said, "My friend's boss thought labor costs were too high. He did some kind of a study and decided to buy convenience food items and fire her."

"I hope that doesn't happen here," said Jules, "but I know our boss wants to save money. I just hope he remembers the food we produce is great. Personally, I don't think that ready-made food is as good as what we make here."

1. What do you think the manager should have said to the cooks when he decided to review menu items to determine if production costs could be lowered by purchasing convenience food products?

2. If the manager determines that some menu items should be purchased as convenience food, eliminating the need for that labor, what should he say to the employees?

THE IMPORTANCE OF QUALITY STANDARDS

Purchasers must ensure that they are obtaining the proper quality of products and services for their operation. Vendors usually offer products and services in a variety of different quality levels. A challenge for the purchaser, then, is to determine quality standards for the products and services required. Quality standards are the factors that are used to compare an actual product or service with the desired product or service. For example, the size of an olive is one factor in determining its quality. The desired location of knives, forks, and spoons on a table is a quality standard for service. It is important to consistently ensure that these standards are met.

What Is Quality?

The concept of quality can be difficult for some purchasers to define. Some may say, "I know it when I see it." They may make a decision about quality when they see products delivered by the vendor. Then it is often too late to take more than limited corrective actions. Refusing the items can disrupt production and disappoint customers. Negotiating a lower price for a product of inadequate quality is never a "deal."

In fact, purchasers must determine and effectively communicate quality requirements with vendors to best ensure that quality standards will be met when products are received. Chapter 1 stated that quality relates to the intended use of a product or service and its value or worth. The better a product can do what it is supposed to do, the better its quality. This definition requires that a buyer must first define what a product will be used for. Then the proper quality of product becomes the one most suitable for its intended use at the lowest cost.

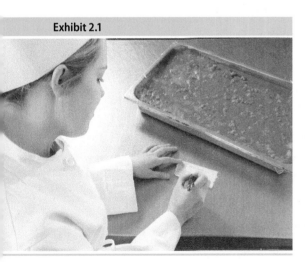

Exhibit 2.1

A cook is preparing spaghetti sauce with a recipe requiring tomato products, ground beef, vegetables including onions and green peppers, and several seasonings (*Exhibit 2.1*). What market form of tomato products should be used? Market form relates to alternative ways that food products can be purchased. Some examples of market forms for tomatoes include fresh whole tomatoes, tomato pieces of relatively uniform or irregular sizes, tomato sauce, or tomato puree. As a second example, bread can be purchased in several market forms including fresh baked either sliced or unsliced, or frozen preweighed dough portions.

Perhaps the cook preparing spaghetti sauce is employed by a high check average establishment. It offers higher-priced meals because of the higher costs of products, service, and other features of the dining experience. Its customers believe that "fresh is best," and the higher selling prices help offset high labor costs involved with processing fresh food.

Therefore, no canned tomato products will likely be used in the spaghetti sauce recipe. The operation will likely purchase tomatoes in a fresh, whole market form. However, if the cook works in a family-service restaurant featuring a wide variety of lower-priced meals where convenience food products are frequently used, there may be no fresh tomato products in the sauce.

Why Is Quality Important?

Purchasers must know the intended use of a product to understand its required quality. In the preceding examples, fresh tomatoes may be used for numerous products in high check average establishments. They may be used only in fresh salads or as plate garnishes in another types of operations.

Customers increasingly demand value when they visit restaurant and foodservice operations. It is just as important for purchasers to seek value when they buy products for their establishment. Customers and buyers both must ask, "Is the product I am considering really worth what it costs?" Additionally, many customers and purchasers want to get more than what they are paying for, and then the definition of value is expanded.

QUALITY IN THE RESTAURANT OR FOODSERVICE OPERATION

To this point, quality has been discussed in the context of the products that are purchased. However, an organizational definition of quality is also important. Quality is the consistent delivery of products and services according to expected standards. For example, if the purchasing team decides that 93 percent lean fresh ground beef is required, that is the quality that should always be purchased. If the dining-room team decides that a glass of ice water should be presented to guests when the server first approaches the table, that procedure should always be followed. This goal is always difficult to attain, but it is impossible to accomplish if the products required are unavailable because of poor purchasing. Buyers must purchase products meeting quality requirements to help the operation meet its overall quality commitments.

Some managers use the term quality assurance to refer to all activities that an organization uses to attain quality. Several of these activities relate to purchasing:

- Considering the products that provide the best value for customers
- Defining quality and developing product specifications that identify quality standards
- Evaluating vendors to ensure that they consistently deliver the proper products at a fair price
- Emphasizing the importance of maintaining quality standards

---

Manager's Memo

There are four different costs of quality:

- Prevention costs, such as the cost of developing a purchase specification that describes a product of proper quality for its intended use.

- Appraisal costs, such as the cost of inspecting incoming products to ensure that they meet quality requirements.

- Internal failure costs, such as the cost of errors and rework created by using inappropriate products or incorrect work methods.

- External failure costs, such as the costs incurred by using products that do not comply with product specifications. These costs include dissatisfied customers and frustrated employees who must produce menu items with improper ingredients.

- Training employees to perform purchasing activities
- Inspecting to ensure that quality standards are met when products are delivered
- Determining corrective actions that address purchasing defects
- Obtaining feedback to improve purchasing

Another quality concept, **total quality management**, relates to the pursuit of organization-wide quality. The emphasis is placed on improving processes and procedures rather than identifying defects. Effective purchasers improve existing processes and discover new ones to help the establishment meet quality requirements. Increasingly, this involves obtaining assistance from vendors who provide added value by offering their knowledge, experience, and information to help the operation better serve its customers.

ECONOMICS OF QUALITY

Some managers might think that since customer value is a priority, the best strategy is to reduce selling prices. For example, wouldn't a dinner with a reasonable menu selling price of $35 be a great value if it were priced at $25? Unfortunately, if the organization's cost to produce that item was $26, the operation offering such a low price would be unprofitable and would likely go out of business.

Customer value is achieved by considering competitive alternatives. Customers paying $35 for a meal will consider it a value if it is better than any other meal they can purchase at that price. Operations must consistently provide better value for customers than their competitors.

Purchasing staff help customers receive value. First, they ensure that the products purchased help customers enjoy their experience. For example, the quality of ingredients used to prepare an entrée is important. Managers must determine what their customers want. Then those who purchase must help define these needs and ensure that products meet these standards.

Purchasers also help achieve quality by eliminating excessive costs as the right quality rather than the highest quality is purchased. This is not a suggestion to "buy cheap." Instead, it reinforces the quality definition cited earlier: proper quality relates to suitability for intended use. This depends on many factors, including how the ingredient will be used and what customers want. Savings made from effective purchasing yield reduced costs. These savings can then be passed on to the customer to provide better value perception, or they can also be used to help the operation remain financially successful.

Manager's Memo

There are three basic types of purchasers:

- **Price-conscious purchasers:** They are concerned about price ("the cheaper the better"), and their primary purchasing goals relate to buying the least-expensive products.

- **Quality-conscious purchasers:** They are not overly concerned about costs. Instead, they want to purchase products of the highest possible quality. Some of these purchasers believe that "you get what you pay for," and they believe that higher prices represent greater quality. They may also believe that higher costs can be passed on to the customers.

- **Value-conscious purchasers:** They recognize and study the relationship between product price and quality. These purchasers recognize that neither the lowest or highest price nor the lowest- or highest-quality product is likely needed. Instead, the right product is the one that represents the greatest value based on price and suitability for intended use.

Quality Standards

Quality standards identify and communicate required product characteristics and specifications to the operation's staff and its vendors. They are developed in recognition of the operation's concept, location, customers, and competition. For example, the product and service needs of a casual dining establishment located in a strip mall differ significantly from those of an upscale steakhouse in a luxury hotel. While each operation may have similar menu offerings, the level of food quality, service, and environment will differ based on the quality standards required by its customers.

BENEFITS OF QUALITY STANDARDS

Quality standards describe the products and services needed by the operation. There are several benefits of properly written and recorded quality standards:

- They provide a written record of purchasing criteria so the operation can control the quality and cost of all purchases.

- They communicate product and service standards and requirements to employees and vendors to help prevent ordering and shipping errors.

- They identify specific requirements for products or services identified in requests for proposals sent to vendors.

- They allow purchasers to define terms with vendors to establish a replacement policy for products that do not meet quality requirements.

- They improve the ability of employees to identify and prepare menu items.

DETERMINING QUALITY STANDARDS

Determining and writing accurate quality standards can be a complex process that requires close attention. A single person such as the chef or a group including the manager, chef, and others from the restaurant or foodservice operation may define the establishment's quality requirements (*Exhibit 2.2*).

Exhibit 2.2

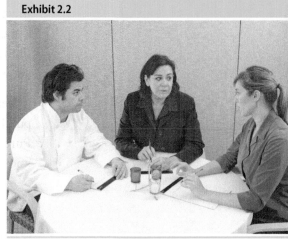

Others who may help determine and write quality standards include purchasers, suppliers, and external consultants. Purchasers typically make recommendations for quality standards and often bring unique knowledge to the process. They are often knowledgeable about product quality levels, grades, common market forms, availability, relative value of different brands, and as purchased (AP) versus edible portion (EP) costs. The term as purchased (AP) refers to the weight of a product before it is processed, prepared, or cooked. The term edible portion (EP) refers to the weight of a product after it is processed, prepared, and cooked.

Exhibit 2.3

ASSISTANCE IN WRITING QUALITY STANDARDS

- American Cutlery Manufacturers Association
- American Institute of Banking
- American Seafood Distributors Association
- Foodservice Equipment Distributors Association
- National Livestock and Meat Board
- National Pasta Association
- National Poultry & Food Distributors Association
- U.S. Department of Agriculture
- U.S. Department of Commerce
- U.S. Food and Drug Administration
- Wine & Spirits Wholesalers of America, Inc.

Some quality standards have already been developed and are available in government guidelines and industry publications. *Exhibit 2.3* lists several industry organizations with information that can help you get started in determining and writing your quality standards. These resources are available to the public and can be reviewed, reproduced, or used as templates. It is a good idea to review these resources when you determine quality standards to see if any of them apply to your operation. While there is no designated system that will work for every single operation when applying these standards, use of all available resources, including the Internet, will help you create your operation's standards.

As an example of differing needs for different establishments, consider a casual dining operation that may determine that a choice grade of meat and two-ply paper napkins will be acceptable for its customers. In contrast, an upscale steakhouse may want prime-grade meat and thick, white linen napkins. Managers in each operation must determine the level of quality needed for the products and services they will purchase, and then they must identify the specifications for that quality.

The owner or manager of an independent operation typically determines quality standards for food products, often working closely with the chef. In a chain operation, top management and corporate-level departments such as quality assurance, research and development, and purchasing likely develop quality standards. However, some chain operations allow individual units to use local vendors for certain products or services. These products or services must comply with the operation's established quality standards. For example, some chain operations may designate a certain grade of fresh steak for use in Philly cheese steaks. To preserve quality and freshness, the operation may allow local units to order the same quality steaks from a local vendor.

Others who may help determine and write quality standards include purchasers, vendors, external consultants, and other company staff. Purchasers typically make recommendations and often bring unique advisory knowledge to the process.

DEFINING QUALITY WITH PRODUCT SPECIFICATIONS

Recall from chapter 1 that product specifications identify the required characteristics of a particular product or service, and they are used to implement quality standards. They do so by communicating product and service information to staff and vendors. Quality standards speak generally to what is necessary, and product specifications provide details about specific products.

Product specifications for a specific product such as ground beef vary for different establishments. Some may be very detailed and formal and provide precise information. Examples of detailed requirements include an item's packaging, quality grade, count, size, temperature or processing requirements, and shipping and inspection methods. Government facilities, hospitals, and large chain operations that work with approved vendors are examples of operations that might use these types of specifications.

Smaller independent operations might use more informal specifications. These establishments might list only a few requirements such as a product's exact name, intended use, and portion size. Each operation will determine product specifications and document them in a way that is appropriate for its business and satisfies its quality standards. For example, product specifications should be included in the general information sent to approved vendors including vendor handbooks and in information provided to those who must recognize and accept quality requirements as part of the receiving process.

Purposes of Product Specifications

Product specifications are an important communication tool. They help ensure that managers, production staff, purchasers, and vendors have the same understanding about quality needs.

Effective product specifications meet several requirements:

- They are as simple and short as possible while providing an accurate product description.
- They are capable of being met, whenever possible, by several vendors to encourage competitive bidding: a strategy for comparing vendors' prices for products of acceptable quality to determine the lowest price.
- They are representative of currently available products to minimize customization costs.
- They can be verified on delivery to ensure that proper quality is received.

Uses of Product Specifications

Product specifications are useful at different stages of production. Specifically, they are used during purchasing and receiving.

PURCHASING

Product specifications allow several vendors to quote prices for the same quality product or service. This makes it easier to evaluate prices when competitive bidding is used.

THINK ABOUT IT . . .

A buyer asked three vendors to quote a price for beef without indicating the product specifications. The vendors all submitted different prices.

How would the buyer determine which vendor should get the purchase order?

Product specifications can be described in several ways:

- **Exact name:** When applicable, you should use the exact name of the item or service you want to buy. For example, if you are writing a specification for grapes, you may receive the wrong ones if you write only "grapes" in your specification. Instead, you should write the exact grape you need, such as "grapes, Thompson seedless." Using exact names helps ensure that you receive the correct item, avoids frustration and misinterpretation for you and the supplier, and keeps customers satisfied.

- **Brand name:** Purchasers who specify a specific brand of ketchup are indicating a quality preference. It is probably based on their experience with the product or its reputation. A packer may produce more than one quality of a product such as green beans and sell each product under a different name for a different price. One advantage to using a brand name for a purchase specification is that the specification is quick and easy to write. However, there may be only one vendor in a local area that can provide the desired brand-name product, and then competitive bidding is not possible.

- **Certification with industry specification:** The U.S. Department of Agriculture's Institutional Meat Purchasing Specifications (IMPS) and the Meat Buyer's Guide produced by the North American Meat Processors Association (NAMP) are examples of this type of specification. When a purchaser specifies, for example, NAMP #1184D, that number identifies a beef loin, top sirloin cap steak that is boneless and meets specific quality standards. U.S. grading standards are additional examples of widely circulated and recognized trade specifications that are available for many products.

- **Careful description of product:** Many products cannot be quickly summarized by a brand name or a trade-recognized product number. Fresh seafood, dairy products, and bakery items are among the products for which written purchase specification statements are needed.

- **Use of samples:** Samples of products currently used by an operation may serve as product specifications. Consider an establishment that produces specialized bakery products (*Exhibit 2.4*). The purchaser may investigate the possibility of buying these items ready-made, and samples may be given to possible vendors to identify the quality standards required.

Exhibit 2.4

Using product specifications has advantages for the purchaser and the operation. Detailing quality standards requires that the purchaser be very familiar with every characteristic of all products, from establishing the most important quality concerns to ensuring that the desired quality of product is available.

Vendors also benefit when product specifications are used. For example, there will be fewer communication problems from products delivered that do not meet quality requirements. Also, vendors know they are less likely to be underbid by a competitor who quotes a lower price for a lower-quality product. When vendors quote prices for products of the same quality, all vendors have a better chance of being awarded the order.

Product specifications must be updated when needs change because of evolving customer preferences and new marketplace alternatives. Also, revisions may be needed when products are used for purposes not considered when the current product specifications were developed. When specifications are used and competitive bidding systems are in place, all vendors can quote prices on the same quality of product. This helps eliminate one reason for price differences.

RECEIVING

It does little good for an operation to develop product specifications if they are not used at the time of receiving. This is the opportunity to confirm that quality standards have been met.

Experienced purchasers know they are likely to pay for the quality of products they order, even if that quality is not received. Vendors must know an operation's product specifications if they are to deliver proper quality products. However, if receiving staff do not know specifications or do not check incoming products against them, quality variations can still occur. Receiving staff must ensure that the products being received meet standards. Then the operation will receive what it paid for: an item that represents value for the organization and enables it to provide customer value.

Specification Development Responsibilities

Purchasing staff and user department staff can both assist as specifications are developed. Also, vendors can be consulted.

ROLE OF PURCHASING STAFF

Purchasers in large-volume operations can do much to help develop product specifications. They can research, communicate about, and develop these purchasing tools because those with direct operating responsibilities typically have less time for these tasks:

- They can study the exact needs for items to be described in the specifications. Effective buyers keep current by reading industry publications, meeting with vendors, and attending trade shows. They can make suggestions as product usage questions are addressed.

- They can study alternative products and vendors. Discussions with existing vendors and requests for referrals to other vendors may be helpful.

- After potential vendors are identified, purchasers can obtain information and product samples, if necessary, for evaluation.

> **Manager's Memo**
>
> Product specifications may not be required for every product purchased. They should first be developed for the relatively few items that represent the largest purchasing costs. For example, expensive meat and seafood items are normally of greater concern than inexpensive condiments and lower-cost spices, herbs, and seasonings.
>
> Purchasers working for organizations without product specifications may create a schedule for developing them. For instance, the organization may decide to create one specification every month. A scheduled approach will ensure that, over time, the organization can benefit from the use of product specifications.

- They can help evaluate current products for which specifications are being developed or revised and new products for which specifications do not exist. They can help manage taste panels with managers, employees, and even customers.
- They can develop drafts of product specifications. General information from vendors and trade organizations along with specific characteristics suggested by production staff can be useful as they do so.
- They can share drafts of proposed product specifications with vendors to obtain feedback and to ensure that the resulting specifications do not limit the number of vendors who can provide products.
- They can implement the use of product specifications.

ROLE OF EMPLOYEES

The employees in the departments that will use the products will know about their intended uses. They will also likely have suggestions about "good" and "bad" features of existing products and can identify important quality characteristics. Staff members may be able to suggest potential supply sources or may know persons in other operations who can. They can also evaluate alternative products, review early drafts of specifications, and note concerns that should be addressed with purchasing staff or with potential vendors.

ROLE OF VENDORS

Those who purchase can benefit from technical information and support provided by vendors. Vendors are experts in the products or services they provide, and their assistance as specifications are developed provides value.

Some purchasers are cautious about using vendors for specification development. They believe there is a risk in providing some confidential information such as advance notice of new menu item rollouts. Also, vendors not involved in the specification development process may believe their relationship with the property is inferior. If they choose not to bid on the products, competitive pricing benefits will be lost.

Specification Information

Those who purchase must tell vendors what they need to help ensure that the operation receives the right products. Certain quality features are commonly included in product specifications.

EXACT NAME OF ITEM

Use the exact name of the product being purchased to help ensure the correct item will be purchased, and to prevent frustration and misinterpretation for the buyer and the vendor. As previously mentioned, a specification for grapes is improved significantly if "grapes, Thompson seedless" is used to identify the product.

As a second example, consider purchasing chicken. Those who order chicken must specify the type that is needed. Choices include grilled chicken, boneless chicken, fillets, chicken wings or breasts, and whole birds, to name just a few. The buyer needing boneless, battered chicken nuggets should begin the specification with the correct name of the product. Doing so will help reduce the possibility of receiving chicken in some other market form.

INTENDED USE OF PRODUCT

The intended use describes how a product is meant to be used, developed, or consumed. It is among the most important characteristics to consider when product specifications are developed. For example, buyers may use some items that are pre-portioned and individually packaged because they are more cost-effective than purchasing the item in bulk.

For example, when breakfast is served, jelly can be portioned into open jelly dishes placed on each table. However, jelly that is not consumed must be thrown out. The use of jelly in portion-control packets, or individual servings, will allow unused packets to be re-served. In addition, the contents of an opened jar will lose quality much faster than jelly in individual packets that are not opened until consumption. Therefore, the intended use of the jelly drives its desired quality features.

PACKAGING

Packaging alternatives are just as numerous as product choices. Selection factors typically focus on the type of item, weight, preservation needs, intended use, and the amount or portion size of the item within the overall package.

As in the jelly example, product use is an important packaging concern. A quick-service restaurant will likely use individual ketchup packets, while a casual eat-in diner may place small ketchup bottles on the tables.

Packaging must consider the type of product and how fragile it is. Packaging for items such as eggs, dairy products, and other highly perishable items must protect them from loss of visual appeal, contamination, temperature abuse, moisture, and crushing while being handled or stored.

Packaging for frozen meat, poultry, and seafood must withstand the storage and transportation of very cold items. Loss of quality and food safety problems can occur when these factors are not considered. Carefully packaged products maintain their culinary quality characteristics and their appearance. They have a comparatively longer shelf life: the amount of time a product remains suitable for use.

PURCHASE UNIT SIZE

Specifications may include the required size of an item or package. Size measurements are indicated in terms of weight, volume, or count. Flour can be purchased in bags of 5, 10, 25, 50, or 100 pounds. Milk can be purchased in one-half pint (one cup), pint, quart, gallon, and 5-gallon containers. Shrimp can be purchased by count, for example, 36 to 42 shrimp per pound.

Exact weight measurements can be provided for such items as flour or rice. Weight ranges, however, for products such as a side of beef or a whole turkey are necessary. For example, a 4-ounce hamburger patty may be purchased with an allowance of $\frac{1}{4}$ ounce. This means that weights between $3\frac{7}{8}$ ounces and $4\frac{1}{8}$ ounces are acceptable. A fresh whole chicken may be purchased with a 2.5-pound weight requirement. This product may have a weight allowance of 2 ounces, or 1 ounce more or less than the 2.5-pound requirement.

GRADE

The U.S. Department of Agriculture (USDA) provides quality grading for numerous food items including beef, poultry, and eggs. Grading relates to a voluntary assessment of food against predetermined quality standards. A higher-graded product will normally cost more than a lower-graded product. *Exhibit 2.5* reviews three grading standards for beef. Inspection of meat and poultry products is generally required to ensure that these items are fit for human consumption.

The U.S. Department of Commerce offers voluntary inspection and grading services for fish, shellfish, and other fishery products.

Exhibit 2.5

U.S. GRADES OF BEEF

USDA Prime

Prime-grade beef is the ultimate in tenderness, juiciness, and flavor. It has a lot of marbling, or flecks of fat within the lean, that increases its flavor and juiciness.

USDA Choice

Choice-grade beef has less marbling than prime-grade beef but is of very high quality. Choice roasts and steaks from the loin and rib will be tender, juicy, and flavorful.

USDA Select

Select-grade beef is very uniform in quality and somewhat leaner than higher grades. It is fairly tender, but because it has less marbling, it may lack some of the juiciness and flavor of the higher grades.

MARKET FORM

Specifications should describe the desired market form of the product. For example, those who purchase carrots should specify fresh, canned, or frozen carrots, among other types available.

A market form can also address preservation needs. Purchasers may desire vacuum packaging, with no oxygen in the package that can hasten spoilage. For some applications **individually quick frozen (IQF)** products may be desired. The IQF process is mostly used with fish or fruit, and it involves blast-freezing food in individual pieces before packaging. When this method of preservation is used, the taste, texture, and nutrient values of the food items are better maintained.

COLOR

If an item is available in different colors, buyers should specify the color they desire. For example, a purchaser can choose between green beans and yellow beans, white grapes and red grapes, or white-shelled eggs and brown-shelled eggs.

In addition to how a product looks, some products taste different depending on their color. For example, most white grapes have a distinctly sweeter flavor than red grapes. Therefore, the color of grapes should be specified based on the desired flavor of the menu item in which they will be used.

PLACE OF ORIGIN

A product specification may indicate a desired place of origin. Examples include Florida oranges, California walnuts, New Zealand lamb, and Maine lobster. There are several reasons why a product's place of origin may be important:

- The texture and flavor of certain products are specific to their region of origin.
- The operation's menu may state that the item comes from a particular place.
- Purchasers may indicate that they desire products from a nearby location to help guarantee an item's quality and freshness.

ACCEPTABLE SUBSTITUTES

Some purchasers provide information on the specification that identifies acceptable substitutes for the products that were originally requested. Doing so can save time and effort by the vendor to contact the buyer if an item is unavailable.

Another advantage arises when stockouts occur at the operation, because the substitute may be more readily available. A **stockout** occurs when an item is no longer available in inventory.

Purchasers must understand the recipes in use in order to avoid purchasing unacceptable substitute items. An added expense of identifying acceptable substitutes relates to the time needed to test substitutes to ensure they are compatible with quality standards, production, and service needs.

While stockouts are never good, hastily substituting an item as a quick fix for a stockout does not solve the problem leading to the inventory shortage. Chapter 3 addresses procedures for managing the quantity of products purchased.

Finally, using substitute ingredients to prepare popular menu items may affect customers' image of the operation's quality standards. If acceptable substitutes are identified, it is always best to ensure that the item still falls well within the guidelines stated in the quality standards.

TEMPERATURE CONTROL PROCEDURES

Purchasers may specify the method of handling for a product by requesting certain temperature controls. A purchaser might, for instance, insist that all dairy products be delivered at or below 41°F (5°C) to preserve freshness and retain quality. This is important because perishable products usually deteriorate and quickly become unsafe outside certain temperature levels. As this occurs, the preparation of menu items may be affected.

Specific instructions that relate to food safety and quality are important. Meat, poultry, fish, produce, dairy, some beverages, and other perishable food categories require specific temperature controls. Temperature control procedures are critical in foodhandling. If frozen food is ordered, the food should be solidly frozen when delivered, and not even slightly thawed on the outside surfaces. After products are received, it is important to confirm that they are quickly stored to avoid problems with food safety and freshness.

Specification Format

Many hospitality organizations use a template of basic information for the products for which product specifications are developed. An example is shown in *Exhibit 2.6*.

Exhibit 2.6 notes many details normally addressed in a purchase specification. It also includes one feature less commonly included: information about the establishment's quality inspection procedures. Including product inspection procedures on the specification emphasizes that the operation is serious about making sure quality requirements are met. Employees will do so by carefully checking products as they are received.

Exhibit 2.6

SAMPLE PURCHASE SPECIFICATION FORMAT

Product name: _____ Specification no. _____

Menu item name (if applicable): _____

Product's intended use: _____

_____

General product description: _____

_____

Specific information (as applicable)

Count/portion size: _____

Grade: _____

Weight: _____

Variety, style, type, color: _____

Market form: _____

Packaging requirements: _____

Purchase unit size: _____

Place of origin: _____

Temperature control procedures: _____

Acceptable substitute: _____

_____

Other special information: _____

_____

Quality inspection procedures: _____

_____

Other requirements and general information: _____

_____

Specification implementation date: _____

Exhibit 2.7

DEVELOPING AND IMPLEMENTING PRODUCT SPECIFICATIONS

Step 1 — Determine Needed Products

Step 2 — Learn about Available Products

Step 3 — Match Specifications of Available Products with Needed Products

Step 4 — Determine Which Available Products Best Meet the Operation's Needs

Step 5 — Create Draft of Product Specification Form

Step 6 — Request Advice about Specification from Production Staff

Step 7 — Revise Specification as Needed

Step 8 — Send Specification to Potential Vendors

Step 9 — Use Specifications When Receiving Products

Developing and Implementing Specifications

Exhibit 2.7 suggests steps useful in developing and implementing specifications. The steps apply equally to products already being purchased for which no specifications exist, and to new products considered for purchase.

The following points review the steps in *Exhibit 2.7*:

Step 1. Determine needed products

Ideally, product specifications would be developed for every item in every recipe. The ingredients, then, will be located on recipe cards or in electronic files. In practice, many managers develop detailed specifications for some ingredients including those that are expensive, purchased in large quantities, perishable, or have other special control concerns. They might purchase other ingredients such as spices, baking items, and some convenience food products by brand name (which is also a specification). Still other items, such as supplies including paper goods and baked products including fresh bread and rolls, might be purchased from vendors with whom they have had experience in consistently receiving products of the proper quality.

Step 2. Learn about available products

Those with purchasing responsibility typically review available products. They do not ask manufacturers to produce special items for the operation's use, although some large-volume purchasers are able to do this. Available sources of information include samples from potential vendors, information from trade magazines and trade shows, and Internet reviews.

Step 3. Match specifications of available products with needed products

Items identified in step 2 should be reviewed against the products needed to determine which might fulfill the operation's needs. Reviews of specifications supplied by vendors are one way to do this. Production staff may also prepare small quantities of standardized recipes using potential ingredients and evaluate the results with taste tests.

Step 4. Determine which available products best meet the operation's needs

At this point, buyers should know what they need and which products best meet their needs. Discussions and decisions of production staff and managers should lead to agreement about the best specifications for products used by the operation.

Step 5. Create draft of product specification form

This step will probably need to be done only once. Most operations use the same specification format for each item. For example, consider the specification format shown in *Exhibit 2.6*. It allows buyers to provide a wide range of specific information about a desired product. However, there are probably few, if any, items for which every factor is applicable. Instead, just the important quality features for a specific item are addressed in the specification; other features are left blank for that product.

Step 6. Request advice about specification from production staff

The analysis in previous steps should have yielded a specification that accurately reflects the organization's quality standards for the product. However, further evaluation can still be helpful. Perhaps, for example, potential vendors may be asked to review the specification.

Step 7. Revise specification as needed

The careful listing and review of the specification factors should have yielded a product specification that best meets the quality needs of the operation. The document should be word-processed and carefully edited to ensure there are no errors that might create communication problems as the specification is implemented. The specification may need formal approval from the owner or higher-level manager in some establishments. If so, this step will complete the specification development process.

Step 8. Send specification to potential vendors

Those who will be asked for price quotations should receive a copy of specifications. These documents may be sent electronically, hard copies may be given to a vendor's representative, or copies may be included in a handbook given to all vendors.

Step 9. Use specifications when receiving products

Current and accurate specifications identify the quality standards required for specific products being purchased. They also help receiving staff confirm that incoming products meet quality requirements.

Exhibit 2.7 also indicates that the process of implementing product specifications is ongoing. The availability of new products, changing customer preferences, and menu revisions requiring new ingredients are all examples of times when specifications may need revision.

Manager's Memo

The product specification process described appears relatively easy. However, it is made more difficult because a single item such as tomato sauce might be used in several recipes.

A basic purchasing principle suggests that the number of different ingredients purchased should be minimized. Reasons involve available storage space, meeting minimum order requirements, and the need to purchase from different suppliers. Therefore, those developing product specifications should try to use the same products in as many recipes as possible.

However, there may be times when this cannot be done. The operation may need, for example, one size of shrimp for use in mixed seafood dishes and a larger size for shrimp cocktails. Products of more than one quality characteristic, such as size or market form, may be needed to satisfy menu requirements. However, decision makers should be challenged to minimize the use of different varieties of a single ingredient whenever possible.

MAKE-OR-BUY ANALYSIS

One of the most important projects a purchaser and his or her team can undertake is developing a make-or-buy analysis. A **make-or-buy analysis** is a study that suggests whether a product should be prepared "from scratch" on-site, or purchased as a partially or fully processed item. Determining what should be created internally versus what should be bought ready-made may seem to be a simple task. However, there are many factors to consider carefully, and the quality and cost concerns that must be studied have important impacts on the operation.

Make or Buy Responsibilities

In large organizations, full-time purchasing staff members are often responsible for make-or-buy analyses, but they must involve others in the study. In small operations without specialized purchasing assistance, make-or-buy decisions are typically made by managers, supervisors, or others in the operation.

Make-or-buy analyses are done to discover how quality and cost-of-production concerns of selected menu items can best be met. In many cases, the higher purchase costs of convenience food products are more than offset by lower labor costs. However, quality concerns are also important; convenience food items cannot be used if their quality is unacceptable.

Factors Impacting Make-or-Buy Analysis

Managers frequently are confronted by problems that must be resolved, others that would be "nice" to address, and still others causing challenges of which they are unaware. An overriding concern is always to increase value for the customer while reducing costs. However, these concerns will never be addressed if managers consider alternatives only "when they get around to it." Instead, they must continually be alert to better ways to do things. Make-or-buy analysis provides a good way to review customers' quality concerns and the property's cost concerns.

THE CASE FOR ON-SITE PRODUCTION

Numerous issues should be considered as make-or-buy decisions are made. *Exhibit 2.8* identifies some questions that might prompt a make-or-buy analysis when products are currently produced by employees.

Owners and chefs in some operations take pride in the fact that they offer unique products, and they do not want to consider convenience food substitutes. This is especially true of their **signature dishes**: menu items that customers associate with a specific operation, such as one-pound pork chops or "mile-high" pie. An establishment may be known for its tangy barbecue sauce or spicy buffalo wings. These items are not likely to be candidates for make-or-buy analysis.

Manager's Memo

Concerns about the quality and cost of preparing food on-site or using a convenience food alternative are always most important in a make-or-buy analysis. Typically, convenience food products cost more than the ingredients required to make the same product on-site if quality is the same. For example, pre-portioned hamburger patties cost more than bulk ground beef. However, when convenience food items are used, labor costs should be reduced because less preparation time is needed.

Those doing make-or-buy analysis must carefully consider all costs and must be sure that the quality of alternative products is the same or very similar.

Exhibit 2.8

QUESTIONS THAT PROMPT MAKE-OR-BUY ANALYSIS WHEN PRODUCTS ARE PRODUCED ON-SITE

- Are changes in production volumes causing staff difficulties?
- Are prices for necessary products or ingredients increasing?
- Is there an interest in increasing the variety of menu items without increasing labor costs?
- Is new (expensive) equipment necessary to continue on-site production?
- Is it difficult to maintain a consistent source of supplies?
- Is there a limited number of vendors available?
- Are alternative products available in the marketplace?
- Does purchase from an external vendor impact other items? For example, is a sauce an ingredient in several menu items?
- Is equipment or space available to store products purchased in other market forms?
- Are there concerns about returning to on-site production if convenience food products are found unacceptable?
- Will the quantities of convenience food items that might be purchased be of interest to vendors?
- Will future costs of on-site production change? If so, why and how much?

THINK ABOUT IT . . .

Some managers think the nutritional content of food is greater when items are prepared on-site rather than purchased as a convenience food.

What are factors that can reduce the nutritional content of items prepared on-site?

THE CASE FOR CONVENIENCE FOOD PRODUCTS

Some buyers find that their quality standards are easily met when purchasing convenience food products. They cite several advantages:

- **Consistency:** Convenience food items are prepared, portioned, and packaged the same way every time. Therefore, there is a consistent level of quality in each portion of product every time it is prepared.

- **Cost-effectiveness:** Convenience food products are delivered partially or completely processed (*Exhibit 2.9*). Therefore, managers can better plan and schedule labor, and the costs of highly skilled employees to prepare these items is reduced. Also, if the items are pre-portioned and prepared to order, there will be less waste and leftovers. Pre-portioned items generally have an increased edible yield, or the amount of a product that can be consumed. This means there will be a more reliable quantity of usable product available.

- **Time-effectiveness:** Convenience food products free up the time otherwise needed to supervise employees preparing and handling food. Supervisors can be more productive working to increase sales volume and improve customer relations by spending more time in dining areas.

- **Space savings:** The ability to prepare menu items with less equipment, supervision, and storage space for leftovers means possible space savings in preparation and storage areas. This freed-up space can provide more room for other purposes.

Exhibit 2.9

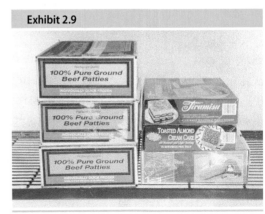

An operation is currently purchasing a convenience food product from a vendor, and the managers want to determine whether they should continue doing so. Questions to consider when this decision is made include those in *Exhibit 2.10*.

Exhibit 2.10

QUESTIONS THAT PROMPT MAKE-OR-BUY ANALYSIS WHEN CONVENIENCE FOOD PRODUCTS ARE PURCHASED FROM VENDORS

- Have product quality requirements changed?
- Have volume requirements changed?
- Are there problems with the consistency of products that are now purchased?
- Are purchase costs higher than anticipated?
- Has the operation's need for the product changed?
- Are there vendor relationship difficulties?
- Are there concerns about reversing the decision if unanticipated problems with on-site production arise?

The list of factors in *Exhibits 2.8* and *2.10* suggest two very important concerns that are part of every make-or-buy decision:

- Which alternative consistently provides the product of appropriate quality from the customers' point of view?
- Assuming equivalent (acceptable) quality, which product alternative is least expensive?

The make-or-buy analysis process discussed in the next section addresses these two questions. Experienced purchasing professionals know that careful analysis is needed. They also know that the more the decision impacts customer value and costs, the more important their decisions become.

Steps in Make-or-Buy Analysis

Exhibit 2.11 previews the make-or-buy analysis process. It consists of 10 steps.

Before discussing *Exhibit 2.11*, remember that the quality of convenience food items must be assessed before their costs are determined. In fact, the first six steps in the exhibit relate to quality aspects of the decision, and only two steps (7 and 8) directly concern cost aspects. This reinforces a point made earlier: Make-or-buy analysis is not a decision about cost alone. Instead, it is a decision about quality and costs. It does little good to determine the costs of product alternatives if the product cannot be used because of unacceptable quality.

Now *Exhibit 2.11* can be reviewed in detail:

Step 1. Determine need

Need relates in part to intended use. However, it can also relate to the quantity of product needed. For example, if a new menu item will be available during a short holiday period, significant time to undertake a make-or-buy analysis may not be cost-effectively spent.

Step 2. Assess quality requirements

How should the quality of the product prepared by employees be described? What type, quality, and amount of ingredients are used? What is the portion size? What are the most important factors suggesting the need for a make-or-buy analysis? This step is critical because the result should be a product description that provides a product standard against which to evaluate alternatives. If desired quality cannot be described, it cannot be measured or evaluated in step 5.

Step 3. Identify possible supply sources

Employees may know about possible vendors, and purchasers may have collected information about alternate supply sources. Managers may learn about potential vendors as they visit trade shows, review trade magazines, and discuss challenges with current vendors. Also, Internet searches are an easy way to identify potential sources.

Step 4. Request and receive product samples

Potential vendors of the convenience food product being considered should be informed that the establishment is considering a purchase. When detailed information about the desired product or service is provided (steps 1 and 2), it is easier for potential vendors to assess whether their products might be

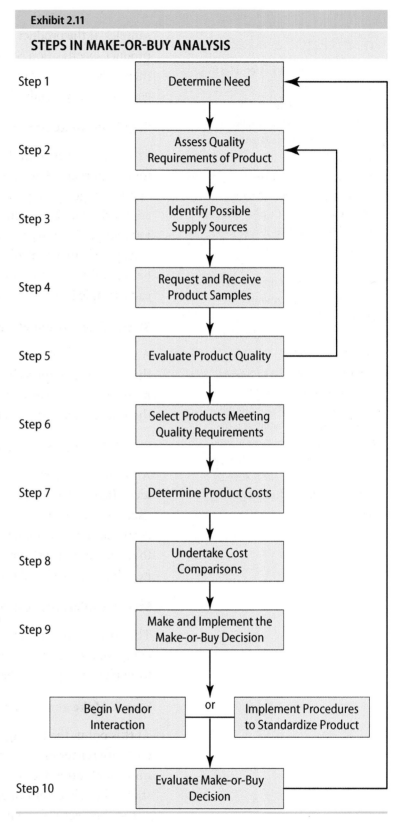

Exhibit 2.11

STEPS IN MAKE-OR-BUY ANALYSIS

Step 1 — Determine Need

Step 2 — Assess Quality Requirements of Product

Step 3 — Identify Possible Supply Sources

Step 4 — Request and Receive Product Samples

Step 5 — Evaluate Product Quality

Step 6 — Select Products Meeting Quality Requirements

Step 7 — Determine Product Costs

Step 8 — Undertake Cost Comparisons

Step 9 — Make and Implement the Make-or-Buy Decision

Begin Vendor Interaction — or — Implement Procedures to Standardize Product

Step 10 — Evaluate Make-or-Buy Decision

useful. Purchasers should know their organization's policies about product samples. If the product will replace one currently produced, the applicable product specification should be provided. If the item will be new to the menu, the purchaser may request samples of alternative products that meet general quality standard requirements.

Step 5. Evaluate product quality

Product samples should be evaluated using the item currently produced for comparison. A team of food-production and purchasing staff, food and beverage managers, and service staff might participate in taste comparisons. Customers may be given samples and asked their opinion. Large organizations considering large-volume purchases may use formal taste panels in a controlled environment. When alternative products are being evaluated, "blind-tasting" helps ensure the brand or the vendor for each sample is unknown during the evaluation.

Step 6. Select products meeting quality requirements

A formal evaluation of product alternatives (step 5) will identify those that meet the property's quality requirements (step 2). It is then necessary to determine the costs of acceptable products and to compare them with items produced on-site.

Step 7. Determine product costs

All significant costs incurred as the item is produced should be identified. What is significant? The cost of utilities needed for an oven used to bake bread may be easy or difficult to determine. Also, these costs may or may not be considered significant. A good rule of thumb is to determine the estimated cost for all expenses incurred to produce an item if it is considered practical (cost-effective and reasonable) to do so.

Step 8. Undertake cost comparisons

The costs for purchasing and preparing a required product should be compared. If the previous steps have been followed, it will be an "apples-to-apples" comparison based on products of equal quality.

Step 9. Make and implement the make-or-buy decision

At this point, the manager or planning team will know the quality and cost differences of the products being evaluated. While these are important, other factors must also be considered. Undependable vendors should have been eliminated in step 3. However, service factors are part of the "big picture" evaluation. Further interaction with the selected vendor will be necessary if a "buy" decision is made. Alternatively, for a "make" decision, procedures must be implemented to ensure that products purchased for on-site production are standardized.

Step 10. Evaluate make-or-buy decision

Exhibit 2.12

Was the decision to produce or buy the product a good one? The phrase "only time will tell" may be relevant to answering this question. Situations that impact the decision do change. As suggested in *Exhibit 2.11,* the make-or-buy process may need to be repeated in the future.

Example of Make-or-Buy Analysis

The make-or-buy analysis process involves many details about quality. However, there is more to be said about costing concerns, using an example of a potential food product purchase.

The Chef's Broiler Restaurant serves a broad variety of grilled items including its famous chef's quarter-pound burger with a selection of gourmet sauces. Currently, bulk ground beef is purchased, and a food-production employee pre-portions the ground beef into quarter-pound portions.

The purchaser has discovered that a ground beef product of the same quality can be purchased already portioned into quarter-pound patties (*Exhibit 2.12*). However, the price per pound is higher than the price currently being paid for bulk ground beef.

A make-or-buy analysis is done using the information in *Exhibit 2.13* on the next page to determine which of the products of equal quality is the least expensive.

When reviewing *Exhibit 2.13,* notice that the purchaser first determined in part A a total ground beef cost of $168.96 for the bulk ground beef currently being purchased. Next the purchaser determined the total labor cost including the hourly rate and benefit percentage for the employee portioning the ground beef into patties: $35.86. Finally, the purchaser determined a total food and labor cost of $204.52 for the 175 hamburger patties that were prepared and sold each day.

Next, in part B, the purchaser determined a total ground beef cost of $186.56 that was incurred to purchase the convenience food ground beef patty. Although the purchase price per pound of $4.24 for the convenience food product was higher than the purchaser cost per pound of $3.84 for the product currently being purchased, the total cost per portion was less.

In part C, the purchaser compared the cost per portion for each alternative and determined that it was $0.10 per portion less to buy the convenience food portion ($1.17 for the bulk ground beef patty −$1.07 for the cost of the convenience food portion). The purchaser then, in parts D, E, and F, determined the savings that would result from purchasing the convenience product for a day, each week, and for an entire year.

Exhibit 2.13

MAKE-OR-BUY ANALYSIS FOR BULK AND PATTY GROUND BEEF

Part A: Cost of On-Site Preparation

- 175 4-oz (AP) hamburgers per day
- Ground beef cost: $3.84 per pound (10-pound polyvinyl package is $38.40)
- Preparation labor time: 2.25 hours (includes making patties and work station setup and cleanup of all preparation trays, utensils, and the work station)
- Preparation labor costs: $12.85 per hour + 23% benefits
- Food cost:

16 oz	÷	4 oz	=	4
(oz in pound)		Portion size		No. patties per pound

175	÷	4	=	44 (rounded)
No. of hamburgers sold		No. of patties per pound		No. of pounds of ground beef needed

44	×	$3.84	=	$168.96
No. of pounds of ground beef sold		Cost per pound of ground beef		Total ground beef cost

- Labor costs:

2.25	×	$12.85	=	$28.91
No. of labor hours		Hourly wage rate		Total wage

$28.91	×	0.23	=	$6.65
Total wage		Benefits %		Total benefits

$28.91	+	$6.65	=	$35.56
Total wage		Total benefits		Total labor cost

- Total cost (175 hamburgers):

$168.96	+	$35.56	=	$204.52
Total food cost		Total labor cost		Total hamburger cost

- Per-portion hamburger cost:

$204.52	÷	175	=	$1.17 (rounded)
Total hamburger cost		No. of hamburgers		Per portion hamburger cost

Part B: Cost of Convenience Food Alternative

- 175 4-oz (AP) hamburgers per day
- Ground beef cost: $4.24 per pound (10-pound box is $42.40)
- Number of hamburgers per pound (see part A): 4
- Number of pounds of ground beef needed (see part A): 44 pounds (rounded)
- Food cost:

44	×	$4.24	=	$186.56
No. of pounds of ground beef needed		Cost per pound of ground beef		Total ground beef cost

- Per-portion hamburger cost:

$186.56	÷	175	=	$1.07 (rounded)
Total food cost		No. of hamburgers		Per portion hamburger cost

Part C: Per-Portion Cost Comparison

$1.17	−	$1.07	=	$0.10
Cost of on-site prepared hamburger portion		Cost of convenience food portion		Per-portion cost difference

Part D: Daily Per-Portion Cost Difference

$0.10	×	175	=	$17.50
Per-portion cost difference		No. of hamburgers sold per day		Daily per-portion cost difference

Part E: Weekly Per-Portion Cost

$17.50	×	7	=	$122.50
Daily per-portion cost difference		Days in week		Weekly per-portion cost difference

Part F: Annual Per-Portion Cost Difference

$122.50	×	52	=	$6,370.00
Weekly per-portion cost difference		Weeks in year		Annual per-portion cost difference

Manager's Memo

It has been said that "You can't bank a paper savings." In *Exhibit 2.13*, the purchaser estimated an annual savings of approximately $6,370 when the pre-portioned hamburger patties were purchased. However, several assumptions were made:

- The cost of bulk ground beef
- The cost of the pre-portioned patties
- Employee labor costs including benefits
- The time required to pre-portion the bulk ground beef

If any assumptions are wrong or change, the numbers supporting the decision also change. Careful study is required for make-or-buy analysis, and an ongoing review of conditions that impact the results is important.

Since the quality of both product alternatives was acceptable, the purchaser probably makes the decision to buy a convenience food product. However, he or she knows that these savings will never be realized unless the labor hours for the preparation cook are reduced by the 2.25 hours of production labor that were used in the analysis.

Implementing Make-or-Buy Decisions

Completing a make-or-buy analysis is not difficult. However, since savings on paper do not always equal actual savings, managers must "work their assumptions." In other words, they must do what they said they would do when they decided how to calculate the costs. There are sometimes differences between what the make-or-buy analysis assumes and actual practices used after the decision is implemented.

Consider, for example, a make-or-buy analysis that determines that labor costs will be saved if pre-portioned hamburger patties are purchased. The manager or buyer has calculated the number of labor hours, labor costs, and benefits used to prepare the patties. These labor-related costs will no longer be needed because the product will be purchased in a pre-portioned market form.

Pre-portioned hamburger patties of the same quality as the bulk-purchased beef will likely be more expensive. Will labor hours be reduced to make up for the higher purchase costs? If so, the savings suggested by the make-or-buy analysis may occur, and the total costs can be reduced. However, if the cooks' schedules are not revised to reduce labor hours, two things will happen. First, the food costs will be higher because a more expensive market form of ground beef will be purchased. Second, the labor costs will remain the same. The result will be higher operating costs using the pre-portioned patties even though the analysis suggested that the costs would be lower.

As a second example, specialized equipment might be purchased to reduce the labor hours needed to portion patties of beef purchased in bulk. Since equipment costs will increase, this cost must be more than offset by the reduced labor cost. If labor hours are not reduced, equipment costs will be higher, labor costs will remain the same, and the financial impact of the make-or-buy analysis will be more harmful than helpful.

Experienced buyers ensure that all practical details are addressed when a make-or-buy analysis is performed. This will result in a reduced chance of surprises when the decision is implemented. Resistance to change, and some employee's tendencies to defend how things are currently done, represent aspects of make-or-buy decisions that are difficult to consider during the analysis.

However, these employee-related issues can cause significant challenges when decisions are implemented. The best approach is to ask for input from affected employees, including those who will be working with revised products or work methods. First, their input can be helpful. Second, their "buy-in" may reduce the resistance to change that is otherwise possible.

THINK ABOUT IT . . .

Assume you were a cook and you prepared shrimp for cooking. The manager has decided to purchase ready-to-cook shrimp and cut your hours.

How would you want to be told about this?

52

Evaluating Make-or-Buy Decisions

Step 10 in *Exhibit 2.11* indicates that make-or-buy decisions should be evaluated. This is easier to do when objective information is available. For example, the number of labor hours saved and the reduced labor costs that result from an analysis can be measured. In contrast, a make-or-buy analysis might be undertaken to "make customers more satisfied" or "keep employees happy." How can these objectives be measured? How can the manager know if, for example, the decision to purchase convenience food was worth the cost? This cannot be determined because a specific value cannot be placed on customer or employee satisfaction.

Systems to track information needed for make-or-buy analysis are frequently not in place. Operations do not typically track the amount of time required to process a case of lettuce, nor would managers know the time needed to portion bulk ground beef into patties. Instead, the times required for these tasks would probably have to be assessed just to develop information needed for the make-or-buy analysis.

It is difficult to evaluate the effectiveness of make-or-buy decisions when special procedures are needed to do so. For example, should a cook be asked to keep track of the time needed to chop lettuce? Should the purchaser, chef, or a manager assume this responsibility?

It is important to evaluate the results of a make-or-buy analysis such as wage or food cost changes. New equipment, revised work processes, and the availability of new market forms of food are examples of factors that can make an analysis out of date.

Busy buyers and managers may, at least subjectively, evaluate changes resulting from a make-or-buy analysis immediately and for a short time afterward. After a relatively short time, however, the new product or process will become the accepted way that things are done.

SUMMARY

1. **Explain the importance of consistently purchasing products of the proper quality, and describe how the establishment of quality standards is an important first step in defining quality needs.**

   Quality relates to the intended use of a product or service. The better a product can do what it is supposed to do, the better its quality.

   Quality is important because customers demand it as they look for value while dining out. Quality standards identify and communicate product requirements to vendors. They are developed in recognition of what the establishment is trying to do to best serve customers. Quality standards are developed by carefully considering what customers want and exploring ways to incorporate these quality needs into products purchased.

OPEN FOR BUSINESS

RESTAURANT TECHNOLOGY

In the past, managers undertaking a make-or-buy analysis had at least two time-consuming tasks: They had to determine alternative supply sources and assess other information required for quality and cost comparisons.

Today buyers can use technology to obtain information needed for make-or-buy decisions. The Internet can be used to research suppliers carrying a wide range of products from frozen desserts to hard-to-find ingredients for regional specialty dishes. Buyers wanting to review and revise recipes have access to numerous electronic recipe sources.

After make-or-buy decisions are made, product inventory assessments, ordering, receiving management, invoice processing, and related tasks can be managed electronically for items to be purchased. Procedures to purchase products and services are increasingly automated. This gives buyers more time for creative decision making.

2. **Explain the role of properly constructed product specifications in communicating product quality needs to vendors, and tell how product specifications are developed and implemented.**

Product specifications indicate the required characteristics of the products buyers want to purchase. They are used to communicate quality requirements and ensure that competitive bids are based on products of the same quality. They are also used to help confirm that the quality of products ordered is the same as products received.

Specifications should be developed by a team consisting of those who purchase and use the products. Information on a specification may include the product's exact name, its intended use, packaging and purchase unit information, grade, and market form. Other information may include color, place of origin, temperature control and, if desired, acceptable substitutes.

A process can be used to develop product specifications. Steps include determining needed products, learning about available products, and matching specifications of available products with needed products. Then it is important to determine which products best meet the operation's needs, create a specification draft, and request advice about the specification from production staff. Finally, the specification development team should revise the specification as needed, seek approval if the establishment requires it, send the specification to vendors, and use them as an important part of the purchasing process.

3. **State the importance of make-or-buy analysis, and describe how the process should be done.**

A make-or-buy analysis helps managers decide whether a product should be prepared on-site or purchased as a partially or fully processed item. Generally, the purchase price of a convenience food is higher than "from scratch" ingredients. However, this price may be offset by reduced labor costs. Determining the cost of both alternatives is an objective of make-or-buy analysis.

There are two primary concerns in a make-or-buy analysis. The first and most important relates to equal quality. After quality concerns are addressed, costs for each alternative become important.

There are 10 basic steps in a make-or-buy analysis. The need for a specific product must be determined and its quality requirements defined. Then possible supply sources should be identified, and vendors should provide samples. The samples are evaluated and those meeting quality requirements are selected. The cost of these products should be determined, cost-per-portion comparisons with on-site preparation should be undertaken, and then the make-or-buy decision can be made. Once implemented, its effectiveness should be evaluated to ensure that critical assumptions of the analysis are put into practice.

APPLICATION EXERCISE

You are the manager and purchaser for an independently owned quick-service restaurant that specializes in burgers. You must update the product specifications for ketchup, cheese, tomatoes, and hamburger meat. Use the purchase specification format shown in *Exhibit 2.6* and the discussion of specification factors that precedes it. Consider the factors that should be included in a purchase specification for each item. Complete one copy of the specification for each of the four ingredients. Consider how to explain your decisions to the owner.

REVIEW YOUR LEARNING

Select the best answer for each question.

1. **What is the best definition of quality?**
   A. Appropriateness for product use
   B. A lower price than similar products
   C. A higher price than similar products
   D. Favorable comparison with other products

2. **What must a purchaser know in order to determine the quality of a product?**
   A. The approved vendor
   B. Its purchase cost
   C. Its intended use
   D. The storage life

3. **Which type of purchaser is concerned about the relationship between price and quality as purchasing decisions are made?**
   A. Price-conscious
   B. Value-conscious
   C. Quality-conscious
   D. Availability-conscious

4. **What document implements an operation's quality standards?**
   A. Purchase specification
   B. Request for proposal
   C. Grading assessment
   D. Purchase order

5. **What is an advantage to using a brand for a purchase specification?**
   A. Every vendor will carry it.
   B. It is quick and easy to write.
   C. Product prices will be lower.
   D. It will never need to be revised.

6. **Why do receiving staff use product specifications?**
   A. To confirm that product prices are correct.
   B. To determine that quality requirements are met.
   C. To determine that the vendor delivered correct products.
   D. To confirm that products are at the correct purchase price.

7. **What item is commonly found in a product specification?**
   A. Market form
   B. Purchase price
   C. Quantity in inventory
   D. Vendor supplying product

8. **What must first be determined when doing a make-or-buy analysis?**
   A. Product inventories
   B. Product availability
   C. Product quality
   D. Product cost

9. **Why is it often difficult to evaluate make-or-buy decisions?**

    A. Systems to collect information are not in place.

    B. Most managers do not think it necessary to do so.

    C. Vendors typically do not provide necessary information.

    D. Technology is not available to make the process manageable.

10. **What should be done if a make-or-buy analysis indicates two labor hours daily can be reduced with a convenience food product, and the decision is implemented because the money should be saved?**

    A. Increase labor hours in another department.

    B. Use the kitchen labor hours for another purpose.

    C. Eliminate the two labor hours from the schedule.

    D. Schedule the hours in case estimates were wrong.

FIELD PROJECT

Quality of alternative products is the first concern when undertaking a make-or-buy analysis. This exercise will help you learn how to assess the quality of two different products.

Purchase two different types of bottled blue cheese dressing. Conduct a taste test of both dressings with classmates, family members, and/or friends using the Salad Dressing Evaluation Form provided.

Step A

For a blind-tasting, make one copy of the evaluation form (part A) for each person who will do the evaluation. Use a blind-tasting method: Place some of each dressing in a white or neutral-colored bowl on a saucer and label each saucer "dressing #1" or "dressing #2." Then ask each evaluator to complete a copy of the evaluation form. Do not tell the evaluators the names of each dressing until they have finished the taste testing.

Step B

After the evaluation is completed, you can complete part B of the evaluation. Do this for each evaluator:

1. Count the number of "Poor" evaluations (column 1), and multiply that number by 1.

2. Count the number of "OK" evaluations (column 2), and multiply that number by 2.

3. Count the number of "Excellent" evaluations (column 3), and multiply that by number 3.

4. Add the total number of points to determine the score given by the evaluator for dressing #1. Repeat the process for dressing #2.

Step C

Finally, complete part C of the evaluation form. Transfer the total points from each evaluator for dressing #1 and dressing #2 to the "Total Points" column in part C. Total the points given by all evaluators for each dressing to determine the grand total points for each dressing.

Step D

The final part of the evaluation form is part D. Which salad dressing is best? Make a decision about the best salad dressing based on the objective information (number of points) in part C of the form. You should also consider the comments provided by each evaluator (also in part A).

A. Salad Dressing Evaluation Form (Chapter 2)

Evaluation date: _____   Evaluator name: _____

Instructions: Check the box that represents your analysis of each factor.

	Dressing #1 Your Analysis			Dressing #2 Your Analysis		
	Poor	OK	Excellent	Poor	OK	Excellent
Evaluation Factor	**(1)**	**(2)**	**(3)**	**(1)**	**(2)**	**(3)**
Color	❑	❑	❑	❑	❑	❑
Texture	❑	❑	❑	❑	❑	❑
Taste	❑	❑	❑	❑	❑	❑
Aroma	❑	❑	❑	❑	❑	❑
General appeal	❑	❑	❑	❑	❑	❑
Overall summary	❑	❑	❑	❑	❑	❑

Comments:

B. Student Analysis

Evaluator name: _____

Dressing #1

No. of "Poor" evaluations: _____ $\times$ 1 = _____

No. of "OK" evaluations: _____ $\times$ 2 = _____

No. of "Excellent" evaluations: _____ $\times$ 3 = _____

Total Points: _____

Dressing #2

No. of "Poor" evaluations: _____ $\times$ 1 = _____

No. of "OK" evaluations: _____ $\times$ 2 = _____

No. of "Excellent" evaluations: _____ $\times$ 3 = _____

Total Points: _____

C. Dressing Evaluation Summary

Evaluator Name	**Dressing #1 Total Points**	**Dressing #2 Total Points**
1. _____	_____	_____
2. _____	_____	_____
3. _____	_____	_____
4. _____	_____	_____
5. _____	_____	_____
Grand Total Points	_____	**Grand Total Points** _____

D. Which salad dressing is best? Why?

3

Purchase Quantity Requirements

INSIDE THIS CHAPTER

- Importance of Purchase Quantities
- Factors Affecting Purchase Quantities
- Forecasting Purchase Quantities
- Effect of Product Yields on Purchase Quantities
- Determining Quantities to Order
- Nontraditional Methods for Determining Quantities

CHAPTER LEARNING OBJECTIVES

After completing this chapter, you should be able to:

- Explain why purchasers must carefully consider the quantities of products to purchase.

- List important factors that affect the quantity of products purchased.

- State procedures helpful in forecasting product needs.

- Explain how product yields affect purchase quantities.

- Describe traditional systems used to calculate purchase quantities.

- Identify and discuss two nontraditional purchasing methods that impact the quantities of products to be purchased.

KEY TERMS

CASE STUDY

"If you like new problems every day, this is the place to work," Leron said to Brandon. The cooks at Joliet Palace Resort were complaining about the new manager.

"I like challenges," Brandon replied, "if they can be resolved. Whatever we suggest will never be accepted."

Leron added, "What manager buys a lot of products if they are on sale and very few if not? The menu requires certain quantities. We can prepare items only when we have the ingredients. Thinking of other items to serve creates a lot of stress."

"We need a purchasing system that gives us the products we need to prepare menu items," Brandon said.

1. In addition to not being able to produce menu items, what other problems might arise when products are not available?

2. If you were the manager, what procedures might you use to ensure that the correct quantity of products is always ordered?

IMPORTANCE OF PURCHASE QUANTITIES

Most restaurant and foodservice operations have a menu that requires the same products to be purchased again and again. One possible exception might be a catering business where the only revenue source is special events that require special menus. Even these operations typically offer preplanned menu suggestions that feature items used in the past. They often have inventories of nonperishable products for the preplanned menus.

There is a relationship between the number of forecasted customers and production requirements. There is also a relationship between product inventory levels and the quantities that must be purchased to meet production needs.

Buyers typically use different procedures to determine necessary purchase quantities for different products. Highly perishable items such as fresh dairy products and produce, for example, are typically purchased in amounts that can be used within several days. In contrast, frozen, dry, and canned food items can be purchased in amounts that will last several weeks or longer. Other products, such as cleaning supplies and paper goods, can be purchased in quantities that will last for months or even longer if a purchaser wishes.

Excessive Quantities

Several problems can arise when products are purchased in larger quantities than necessary:

- Large purchases impact cash flow. Products in inventory for long periods must be paid for before they are used. These payments require cash that could be used for other purposes.
- Buying ahead can impact flexibility. Purchasers may be less interested in taking advantage of special discounts when ample quantities are already on hand.
- More space must be available to store the extra products.
- There is an increased risk of employee theft, or pilferage which is stealing small quantities of products over a relatively long time period.
- The quality of perishable products may be decreased.
- There is an increased risk of product damage or destruction.
- Handling costs increase. For example, more time is required to conduct inventories and to perform storage cleaning duties if products must be moved.

Are excessive inventory quantities ever acceptable? Ideally, the answer is no. However, more products may need to be purchased if managers do not use effective forecasting procedures. Also, additional products may be needed if deliveries are frequently late or when shortages occur. Effective customer forecasting and vendor selection can reduce these problems and allow purchasers to maintain proper inventory levels (*Exhibit 3.1*).

Exhibit 3.1

Inadequate Quantities

Inadequate purchase quantities can lead to stockouts that create several problems:

- An inability to meet production requirements
- The need to revise production plans to compensate for stockouts
- The possibility of disappointed customers who may visit just to enjoy a favorite item that is unavailable

Problems arise when there are too many or too few products available in inventory. Both of these problems occur when the proper quantity is not ordered.

FACTORS AFFECTING PURCHASE QUANTITIES

Most buyers do not order each item in their inventory when it reaches an ideal order point. They would not, for example, order canned green beans on Wednesday and canned peaches on Friday because these are the ideal times.

They do not place separate orders for each product because of the extra time it would take to make contact with vendors and decide from whom to purchase. Costs would also increase because of the wages paid to employees to do these tasks and because of the expenses involved with processing additional invoices for payment. Placing a lot of separate orders means there would likely be many deliveries from many suppliers each day. The time needed for purchasing, receiving, and related processing costs would be excessive, and the inventory counts of each product would need to be ongoing.

Instead, items are typically divided into several product categories, and all or most products of one type are ordered at the same time. For example, all fresh produce, fresh meat, and dairy products may be grouped into their specific categories. Then orders are planned for all items in these categories at the same time. The same vendor is often selected to supply all products needed in a specific category. This likely means that the quantity of each product ordered will be greater or less than the amount that would have been purchased for just that product at the ideal time.

THINK ABOUT IT . . .

A vendor is changing product lines and wants to sell some frozen shrimp. You normally pay $10.55 per pound. The vendor offers the same shrimp for $7.75 a pound. You have available freezer space.

What would you do?

Manager's Memo

Nontraditional purchasing systems do not always consider the quantity of products to be shipped to an operation on a single delivery. Some systems consider the total quantity of products the purchaser will commit to buy over longer time periods. For example, products may be delivered over many months on a frequent, even daily, basis to minimize storage and other inventory management problems.

These systems require purchasers to think about purchase quantities in a new way. The quantity of product committed to and delivery frequency become separate negotiation concerns. Purchase quantities, then, do not necessarily refer to the amount of product to be delivered at one time for prompt use.

Managers must consider inventory safety levels when ordering quantities of products. The inventory safety level is the amount of a given item that should be available at all times. There are several reasons why a carefully determined safety level should be maintained:

- To ensure that products are available if vendor delivery schedules are not maintained
- To reduce the impact of incorrect production forecasting that results in greater customer counts than expected
- To enable replacement of products that may be found unusable
- To help deal with miscounts in the quantities of products actually available
- To provide a cushion against product theft or pilferage

These concerns are valid. However, managers should develop systems to reduce these kinds of problems. Then inventory safety levels will not need to be excessively large, and cost, storage, and lowered quality will not need to be addressed.

Several other concerns may be important when purchase quantities are determined:

- **Minimum orders:** Many vendors specify that a minimum dollar value of products must be delivered in each order to make the cost of delivery worthwhile.
- **Expected changes in price:** When product prices are increasing, purchasers may buy in larger quantities to reduce the need to purchase additional quantities at higher prices. Conversely, when market prices are decreasing, buyers may purchase in smaller quantities. This will allow them to take advantage of lower prices on future purchases.
- **Products on sale:** Larger quantities may be purchased when, for example, vendors or manufacturers offer close-outs. This is a strategy used by vendors or manufacturers to quickly sell unwanted inventory by reducing prices. Examples include short-term promotional discounts to introduce new products or to sell products with outdated packaging.
- **Trial orders and samples:** Small quantities of products may be ordered when new menu items are being considered. A proposed item might, for example, be offered as a "daily special" on several occasions to assess customer interest.
- **Parts and supplies being discontinued:** Items related to equipment being discontinued by the manufacturer may be purchased in a large quantity. Doing so will expand the useful life of the equipment. It also makes financial sense because, if available, these items will likely need to be purchased from other sources in the future.

FORECASTING PURCHASE QUANTITIES

Most methods used to determine the quantities of food products to purchase consider production needs. As more menu items are produced for more customers, inventory levels are depleted, and additional quantities must be purchased. The food purchasing methods described in this chapter are directly or indirectly driven by forecasts, or estimates, of business volumes.

There are some exceptions to the relationship between production and purchasing volumes. Consider, for example, the custodial supplies used to clean public spaces (*Exhibit 3.2*). These areas must be cleaned frequently without regard to the number of customers. Exterior window cleaning and parking lot maintenance supplies are also purchases that typically depend on other factors.

Wise purchasers understand that the inventory levels for these nonperishable products are still important. However, judgment errors will not result in the waste that occurs when perishable products must be thrown out.

The method used to make an accurate production forecast is relatively straightforward. Managers can track **sales histories**, or the number of each specific menu item that is sold. They make adjustments for factors that will likely impact sales in the future. They can then use this information to estimate customer counts for future periods. With this forecast, they can determine the quantities of products that must be ordered.

Manual Forecasting Systems

Traditionally, and in some operations today, forecasting calculations are done manually. A manager can forecast the number of customers, the number of each menu item to produce based on likely purchases, or the amount of revenue anticipated for a specific time period.

Learning to make accurate production forecasts is a critical management skill. A production forecast is important because it tells managers how many of each menu item will likely be sold. If this is known, managers will know how much of each ingredient must be on hand. Managers cannot predict exact sales for any future period. Their production forecasts can, however, realistically estimate the number of menu items they will sell. To create an accurate production forecast, managers use information from the past, present, and future.

PAST SALES TRENDS

What has happened in the past is often a good indicator of what is likely to happen in the future. The further back past sales can be tracked, the more accurate forecasts will be. For example, a manager who knows the number of

Exhibit 3.2

Manager's Memo

Vendors can offer service and information that impacts a purchaser's decision about the quantity of products to order. When vendors do this, purchasers gain value in their relationship with the vendors.

For example, purchasers will not know about close-out specials unless they are informed. They cannot take advantage of trial orders or obtain samples unless their vendors allow these typically costly requests. Rigid definitions of minimum orders for delivery may be flexible in some instances. Vendors may share advance information about potential changes in market prices with purchasers who keep up with changing market conditions.

Purchasers should ask vendors about how they can save purchase dollars without reducing quality. The answers they receive may be surprising and very useful.

steak sandwiches sold on each of the past 25 Thursdays can more accurately forecast the number to be sold this Thursday than if he only had information about last Thursday. Estimates of the quantities of menu items to be sold are used to determine the quantity of food to purchase.

Modern point-of-sale (POS) systems allow managers to keep excellent records of menu item sales. Some types of historical sales data are useful when forecasting future sales:

- The prior day's sales
- The average achieved sales for the prior five *same* days (for example, Sundays or Tuesdays)
- The prior week's average daily sales
- The prior two weeks' average daily sales
- The prior month's average daily sales
- The actual sales achieved on the same day for the prior month or year

Exhibit 3.3 shows a typical historical menu item sales report that can be generated by a POS system. This report can help managers estimate the number of specific menu items they should expect to sell on a specific day.

Exhibit 3.3

MENU ITEM SALES HISTORY FOR: MONDAY, JANUARY 2

Menu Item	Last Monday Sales	Average Prior Five Monday Sales	Average Daily Sales Last Week	Average Daily Sales Last Month
Sirloin Steak	28	25	22	23
Perch	12	13	14	13
Pork Chops	15	18	14	16
Fried Chicken	39	34	36	31
Lasagna	49	51	46	53

CURRENT SALES TRENDS

Past sales trends should always be compared with the most recent trends. For example, a manager knows that for the past eight months, revenues have increased 3 percent each month over the same period last year. However, in the last two months, the increase has been closer to zero. This may suggest that the revenue increase trend has slowed or even stopped. Good managers always modify historical trends by closely examining current conditions. Other factors that can impact current sales trends include weather predictions, holidays, and activities in the area. Weather impacts customers' interests in and abilities to visit dining establishments, and more people typically dine out on holidays and when there are activities in the area.

FUTURE SALES TRENDS

The evaluation of possible future conditions is also important when developing sales forecasts. Examples include the opening of new competitive establishments, specially featured menu items and planned promotions, and significant changes in operating hours. Local media and trade or business associations, including the chamber of commerce, are sources of information about circumstances that could affect sales. For example, these sources will likely know when groups of out-of-town visitors will be attending meetings in the area.

PUTTING IT ALL TOGETHER

When all past, current, and future sales trends have been evaluated, managers can make accurate production forecasts. An example of a report that provides this information is shown in *Exhibit 3.4*. This report expands on *Exhibit 3.3* to include the manager's estimates of the number of each menu item that will be sold on one day (Monday, January 2). The estimates are based on historical sales information adjusted by current information such as activities in the area and holidays during the production period.

Exhibit 3.4

MENU ITEM PRODUCTION FORECAST FOR: MONDAY, JANUARY 2

Menu Item	Last Monday Sales	Average Prior Five Monday Sales	Average Daily Sales Last Week	Average Daily Sales Last Month	PRODUCTION FORECAST FOR: Monday, January 2
Sirloin Steak	28	25	22	23	29
Perch	12	13	14	13	14
Pork Chops	15	18	14	16	19
Fried Chicken	39	34	36	33	44
Lasagna	49	51	46	53	54

Note that the manager has considered all available data and then, in the last column, has estimated the number of each item that should be prepared on the specific date. The sales information reviewed in *Exhibit 3.4* is for only one day, Monday, January 2. Past, current, and future sales information for the remaining six days in the week should be developed as well. The manager can then develop a weekly forecast such as that shown in *Exhibit 3.5*. This report summarizes the production forecasts, such as the last column in *Exhibit 3.4*, for the following week.

Exhibit 3.5

WEEKLY PRODUCTION FORECAST FOR: JANUARY 2–JANUARY 8

Menu Item	Monday Jan. 2	Tuesday Jan. 3	Wednesday Jan. 4	Thursday Jan. 5	Friday Jan. 6	Saturday Jan. 7	Sunday Jan. 8
Sirloin Steak	29	28	30	35	55	55	25
Perch	14	15	17	20	35	35	10
Pork Chops	19	20	20	25	35	40	15
Fried Chicken	44	40	40	45	55	55	40
Lasagna	54	55	55	55	65	65	50

After the production forecast for the entire week is developed, the manager can use it for three purposes:

- To determine the amount of each ingredient that must be in inventory to prepare the forecasted number of menu items.

- To inform cooks about the number of items that should be prepared.

- To schedule production employees. When schedules are developed, the forecast of meals is often converted into revenue dollars. This is done by multiplying the total number of menu items by their selling prices to determine total revenues.

MENU ITEM POPULARITY INDEX

Manual systems can also generate additional specific information that is useful to some managers. For example, they might wish to know the menu item popularity index, or the percentage of customers likely to order specific menu items. This detailed information makes it easy to determine purchase quantities.

Consider the following example:

- Forecasted number of customers during evening meal periods next week based on previous five weeks = 670

- Percentage of customers who ordered steak entrée based on sales records for last five weeks = 9 percent

- Estimated number of steak entrées to be purchased by evening meal customers next week = 60 (670 forecasted customers × 0.09 steak purchase percentage = 60 steaks sales estimate)

In this example, the forecast for customers served in the next week, the order period for steaks, is 670. That estimate is based on the average number of customers during the evening meal period for the past five weeks. Since no out-of-the-ordinary events are anticipated that will affect customer counts, the base of 670 customers is used.

Sales trend information also reveals that approximately 9 percent of evening meal customers order the steak entrée. Therefore, the estimated number of steak entrée portions, 60, is easily determined. This process can be repeated to calculate the number of other entrée portions to be ordered. Managers can use a spreadsheet program to make the calculations quickly.

With forecasts of production needs for menu items, purchasing staff have basic information for making effective purchase quantity decisions. However, the buyer still must answer one question: How does the current amount of product in inventory affect the quantity that must be purchased?

If products needed are typically ordered based on a par level inventory system, the purchaser must determine whether the amount needed will affect the quantities normally ordered. A par level inventory system is one in which there is a specified quantity of products that should always be in inventory. For example, if a par of eight cases of string beans has been set and there are four cases available, four additional cases should be purchased, plus the number of cases used between order and delivery. The par inventory system is explained later in this chapter.

If products needed are managed under a minimum–maximum inventory system, the buyer must determine whether the amount needed will cause the inventory level to reach the order point. The minimum–maximum inventory system requires the buyer to determine the minimum and maximum quantity that inventory levels must fall between. The minimum–maximum inventory system is discussed later in this chapter.

Computerized Forecasting Systems

Manual forecasting systems often use information generated by a basic POS system, which all but the very smallest operations have. However, systems that provide much more electronically generated purchasing information are also available.

MANAGER'S MATH

Your POS system has generated the following sales information for the past two weeks. You want to use it to develop the sales forecast for the next two weeks and determine the quantity of food to purchase.

Complete the information in the table:

Two-Week Sales Report
(Estimated Customers = 625)

Menu Item	No. Sold (Previous Two Weeks)	% of Total Sales	No. Sold (Next Two Weeks)
Shrimp Plate	201		
Sirloin Steak	125		
Lamb Chops	80		
Venison Fillet	65		
Total Sales	**471**	**100**	**625**

Answer:

Menu Item	No. Sold (Previous Two Weeks)	% of Total Sales	No. Sold (Next Two Weeks)
Shrimp Plate	201	42.7	267
Sirloin Steak	125	26.5	166
Lamb Chops	80	17.0	106
Venison Fillet	65	13.8	98
Total Sales	471	100	625

Advanced POS systems can track the sale of every menu item to determine the quantity of ingredients that should have been used to produce it. This information can be used for food cost control purposes. It answers the question, "To what extent does actual product usage match what product usage should have been, based on actual sales?"

Computerized systems require that standardized recipe software be interfaced with the POS system. **Standardized recipes** provide detailed instructions, including the amount of every ingredient, to produce a food or beverage item. They help control food and beverage costs and ensure that quality and quantity standards are met.

The number of customers ordering each menu item is easily determined. This information is used to calculate the quantities of ingredients that should have been used.

Pleasant Town Café's standardized recipe for chili requires two ounces of tomato sauce in each portion, and meatloaf requires one ounce in each portion. Tomato sauce is not an ingredient in any other dinner item served at the establishment.

Chili and meatloaf, along with all other dinner items ordered, are entered into the POS system when orders are placed by the servers. Since the numbers of customers ordering chili and meatloaf are known, the quantity of tomato sauce in these items can be calculated:

38 chili servings	×	**2 oz tomato sauce**	=	**76 oz**
28 meatloaf servings	×	**1 oz tomato sauce**	=	**28 oz**
		Total tomato sauce used at dinner		**104 oz**

The total quantity of tomato sauce for each evening meal period is automatically combined with total amounts for breakfast and lunch items. For example, tomato sauce is used with breakfast omelets and for casserole dishes served at lunch. The total amount of tomato sauce for all meal periods during a specific time period such as one week can be determined. Then the amount is converted into purchase units such as number of cases, which each contain six #10 cans.

All menu items requiring tomato sauce prepared according to their standardized recipes should use 2,475 ounces of tomato sauce for the one-week time period selected:

2,475	÷	**96**	=	**26 (rounded)**
Ounces		**Ounces per #10 can**		**#10 cans to be used**

26	÷	**6**	=	**4.3**
#10 cans to be used		**#10 cans per case**		**Cases to be used**

This information can help the manager in two ways:

- The manager learned that the amount of tomato sauce available in inventory should be reduced from the current level. This amount can be confirmed for control purposes.
- The lowered inventory level can be considered when the quantity of tomato sauce to order is determined.

Computerized systems do not replace the need for managers and buyers to use judgment in purchase quantity decisions. However, these systems do provide a benchmark of information to help determine the quantity of product that will be needed to rebuild inventory levels.

EFFECT OF PRODUCT YIELDS ON PURCHASE QUANTITIES

The purchasing task would be very easy if all products purchased were cooked without any preparation. For example, frozen pre-portioned 4-ounce hamburger steaks do not have any preparation, or precooking, loss. With many food items, however, some of the product is lost during cooking or preparation, such as when coring a fresh, whole pineapple.

Product Yield Calculations

The quantity to purchase is relatively easy to determine when there is no precooking processing. Consider the 4-ounce frozen portions of hamburger steak noted previously:

$$\begin{array}{c}\text{Estimated}\\\text{portions}\\\text{required for}\\\text{order period}\end{array} - \begin{array}{c}\text{Number of}\\\text{portions}\\\text{in}\\\text{inventory}\end{array} = \begin{array}{c}\text{Quantity of}\\\text{4-ounce}\\\text{portions}\\\text{required}\end{array}$$

Buyers may want to order more than needed to allow for errors in customer forecasts and portions that are mishandled, among other reasons.

Purchasers typically buy pre-portioned meat products by the pound, and there are four 4-ounce portions per pound (16 oz ÷ 4 oz = 4 portions per pound). Standard packaging containers may be 10-pound boxes or bags (10 lb × 4 portions per lb = 40 portions per container) or 25-pound boxes (25 lb × 4 portions per lb = 100 portions per container). The quantity purchased matches the quantity needed for service.

Many products, however, do not have a 100 percent edible yield. Then it is more difficult to determine the quantity of items to purchase, even when the number of portions is known.

RESTAURANT TECHNOLOGY

Basic information from POS systems can be used to estimate the quantity of each menu item sold. One advantage is the ability to control items that are the most expensive or theft-prone or are purchased in large quantities.

Many managers use POS systems to control revenue. For example, if 20 hamburgers were sold and the selling price was $6, the operation should have collected $120 in revenue (20 hamburgers × $6 = $120). The accuracy and time savings compared to manually reviewing hard copy customer checks is significant. Few managers tally customer checks manually today.

Many managers, however, do not use the capabilities of their POS system to provide purchasing information as described in this section. Verifying product quantities used and determining quantities of food to purchase are just as important as controlling revenue.

Exhibit 3.6

For example, the manager of an upscale establishment is planning a banquet for 200 customers. The host has requested that 4-ounce tenderloin filets be served. The operation purchases whole tenderloins weighing 10 pounds (*Exhibit 3.6*) at an as purchased (AP) cost of $17.75 per pound. This entrée is a popular choice, and the buyer and chef have performed yield tests that reveal an approximate 60 percent edible yield. A yield test is a carefully controlled process for determining the amount (weight or percentage) of the AP quantity of a product remaining after production.

Buyers can use yield test data to determine some important information:

- **Production loss:** Production loss is the amount by weight or percentage of a product's AP weight that is not servable. Reasons include trim loss from fat and bones and roasting shrinkage.

  In the tenderloin example, a 10-pound (AP) loin will have a 40 percent production loss:

$$
\underset{\textbf{AP weight}}{100\%} \quad - \quad \underset{\textbf{Edible yield}}{60\%} \quad = \quad \underset{\textbf{Production loss}}{40\%}
$$

- **Weight after processing and cooking:** The loin will weigh only 6 pounds after on-site trimming and roasting:

$$
\underset{\textbf{AP weight}}{10\,\text{lb}} \quad \times \quad \underset{\substack{\textbf{AP weight} - \\ \textbf{Production loss}}}{(100\% - 40\%)} \quad = \quad \underset{\substack{\textbf{Weight after} \\ \textbf{processing}}}{6\,\text{lb}}
$$

- **Amount of product to purchase when there is no inventory:** The purchaser knows that only 60 percent of the quantity of whole tenderloins purchased will be servable. The amount to be purchased for the event can be calculated assuming none is currently available:

$$
\underset{\textbf{Portions}}{200} \quad \times \quad \underset{\substack{\textbf{Per} \\ \textbf{portion}}}{4\,\text{oz}} \quad = \quad \underset{\substack{\textbf{Total amount} \\ \textbf{to be served}}}{800\,\text{oz}}
$$

$$
\underset{\substack{\textbf{Total amount} \\ \textbf{to be served}}}{800\,\text{oz}} \quad \div \quad \underset{\substack{\textbf{Edible yield} \\ \textbf{percentage}}}{0.6} \quad = \quad \underset{\substack{\textbf{As purchased} \\ \textbf{amount required}}}{1{,}334\,\text{oz (rounded up)}}
$$

$$
\underset{\substack{\textbf{As purchased} \\ \textbf{amount required}}}{1{,}334\,\text{oz}} \quad \div \quad \underset{\textbf{Per pound}}{16\,\text{oz}} \quad = \quad \underset{\substack{\textbf{As purchased amount} \\ \textbf{required in pounds}}}{83\,\text{pounds (rounded up)}}
$$

Since each tenderloin weighs approximately 10 pounds, the purchaser will need to buy 9 loins:

$$
\underset{\substack{\textbf{As purchased amount} \\ \textbf{required in pounds}}}{83\,\text{lb}} \quad \div \quad \underset{\textbf{Per loin}}{10\,\text{lb}} \quad = \quad \underset{\textbf{To be purchased}}{9\,\text{loins}}
$$

- **Amount of product to purchase when there is some product in inventory:** The operation has four whole 10-pound loins in storage that are not needed for another purpose. It must then purchase five additional loins to meet banquet production requirements:

$$\underset{\text{Loins needed}}{9} \quad - \quad \underset{\text{Loins available}}{4} \quad = \quad \underset{\text{Loins to purchase}}{5}$$

- **Cost per servable pound:** The cost per servable pound is the cost of one pound of product that can be served to customers. In the tenderloin example, the whole tenderloin costs $17.75 (AP) per pound and has a 60 percent yield. The cost per servable pound is $29.58:

$$\underset{\substack{\text{AP price} \\ \text{per lb}}}{\$17.75} \quad \div \quad \underset{\substack{\text{Edible} \\ \text{yield \%}}}{0.60} \quad = \quad \underset{\substack{\text{Cost per} \\ \text{servable pound}}}{\$29.58}$$

Purchasers rely on information about product yields and production losses as they determine purchase quantities. What can they do to help ensure that an item's yield is similar each time it is purchased so production quantities, costs, and selling price calculations are reasonably accurate?

Several strategies are helpful. Each may involve a management rather than a buyer's responsibility. However, each is especially important as the buyer's input about actual product costs is shared with production managers:

- Conduct yield tests. Yield depends on a product's grade, AP weight, and pre-preparation and preparation methods including cooking times and temperatures. Purchasers working with managers and food production staff can obtain samples, conduct yield tests, and make decisions about products purchased.

- Incorporate yield test results into purchase specifications, share them with potential vendors, and require that price quotations be based on the quality described.

- Ensure that operating controls are used consistently. For example, when incoming products are received, they must be checked against purchase specifications. Ovens must be checked to ensure that desired temperatures are maintained, and cooking times and temperatures must be closely monitored (*Exhibit 3.7*).

- Consider use of industry standards such as the U.S. Department of Agriculture's Institutional Meat Purchase Specifications (IMPS) and other standards developed by the North American Meat Producers Association (NAMP).

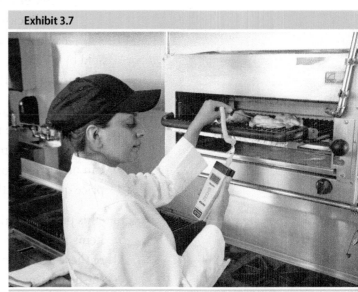

Exhibit 3.7

DETERMINING QUANTITIES TO ORDER

Once the quantity of products needed is known, it is time to consider the quantity to order. Traditional purchasing methods are used to obtain items for immediate use and for longer-term requirements.

Quantities for Immediate Use

Perishable products such as bakery and dairy items and fresh produce are purchased in relatively small quantities because they must be used quickly. Less-perishable items such as frozen food, canned and dry food, and supplies used by staff in various departments can be purchased for immediate use, or they can be stored for longer-term use.

The quantities of perishable products to be purchased depend on products in inventory that must be checked. As discussed earlier, an estimate of quantity used during the time period from order to delivery is also needed.

A purchaser believes that 8 cases of fresh 6-ounce steaks will be used during the three days for which an order is being placed. The purchaser may have determined this through a formal forecasting process, or the business may have a very predictable business volume.

The buyer checks the inventory in the walk-in refrigerator and sees there are 1.5 cases available:

8.00 cases	−	1.50 cases	=	6.50 cases
Quantity needed for order period (3 days)		Quantity currently available		Quantity to purchase

The purchaser knows that there will be an add-on charge if the vendor is asked to split cases. Therefore, he rounds up and orders 7 full cases. A **split case**, also called a broken case, is a case of less-than-full purchase unit size sold by a vendor, such as five #10 cans of peaches rather than a full case containing six #10 cans.

This process for determining the quantity of steaks to purchase can also be used to calculate the quantities of other perishable items. After the purchaser knows the required quantities of each item needed for the order period, he can order the products. This involves selecting the vendor based on lowest price quoted for the quality of steaks described in the purchase specification.

This process works well when buyers can accurately estimate the quantity of items needed for the order period. In many operations, the general usage rates of these products are known. For example, business may be relatively slow at the beginning of the week, Monday through Thursday, and much busier on the weekend, Friday through Sunday.

Buyers know the normal usage rates for perishable products during the first part of the week. They use the process described to determine quantities for orders to be placed on Friday or Saturday for Monday delivery. One challenge is that the quantity of products available at the end of the weekend will not be known when this order is placed. Many buyers use a conservative estimate and may assume zero inventory on Monday morning, ordering the entire quantity needed for the first of the week.

The purchaser will then place an order for perishable goods on Thursday for delivery on Friday. The estimate of higher weekend usage will be known, and the quantity available when the order is placed can be determined. This is factored into the purchase quantity decision.

The quantities of products routinely ordered must be adjusted as business volume varies. Additional quantities will be needed when volume is expected to increase because of celebrations, holidays, and other activities. Conversely, volume estimates will be reduced at other times because of, for example, poor weather or slower business.

Exhibit 3.8

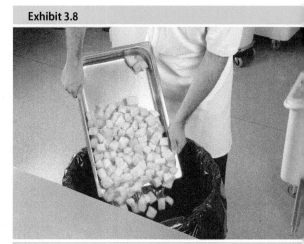

Professional purchasers are always alert for the need to revise the usual quantities of products ordered. They consider situations such as excessive spoilage or waste (*Exhibit 3.8*), which suggest quantities should be reduced. They also consider frequent stockouts or emergency orders, which suggest quantities should be increased.

Generally, purchasers with experience in a specific organization can establish routine purchase quantities for perishable products. They can then adjust these quantities as necessary, considering changes in estimated business volumes.

Par Level Inventory System

A par level inventory system is one in which purchase quantities are calculated on the basis of the number of purchase units required to return inventory to a predetermined level. The system is often used for perishable products, alcoholic beverages, dish-washing and other chemicals, and linen supplies.

The quantity of product used as the par level is determined based on usage rates, experience, trial and error, and other factors including stock safety levels.

Bess, the manager and buyer for Desert Shadows Grill, has established a par level of 10 cases (24 bottles per case) of Western Waters beer. She orders the item on Tuesday for delivery on Thursday. Before ordering, Bess counts the number of cases available and rounds down to the nearest full case. For example, this week she has 4 full cases and an open case with 7 bottles. Since only full cases are included, she notes 4 cases in inventory.

Bess also knows that she normally uses about 1 case of Western Waters beer on Tuesdays and Wednesdays, which are the two days between order and delivery. This rate was confirmed when she forecasted the number of customers using sales trends for the order period. Therefore, she believes her usage estimate of 2 cases will not yield a stockout.

She uses this information to determine the need to order 8 cases:

10 cases	−	(4	−	2)	=	8
Par level		Number of cases available		Number of cases used before delivery		Number of cases to order

Bess was able to make an easy and fast determination about cases to order by considering:

- The established par level
- The number of cases currently available
- The number of cases likely to be used between order and delivery

The par level inventory system has advantages, namely that it is fast and simple. These must be countered with the potential disadvantage of stockouts. Stockouts can occur if the par level is set too low, the usage rate is higher than expected, or the purchaser cannot expedite another delivery if problems occur. Examples include an unanticipated special event or higher-than-expected usage before delivery.

Par level inventories do not typically create ongoing problems with excessive quantities on hand because wise buyers decrease par levels if they notice an increase in inventory levels. Likewise, if there are numerous times when low quantities are found immediately before delivery, this will be noticed. Then anticipated usage rates can be reconsidered and par levels adjusted. The process is a trial and error method that works well over time in many operations.

Minimum–Maximum Inventory System

Restaurant and foodservice buyers require nonperishable products, which are often purchased in quantities to last several days or weeks, or even longer. However, the factors affecting purchase quantities discussed earlier apply to these items. These factors include cash flow, storage space, and increased chance of theft.

The minimum–maximum inventory system uses several concepts that are helpful for purchasing nonperishable products and controlling them in inventory. The purchaser must determine, for each product in the system, the minimum below which available quantities will not fall and the maximum above which quantities will not rise. Procedures involve determining the quantity that should be ordered to bring the inventory level back to the maximum amount when the order is received.

Several conditions should be met when the minimum–maximum inventory system is used:

- Purchase specifications exist for the products, and their quality requirements do not change.
- The vendors' product prices are relatively constant.
- The products are used in relatively consistent quantities.
- The products are expensive and therefore require more extensive purchasing and inventory controls.
- The same type of products will be used in the future.
- The products are not extremely perishable.
- Reasonable maximum quantities do not present storage space problems.
- Inventory and storage procedures are in place to help ensure that stock is rotated and theft or pilferage is minimized.

The minimum–maximum inventory system is best used to control high-volume, expensive, and nonperishable products. It is not typically applicable to inexpensive, low-volume, or perishable products. Instead, the par level inventory system is often used for these items.

Several concepts must be understood as the minimum–maximum inventory system is discussed:

- **Purchase unit:** The purchase unit is the standard size of the package or container in which the product is typically purchased. For example, many canned fruit and vegetable products are purchased by the case with six #10 cans per case, and frozen shrimp may be purchased by the case (10 5-pound boxes or bags per case).
- **Product usage rate:** The purchase usage rate is the number of purchase units, such as cases, that are used during a typical order period.
- **Order period:** The order period is the time (number of days or weeks) for which an order is normally placed. For example, canned goods may be purchased once monthly, and frozen shrimp may be purchased once every two weeks.
- **Lead time:** Lead time is the number of purchase units typically used during the time between placing and receiving the order. For example, if 3 cases of frozen shrimp are normally used during the days between order and receiving, the lead time for this product is 3 cases.
- **Safety level:** Safety level is the minimum number of purchase units that must always remain in inventory in case of late deliveries or unexpected increases in product usage rates.
- **Order point:** The order point is the number of purchase units that should be available in inventory when an order is placed.

Manager's Memo

Some vendors will not even sell split cases because of the high costs to open cases and remove the quantity ordered. Also, they likely have few opportunities to sell the remainder of the case.

Higher charges for small broken-case quantities are one reason that many low-volume organizations buy from retail outlets such as buyer's clubs. These businesses may sell commercial-sized containers such as #10 cans that contain approximately 12 cups, at a per-can price lower than a wholesale vendor who would prefer to sell by case lot of six #10 cans per case.

For example, an operation uses a large quantity of frozen crab legs, and the product is included in the minimum–maximum inventory system. Managers know the following information:

- Purchase unit: 1 case
- Product usage rate: 28 cases per order period
- Order period: 2 weeks (14 days)

Note: *Daily usage rate = 2 cases (28 cases per order period ÷ 14 days).*

- Lead time: 4 days × 2 cases per day = 8 cases

Note: *Number of cases used during lead time is 8 cases (2 cases per day × 4 days).*

- Safety level: 12 cases

Managers can now answer several questions about the purchase quantities for frozen crab legs.

Question 1: What is the maximum number of cases of crab legs that should ever be available in inventory?

To answer this question, the manager adds the product usage rate to the safety level. The usage rate is 28 cases and the safety level is 12 cases:

$$
\begin{array}{ccc}
\textbf{28 cases} & + & \textbf{12 cases} & = & \textbf{40 cases} \\
\textbf{Usage rate} & & \textbf{Safety level} & & \textbf{Maximum}
\end{array}
$$

Question 2: What is the order point for the crab legs?

The order point is the sum of the number of lead time cases and the safety level cases:

$$
\begin{array}{ccc}
\textbf{8 cases} & + & \textbf{12 cases} & = & \textbf{20 cases} \\
\textbf{Lead time} & & \textbf{Safety level} & & \textbf{Order point}
\end{array}
$$

The order point can be verified because the number of cases available when the order is placed minus the number of cases that will be used before the order arrives is equal to the safety level, which is the minimum number of cases that can be available:

$$
\begin{array}{ccc}
\textbf{20 cases} & - & \textbf{8 cases} & = & \textbf{12 cases} \\
\textbf{No. of cases} & & \textbf{No. of cases used} & & \textbf{No. of cases} \\
\textbf{available when} & & \textbf{until crab legs} & & \textbf{available when crab} \\
\textbf{crab legs are} & & \textbf{are delivered} & & \textbf{legs are delivered} \\
\textbf{ordered} & & \textbf{(lead time)} & & \textbf{(safety level)}
\end{array}
$$

Question 3: How many cases of crab legs should be ordered at the order point?

The product usage rate of 28 cases should be ordered if the order is placed at the order point. This can be verified:

$$20 \text{ cases} - 8 \text{ cases} = 12$$

Order point   Lead time   Cases available at time of delivery

$$12 + 28 = 40$$

Cases available at time of delivery   Cases ordered (usage rate)   Maximum inventory cases

Question 4: How many cases of crab legs should be ordered if an order is placed when there are 23 cases in inventory? (The order point for crab legs has not been reached, but the order is placed with other frozen seafood products.)

Step A: Calculate the number of cases of crab legs that exceed the order point:

$$23 \text{ cases} - 20 \text{ cases} = 3 \text{ cases}$$

Cases in storage   Order point   Excess

Step B: Calculate the number of cases to order:

$$28 \text{ cases} - 3 \text{ cases} = 25 \text{ cases}$$

Usage rate   Excess   Order

The number of cases to order when there are 3 cases in excess of the order point can be verified:

$$23 \text{ cases} - 8 = 15$$

Cases in storage   Lead time cases   Cases available at time of delivery

$$15 + 25 = 40$$

Cases available at time of delivery   Cases ordered   Maximum inventory cases

The previous questions demonstrate that product usage rate, order period, lead time, and safety level can be used to determine key information:

- The minimum number of cases allowable in inventory
- The maximum number of cases allowable in inventory
- The order point in terms of number of cases
- The number of cases that should be purchased if an order will be placed before that product's order point is reached

MANAGER'S MATH

(OPEN FOR BUSINESS)

Use the following information to answer the following four questions:

- Purchase unit for frozen chicken legs: 25-lb case
- Order period: 1 week (7 days)
- Daily usage rate: 3 cases (21 cases per order period ÷ 7 days)
- Lead time: 2 days
- Number of cases used during lead time: 6 cases (3 cases per day × 2 days)
- Safety level: 9 cases

A. What is the maximum number of cases of chicken legs that should ever be in inventory?

B. What is the order point for chicken legs?

C. How many cases of chicken legs should be ordered at the order point?

D. How many cases should be ordered if an order is placed when there are 26 cases in inventory?

Answer:

A.
$$21 + 9 = 30$$
Usage rate cases + Safety level cases = Maximum cases

B.
$$6 + 9 = 15$$
Lead time in cases + Safety level in cases = Cases at order point

C. 21 cases (usage rate)

Proof:
$$15 - 9 = 6$$
Order point − Lead time cases = Cases available at delivery

$$9 + 21 = 30$$
Cases available at delivery + Order (usage rate) = Maximum cases in inventory

D. Step 1: Calculate the number of cases that exceed order point:
$$26 - 15 = 11$$
Cases in storage − Order point cases = Excess cases

Step 2: Calculate the cases to order:
$$21 - 11 = 10$$
Usage rate cases − Excess cases = Cases to order

Proof:
$$26 - 6 = 20$$
Cases in storage − Lead time cases = Cases available at delivery

$$20 + 10 = 30$$
Cases available at delivery + Cases ordered = Maximum inventory

---

The safety level for the product represents the minimum number of purchase units below which quantities cannot fall. These factors should be considered when the safety level is established:

- **The lead time required for reorders:** When fewer deliveries are made, the number of lead-time units must be increased. If delivery timing and schedules are not consistent, minimum inventory levels must be increased to take this uncertainty into account. Buyers should also reevaluate the use of vendors whose services are inconsistent.

- **The product's usage rate:** As the volume of product usage increases, safety levels may also need to be increased. One reason is that more customers are likely to be dissatisfied with stockouts of popular items. Ideally, the manager and team implement plans to reduce or eliminate stockouts.

An ideal safety level will minimize the possibility of stockouts without the need to maintain excessive quantities in inventory. A buyer's experience with vendors and customers can help establish this ideal inventory level for products under the minimum–maximum system.

Several factors also influence the decision about lead times for products. They can be established by considering the amount of time generally required for an order. If usage and safety levels incorporate a "cushion" for unanticipated problems, a small variance in the length of lead time is not critical. However, when usage and safety level quantities are minimized, lead time is of greater concern. Then there is a great likelihood that the buyer will need to contact the vendor because of deliveries that are not made on time.

Several conditions can lengthen product delivery lead times:

- Vendors may not be dependable, and this should be an important factor in deciding whether to continue to do business with them.

The operation may be in a remote location and long delivery delays may be more common.

Market conditions can cause unpredictable problems that affect the availability of products and the potential need for backorders.

There are several possible advantages to use of the minimum–maximum inventory system:

Excessive stock buildup is less likely when the buyer has established a reasonable maximum inventory level.

A carefully planned minimum inventory level provides a cushion against stockouts.

The system is easy to understand, explain, and use.

Actual purchasing performance can be monitored against expected performance. For example, the reasons that actual inventory levels exceed or are less than those established for the system can be investigated. Then corrective actions can be taken when needed.

A careful review of inventory levels (*Exhibit 3.9*) may yield changes in product order quantities that might not otherwise have been implemented.

There are also potential disadvantages to the minimum–maximum inventory system:

It may not always be the best way to calculate required product quantities. There are, for example, computer-assisted systems that provide more detailed and accurate forecasts of purchase quantity needs and timing. These systems are increasingly used by large and even relatively small operations.

The assumptions used to establish the system's safety levels and lead-time calculations may be inaccurate. If so, they decrease its accuracy and can create excessive inventory levels or stockouts.

Quantity purchase discounts may not be possible when maximum inventory quantities are below vendor-specified quantities.

Some staff time is required initially to consider and calculate accurate safety and lead-time estimates.

Other Methods for Determining Purchase Quantities

The widely varied types of operations within which buyers work may require the use of other systems to determine purchase quantities:

Exact requirements system: This method involves the purchase of products in the exact quantities needed. For example, a special banquet may be planned with an entrée not generally used. The exact quantity required for just that event would be ordered on a one-time basis, and no permanent inventory of that product would be desired.

Exhibit 3.9

Manager's Memo

Successful managers know that special attention is always necessary to control the relatively few products for which most purchasing dollars are spent. They know that every product purchased is important. However, items that are expensive, theft prone, and used in large quantities frequently require special attention.

This special emphasis begins when product needs are established, and it continues as purchase specifications and purchase quantities are determined. Special procedures may be in place to manage purchase costs, such as the use of negotiation with potential vendors. Focused control procedures are also used when the products are ordered, received, and stored.

Purchasers seldom have the time to do everything they would like. Therefore, they must establish priorities, and one of these involves the special emphasis placed on these high-cost products.

- **Periodic ordering system:** This method involves a random determination of inventory quantities followed by a decision about the quantity of items that should be purchased. For example, perhaps a large quantity of light bulbs was purchased some time ago, and they are used as needed. At some point, a decision will be made to purchase additional light bulbs. This system can be useful when vendor delivery times are short or when the owner or manager purchases from a buyer's club. A buyer's club is a retail organization in which, after payment of a member fee, persons can purchase food and other products in large-volume package sizes.

- **Cooperative (pool) buying system:** This method involves several operations that combine orders for a similar quality of products and then submit one order to a vendor. This method may not have a direct impact on the quantity of products purchased by a specific organization. However, participants may need to agree to purchase a minimum quantity when they place an order so the total purchase volume will qualify for special discounts.

- **Economic order quantity (EOQ) system:** This computerized method involves the use of mathematical calculations to analyze costs related to factors such as product price, usage rates, and internal handling costs including storage. Then the product order quantity with the lowest total variable costs is selected for purchase. The method can yield lower inventory levels and fewer orders with reduced chances for stockouts.

- **Definite quantity contract system:** Large-quantity buyers may enter into an agreement with a vendor to purchase a definite quantity of products over a specified number of deliveries. Purchasers estimate the quantity required for the contract period by considering anticipated business volumes. Delivery charges, if any, and available storage space are also considered as delivery frequency is determined. This method may be useful when significant quantity discounts are offered. These are likely incentives for the purchaser to make a long-term commitment. The system also has other potential benefits. A consistent supply source is better ensured, and purchasers can reduce the time and effort required to select vendors for more frequent orders.

- **Total requirements contract system:** This method is similar to the definite quantity contract, except that the purchase quantity is not fixed. However, there may be an agreed-upon minimum. For example, a purchaser may have an agreement with a dairy to deliver varying amounts of milk products based on the establishment's sales volumes at the same per-gallon price for a specific time period. The advantages of this system are similar to those for a definite quantity contract. One further advantage, although perhaps at a higher unit cost, is that the buyer can be more flexible. He or she can estimate necessary amounts, negotiate prices, and purchase within a range of quantity needs rather than be locked into a fixed quantity.

- **Open market purchasing system:** For products purchased in small quantities and at minimum value, the calculation of exact quantity needs is less important. For example, a petty cash system may be used to purchase office supplies at a local business in a quantity roughly equal to the rate at which they are used. A **petty cash system** is a cash fund used to make infrequent and low-cost product purchases.

- **Vendor-managed par level systems:** This method is frequently used by vendors of chemicals such as dish- and pot-cleaning supplies and by those selling prepackaged coffee products. The procedures are very similar to the par level inventory system described earlier except that the vendor, not the manager or buyer, determines the quantities needed for purchase. The vendor's representative counts the number of purchase units available in storage, subtracts that quantity from the established par level, and calculates the quantities needed to build inventory back to the par level.

NONTRADITIONAL METHODS FOR DETERMINING QUANTITIES

The purchasing methods in this chapter require the continual ordering of a specified quantity of products for a defined order period. All products in an order are delivered in a single delivery. In the future, large-volume food buyers may use purchasing systems that determine product quantities in very different ways.

There are at least two nontraditional purchasing systems that apply to the restaurant and foodservice industry. Both systems involve a close and ongoing relationship between the buyer and vendor.

Just-in-Time (JIT) Purchasing

Just-in-time (JIT) purchasing is a system in which a purchaser has a long-term commitment with a vendor to make frequent product deliveries. As this is done, the operation can minimize its on-site product storage space and increase its cash flow. The goal of a JIT system is to have the necessary quantity of required products arrive close to the time when they are needed for production. For example, the products required for the next day's production might be delivered the previous afternoon. Some additional products might be available for emergency use unless the locations of the establishment and the vendor are very close.

There are several potential advantages to JIT systems:

- Reduced on-site storage space is needed.

- The establishment will enjoy an improved relationship with the vendor.

- Less time will be needed and fewer problems are likely as interactions with numerous vendors are reduced.

Manager's Memo

The nontraditional purchasing systems being described are not likely in use in any small-volume operation today. However, managers should understand how they work. Some procedures may become more widely used in the near future. Also, creative managers working with their vendors may find ways to use some of the procedures in their current inventory management systems.

Think about how successful operations "go the extra mile" to satisfy their customers. Product vendors are businesspersons also. Those that are successful have the same concerns about meeting the needs of their own customers: restaurant and foodservice operations. Will a vendor work with a buyer to develop special systems to meet the buyer's needs? This question cannot be answered unless it is asked. With knowledge about what they wish to do, buyers can work with suppliers in efforts to help both businesses be successful.

- There will be reduced waste from spoilage.
- There are fewer theft and pilferage problems.
- Less money is tied up in inventory.

Purchasers using a JIT system must carefully select a vendor to make the process most beneficial. Buyers are likely to have concerns about single sourcing, which occurs when a buyer relies on a single vendor as the source of one or more products. The concern relates to alternate sources if a supply is not available from the single source.

There are three other potential concerns about JIT purchasing:

- Production issues and delays can arise if products are not delivered.
- Significant changes in existing purchasing systems would be necessary, and reverting to a traditional system would be challenging if the JIT system is unsuccessful.
- Significant planning is needed to ensure that a JIT system is cost-effective and to develop procedures for its implementation and operation.

Exhibit 3.10 shows some differences between traditional and JIT purchasing systems.

Exhibit 3.10

DIFFERENCES BETWEEN TRADITIONAL AND JIT PURCHASING SYSTEMS

Traditional Purchasing	JIT Purchasing
• Buyers purchase in relatively small quantities.	• Buyers make a commitment to purchase greater quantities.
• Vendors schedule fewer deliveries of greater quantities.	• Vendors schedule frequent deliveries of smaller quantities.
• Products rejected at delivery are reordered.	• Products rejected are redelivered without an additional order.
• Lowest price is the primary purchasing objective.	• Lowest total acquisition costs are the primary objective. Acquisition costs are product costs plus any other expenses such as freight and insurance and less any discounts, incentives, or other price reductions.
• Vendors determine delivery schedule.	• Purchasers determine delivery schedule.
• Purchase involves formal communication (e.g., purchase orders).	• Less formal communication used.
• Innovation is discouraged.	• Innovations are encouraged.
• Significant time is spent on purchasing functions.	• Less time is spent on direct purchasing activities.
• Purchaser–vendor commitment is not a consideration.	• Purchaser–vendor commitment is critical.

How might a JIT system actually work in an operation? Consider the food and beverage operation in a large hotel with a strong base of tourist business in Honolulu, Hawaii. It has a high occupancy rate, meaning a large percentage of rooms are rented nightly, and many hotel guests dine at the restaurants for one or more meals daily. The hotel also has a solid base of local customers who enjoy dining there. Like the hotel guests, they enjoy the great food and service and the scenic ocean views.

Top-level managers and their purchasing staff meet with vendors to explain their potential interest in a JIT system. They are considering a six-month commitment to a single vendor to provide all fruit and vegetables required in the restaurants and other food outlets including banquet operations.

The hotel will require deliveries six days each week, and the vendor must provide an agreed-upon quantity of on-site "backup" products. Numerous other details must also be considered and agreed upon, and product specifications detail the quality requirements of the food items to be purchased.

Exhibit 3.11

Several potential vendors are interviewed about their interest in participating in the JIT program. Each currently provides some products in the hotel's traditional competitive bidding system. The vendors are told that the hotel wants to purchase all of its fruit and vegetable needs (*Exhibit 3.11*) from a single supplier for a six-month period. They are given a list of the approximate quantity of each product that will be purchased.

The hotel's purchasing employees realize that vendors cannot know how much they will have to pay for each product, even in the near term. Therefore, the vendors are asked to quote prices based on an amount above an agreed-upon standard such as the published wholesale market price. For example, one vendor may agree to supply iceberg lettuce for $1.56 above the wholesale market price. Another vendor quotes a price of $1.61 over wholesale for lettuce of the same quality. The vendor chosen will be the one submitting the lowest markup prices for all products covered by the purchase agreement and offering the best service.

There are two basic types of quantity purchases involved in this system. Some produce items such as pineapples, lemons, and limes are used on a fairly consistent basis, and a standing order is established for these items. A standing order is an agreement made between a purchaser and a vendor that the same quantity of a specified product is required for each delivery. Unless adjustments are made, the same quantity will be delivered daily.

Other products, including lettuce and spinach, are typically required in significantly larger quantities than the standing order because of large banquets and other catered events. The quantities of these items will be electronically ordered each day.

THINK ABOUT IT . . .

JIT purchasing is not practical for every establishment. However, buyers using traditional purchasing may use some JIT ideas to improve their operation.

What are two JIT concepts that might be practical for a smaller operation?

Manager's Memo

The JIT and vendor-managed inventory systems share several characteristics:

- They require cooperation between the purchaser and the vendor.
- The emphasis moves away from minimizing cost, perhaps at the expense of the other party, to improving financial benefits for both parties.
- The purchaser and vendor have a shared goal: to assist each other.
- There is an emphasis on continuous improvement for both the purchaser and the vendor to enhance quality and reduce waste.

How will the JIT system work? Products required for the next day's production will be delivered in the afternoon of the previous day. The operation's receiving staff will perform normal receiving tasks. See chapter 8 for information about these tasks. Next, items will be moved into storage areas. They will remain on the transport carts used to move them from the loading dock or receiving area. The next morning products will be transported to production areas, and carts will be returned to the receiving area for that afternoon's delivery.

This example does not detail every procedure in JIT purchasing. It provides an overview of the system and suggests details that might be used by creative managers and buyers looking for ways to improve their purchasing. It also illustrates the mutual commitment between purchaser and vendor that will be necessary, and it suggests the types of value-added services that are important for cooperation.

Vendor-Managed Inventory

With traditional purchasing systems, the operation takes ownership of and responsibility for products when receiving activities are completed. The **vendor-managed inventory** system is different. The vendor retains ownership of products until they are issued to production. At that time, the products are considered purchased and product costs are incurred by the establishment.

The vendor-managed inventory system has potential advantages for the operation and the vendor. The establishment incurs no financial responsibility for the care of or costs of inventory such as spoilage and theft until products are issued. It should also receive high levels of service and improved cash flow. The vendor will likely generate a larger dollar value of product sales to the operation as a single-source vendor. Also, the vendor should obtain significant customer loyalty from the organization.

SUMMARY

1. **Explain why purchasers must carefully consider the quantities of products to purchase.**

   When larger-than-necessary quantities are purchased, money is unavailable for other purposes and cash flow is affected. Also, buyers are less flexible, must have more space to store products, and risk the possibility of theft and pilferage. Other concerns relate to quality deterioration, increased chance of damage, and excessive handling costs.

   When products are purchased in inadequate quantities, it may not be possible to meet production requirements because of stockouts. Additionally, customers may be disappointed and production plans may need revision.

2. **List important factors that affect the quantity of products purchased.**

   Primary factors that affect purchase quantity decisions include estimated customer counts, available storage space, and cash flow. Other reasons relate to minimum order requirements, expected price changes, taking advantage of close-outs, and the need for trial orders and samples.

3. **State procedures helpful in forecasting product needs.**

   Most methods for determining purchase quantities consider production needs, which must be forecasted. When manual systems are used, purchasers consider past, current, and expected sales trends. They develop forecasts that may be based on the percentage of estimated customers likely to purchase each menu item.

   Computerized forecasting systems enable managers to know the quantity of each ingredient that should have been used based on items served. This information allows managers to calculate changes in inventories and provides a check on the quantity of products that must be ordered.

4. **Explain how product yields affect purchase quantities.**

   Many food products have yields less than 100 percent. Therefore, additional quantities based on yield tests must be ordered. Managers help ensure that product yields are consistent when they conduct yield tests, incorporate results into purchase specifications, ensure that all operating controls are used, and use available industry standards.

5. **Describe traditional systems used to calculate purchase quantities.**

   Quantities of perishable products to be used immediately can be easily calculated by subtracting the quantity in inventory from the quantity needed for the order period.

   Par inventory systems are based on the number of purchase units required to return inventory to predetermined levels. Calculations involve subtracting cases in inventory and cases used between order placement and delivery from the required par level.

   Minimum–maximum inventory systems are used to purchase nonperishable and expensive products. Buyers must determine the minimum quantity below which inventory levels cannot fall and the maximum amount above which inventory cannot rise. Buyers must know each product's purchase unit, usage rate, order period, lead time, safety level, and order point.

   Other methods for determining purchase quantities include the exact requirements system, periodic ordering system, cooperative (pool) buying system, and economic order quantity (EOQ) system. Some buyers also use definite quantity contracts, total requirements contracts, open market purchasing, and vendor-managed par systems.

6. **Identify and discuss two nontraditional purchasing methods that impact the quantities of products to be purchased.**

The just-in-time (JIT) purchasing system allows the purchaser to make a long-term commitment with a vendor. Frequent product deliveries, often just the amount required for the next day, are used. Close cooperation between purchaser and vendor is needed. Potential advantages include a reduced need for on-site storage, improved vendor relationships, less need for numerous vendors, and reduced spoilage. There are also fewer theft problems, and less money is tied up in inventory.

In a vendor-managed inventory system, the vendor retains ownership of products in inventory until they are issued. This can result in better service and improved cash flow.

APPLICATION EXERCISE

Shola is the owner, manager, and buyer of a medium-sized bistro. Her establishment is located in a major city, and she has easy access to vendors. She uses a par level inventory system to determine the quantities of many products to order, including most of her bottled wines. She has a relatively constant volume of business, with revenue much higher during the busy season months of May to September, mostly from tourists. She has constant, but much lower, revenue during the remaining months, primarily from local residents.

During the busy season, she sells about 42 bottles (750 milliliters) of Vintners' Choice Chardonnay every week. She orders once a week and likes to have 12 bottles, or one case, on hand at all times for a safety level.

Here are her Vintners' Choice Chardonnay purchases over the last three weeks:

Blue Bay Bistro					
Product	Date	Par Level	No. Bottles Available	No. Bottles Used (Two-Day Delivery)	No. Bottles to Order
Vintners' Choice Chardonnay (750-ml bottle)	6/1–6/15	54	20	12	46 (4 cases)*
	6/16–6/30	54	13	12	
	7/1–7/15	54	28	12	

*There is a lower per-bottle case price (12 bottles per case), so Shola orders four cases (48 bottles). Shola always rounds up to the next higher case count when she places her wine order.

1. How many bottles of chardonnay should be ordered for each of the two order periods 6/16–6/30 and 7/1–7/15 to return the inventory to approximately 54 bottles? Note: *Round up to the next highest case lot (12 bottles per case).*

2. What are three reasons the number of bottles available might have been so low when the order was placed for 6/16–6/30?

3. What are three reasons there might have been so many bottles available when the order was placed for 7/1–7/15?

REVIEW YOUR LEARNING

Select the best answer for each question.

1. How do excessive quantities of products in inventory impact the operation's cash flow?

   A. They increase product cost.

   B. They require an increase in menu item selling prices.

   C. They tie up cash that could be used for other purposes.

   D. They limit the ability of buyers to negotiate for better prices.

2. Forecasts indicate that 530 customers will be served Saturday night and 17 percent will order sirloin steaks. How many sirloin steaks will be served?

   A. 30

   B. 60

   C. 90

   D. 120

3. Some POS systems track sales and determine the quantity of ingredients that should have been used by referencing

   A. purchase requisitions.

   B. production forecasts.

   C. standardized recipes.

   D. yield tests.

4. A meat item costs $14.36 per pound (AP) and has an edible yield of 72 percent. What is the approximate cost per servable pound?

   A. $5.40

   B. $12.95

   C. $15.60

   D. $19.95

5. What is the food cost for one portion of steak (100 percent yield) if a 4-ounce serving is used and the steak costs $12.80 per pound?

   A. $3.20

   B. $6.40

   C. $7.80

   D. $9.10

6. A purchaser wants to order highly perishable products for immediate use. She needs 12 cases and currently has 2.5 cases available. How many cases will she normally purchase?

   A. 8.5

   B. 9

   C. 9.5

   D. 10

7. The purchaser has set a par level of 8 cases of lettuce. One case will be used between order and delivery, and 2 cases are currently available. How many cases need to be purchased?

   A. 4

   B. 5

   C. 6

   D. 7

8. Which products should the minimum–maximum inventory system be used for?

   A. Perishable products

   B. Inexpensive products

   C. Low-volume products

   D. Nonperishable products

9. A petty cash system is typically used with which type of purchasing system?

   A. Open market purchasing

   B. Periodic ordering system

   C. Exact requirements system

   D. Total requirements contract

10. Which purchasing system involves buying food products in relatively small quantities?

    A. Just-in-time purchasing

    B. Definite quantity contract

    C. Cooperative (pool) buying

    D. Total requirements contract

4

Selecting Vendors

CHAPTER LEARNING OBJECTIVES

After completing this chapter, you should be able to:

- Explain the importance of selecting the right vendors.

- List the characteristics of the best vendors.

- Explain how to make vendor selection decisions.

- List and describe alternative purchasing sources.

- Explain the flow of products that are purchased for use in multiunit organizations.

- Describe the procedures for evaluating vendors.

KEY TERMS

account, p. 94

broad-line vendor, p. 99

distributor sales
representative (DSR), p. 95

e-commerce, p. 96

franchisor, p. 102

Hazard Analysis Critical
Control Point (HACCP), p. 91

national account, p. 105

payment card discount,
p. 104

qualified buyer, p. 94

request for proposal
(RFP), p. 90

specialty-line vendor,
p. 99

trade show, p. 94

vendor sourcing, p. 90

CASE STUDY

"You know what?" Jamal, an assistant manager at Seaside Breezes Restaurant, asked Soren, another assistant manager. "I've seen the delivery invoices for our frozen meat, canned goods, and disposable supplies. We could save a lot if we just had one of our dish washers go down to the buyer's club every day and pick up what we need. We have a company van, and it wouldn't take more than an hour. What we spend for one hour of wages would be nothing compared to what we could save," said Jamal.

Soren answered, "I shop there a lot, but I've never thought of using a buyer's club for the restaurant's needs. They really do have the cheapest prices. Let's talk to the boss."

1. If you were the manager, what would your response be?

2. How should the manager determine whether any products should be purchased at the buyer's club?

IMPORTANCE OF SELECTING VENDORS

Recall that a vendor is a business that sells products or services to a restaurant or foodservice operation. Some managers use another term, *service provider*, to refer to those that sell services. This book uses *vendor* for both.

The purchasing system used by an operation can never be successful unless the right vendors are used. These vendors will be just as concerned about their customers, the buyers, as restaurant and foodservice managers are about customers who visit their establishments.

Exhibit 4.1

Wise buyers do not merely shop around until they find vendors with whom they want to do business. Instead, they carefully evaluate potential vendors and select those judged best for them. The vendor selection process is almost continuously evaluated as incoming products are assessed when they are received. Ongoing evaluation continues as purchasing and accounting department employees consider the quality of each vendor's information and services.

Purchasers must work very closely with their vendors to consistently obtain the right quality of products at the best prices. In fact, they must interact almost like partners who help each other attain goals (see *Exhibit 4.1*).

Many managers would not likely use the term *partners* to describe an ideal relationship between them and their vendors. Managers, buyers, and vendors do not, of course, share in the financial rewards of a business. However, a partnership can involve organizations with joint interests who work to mutually benefit from what they do together. Viewed this way, the task of selecting vendors that will work very closely with an operation is very important.

Purchasers in many areas of the country can select from among a number of vendors for many products they buy. However, it is impractical to ask each one for a request for proposal every time a specific product is needed. A **request for proposal (RFP)** is a document that is submitted to approved vendors with the request that they indicate the price they will charge for the quantity of products being ordered. It is also impractical to spread around the business and give each vendor an order once in a while to avoid relying on just one or two vendors.

The best purchasers make effective **vendor sourcing** decisions to determine which vendors will be asked to quote prices for needed products. The concept of vendor sourcing relates to decisions about which from among many vendors will be sent RFPs for products to be purchased. The idea of evaluating vendors before using them is a logical step. However, some buyers use other strategies, such as continually purchasing from the same vendors or always looking for the vendor with the lowest price. Both of these approaches may be acceptable if the evaluation process supports the use of these vendors. However, they are not wise strategies if buyers have not considered a range of vendors to ensure that they are dealing with the best.

Customers cannot be satisfied unless the operation always has the right quality of products in the correct quantities to meet their expectations. Effective vendors enable buyers to best serve their customers. This makes it easy to defend the importance of the vendor sourcing decision.

Vendor sourcing involves making decisions about which vendors will be asked to submit prices for the products needed. However, it also involves developing relationships with other potential supply sources that may be useful in the future. For example, new vendors may be needed as the operation's product needs change or if a preferred vendor goes out of business. It is also possible that, over time, the buyer may experience problems with one or more vendors.

CHARACTERISTICS OF THE BEST VENDORS

Some factors that define a good vendor are easy to identify, whereas others are unique to the needs of the specific operation. For example, some buyers are not concerned about the vendor's location if products are delivered according to an agreed-upon schedule. In contrast, other buyers seek to buy local to keep the money in the community.

Purchasers must consider food safety factors when they make vendor selection decisions:

- Vendors' facilities should be sanitary in regard to storage, handling, and delivery.
- Vendors that supply meat, poultry, and egg products must provide products that have been inspected by the United States Department of Agriculture (USDA).
- Vendors must comply with applicable local, state, and federal laws.
- Vendors should be able to provide a list of references to confirm they are reputable.
- Vendors that are inspected must have a Hazard Analysis Critical Control Point (HACCP) program in place. It is a system that can be used to control risks and hazards throughout the food supply process.
- Vendors that provide refrigerated storage or frozen products must have holding units that can maintain the products at the required internal temperatures.

REAL MANAGER

COMPETITION

When I first went to Company A, I looked at the supplier base and basically began to challenge the status quo. Remember, you want a good relationship with your suppliers, but there's no entitlement. One of the products on the appetizers was mozzarella cheese sticks. Two suppliers had shared the business for years and the price kept going up. I looked at alternatives—five bidders. At the end of the day, we kept the same two suppliers, but took $1 million out of the costs without change to the specs.

Moral: Competition is the spice of life. When you remove it, there isn't the same sense of urgency.

- Vendors' delivery trucks must be able to maintain the required internal temperatures for the products being transported.
- Vendors must have procedures in place to ensure their staff follows proper personal hygiene practices.

Most purchasers consider several key characteristics as they assess vendors:

- Consistently provides the quality of products specified by the buyer
- Offers products at a reasonable price for the required quality
- Meets product delivery schedules
- Offers useful support services
- Takes ownership of problems that occur and responds to the purchaser's needs
- Informs the buyer about order or delivery problems as soon as they occur
- Enjoys a stable financial position, which is important to remain in business
- Uses similar values to ensure ethical business relationships and practices
- Employs a highly motivated workforce to minimize problems from employee turnover or union-related work stoppages
- Has a genuine interest in helping the operation achieve its goals
- Is accessible, providing easy communication with the purchaser

Most of these characteristics can be summarized in this way: Purchasers want vendors that will work cooperatively so both parties can maximize the benefits of their relationship.

VENDOR SELECTION DECISIONS

An operation offering extensive breakfast, lunch, and dinner menus may need to purchase several hundred or more food items. If it also has a bar, many additional alcoholic beverage items are needed.

Food products are typically grouped by categories such as fruit and vegetables, meat, dairy products, and seafood items. Buyers generally evaluate and select several vendors that can supply most, if not all, of the products within each group. They would not, for example, interact with a range of vendors for lettuce purchases, with another set to buy potatoes, and with a third group who sell cauliflower. In much the same way, beverage buyers in many states purchase several brands of alcoholic beverages from distributors who carry them in the area. In other states there is only one source controlled by the state.

Buyers do not, then, use hundreds of vendors to supply the hundreds of products they require. However, buyers for operations offering many menu items would likely need the services of thirty to forty or more vendors. If they wanted to obtain competitive bids from two or three vendors for each category, many more vendors would need to be identified and qualified.

Purchasers must make selection decisions about two basic types of vendors. One type provides products that are routinely purchased, such as ingredients for menu items. The second type sells products needed on a one-time or infrequent basis, such as an oven.

Buyers use relatively routine procedures to obtain frequently purchased products. For example, buyers submit an RFP to indicate the products that are needed. These vendors will have the purchase specifications, so they will know the quality desired. The vendor submitting the lowest price is given the order, the products are delivered, and the vendor is paid.

These same buyers may devote much more time to identifying vendors of other products, including capital equipment items. Capital equipment items are resources valued at a certain amount, usually hundreds of dollars or more, with a useful life of more than one year that are used to create products or provide services. Examples of capital equipment items include dining-room tables and deep fryers (*Exhibit 4.2*).

Procedures for vendor sourcing range from using detailed procedures to learn about or screen unfamiliar vendors to confirming an existing vendor. Some purchasers use one or more vendors for each product as their primary source for a specified time period such as six months. Then they reevaluate the vendors to determine which will be used as the supply sources for the next purchasing cycle of six months.

Purchasers do not make vendor sourcing decisions as frequently as they make decisions about when to buy products or what quantity is needed. However, their decisions about which vendors should be asked to quote prices are among the most important purchasing decisions.

Information Sources

How should vendor sourcing decisions be made? Buyers must first learn as much as possible about potential vendors. Buyers use this information to determine which vendors are most likely to meet the needs of their organization. There are numerous sources of information about potential vendors. One of the most useful is the purchaser's previous experience with them, if any. In fact, some purchasers consider this the most important factor. After identifying a good supply source, purchasers continue to use the vendor unless problems arise.

Exhibit 4.2

RESTAURANT TECHNOLOGY

Electronic technology makes it easy to identify potential supply sources for current and new products required by an operation. A manager wants to buy some deli products, for example. One strategy is to contact local food distributors, including those with whom a buyer normally does business, to obtain information and prices. Another useful technique involves an electronic buying guide. This can provide much information, such as identifying manufacturers and even locating local supply sources for the product.

To learn how this process works, refer to the National Restaurant Association Online Buyer's Guide on the association's Web site. This guide allows visitors to browse by category or name to see product suppliers and click on each to obtain contact information, along with other products and services offered by that company.

People often use this strategy in their personal lives to make buying decisions. They become loyal to specific merchants and do not purchase from others who provide equal or perhaps even greater value. One reason they do this is the comfortable relationships they have developed with favored businesses. For example, a person might always use the same hair stylist.

However, researching possible supply sources should be one of the purchaser's ongoing responsibilities. This activity should be done frequently, not just when there is an immediate and specific need for a new source.

There are many useful sources of information about potential vendors:

- **Reputation:** The purchaser's knowledge of the marketplace in general and those providing specific products in the local area will assist in supply source decisions.

- **Trade publications:** Effective purchasers keep up with industry-related information. For example, they read electronic and print magazines, newsletters, and bulletins. This helps them identify manufacturers, vendors, and others in distribution channels that may be supply sources.

- **Electronic marketing information:** There are numerous buyers' guides offered by industry publications, trade associations, and other food industry sources on their Web sites. These guides allow purchasers to search on the basis of a product, for example, to identify possible sources.

- **Vendor representatives:** Good vendors provide information to their accounts: the organizations to whom they sell products. Purchasers who ask their vendors about companies selling noncompetitive products may learn about useful supply sources.

- **Trade shows and other meetings:** Many trade shows offer opportunities for qualified buyers to learn about vendors and their products. Trade shows are industry-specific events that allow vendors to interact with, educate, and sell to individuals and businesses in the industry. Qualified buyers are persons with the authority to make purchase decisions for their organizations. Professional meetings typically include time for attendees to visit exhibits, meet with vendors, and sample products. Vendors may sponsor events to provide selected buyers with information about their products and services.

- **Employees of the operation:** Staff at the establishment and purchasing peers in other properties, especially if they are part of the same multiunit organization, may have knowledge about potential products and vendors. Cooks who have worked in other operations, for example, might be asked about supply sources used by their previous employers.

- **Other information sources:** Vendor catalogs and even the local telephone directory may be good sources of information. Also, mailing brochures and other information collected and cataloged by the buyer may contain information about potential vendors. The Internet can also provide other sources of information about potential vendors.

Vendor Selection Concerns

Receiving high-quality service is a consistent necessity when interacting with vendors. It occurs as the vendor provides timely and accurate price quotations, meets delivery schedules, and makes it easy for purchasers to contact the distributor sales representative (DSR). This person is the purchaser's most immediate contact with the vendor. The contact person may also be referred to as the salesperson or account executive.

Quality of information provided, and help with problem-solving tasks, are two more examples of services that are difficult to judge before the first rounds of purchasing (see *Exhibit 4.3*). Will high-quality technical advice be provided? To what extent will a potential vendor be interested in providing information to help the operation meet its ongoing challenges? Answers to these and related questions should help purchasers in their decision-making process, especially when a vendor has a similar reputation with many other purchasers.

Some purchasers conduct on-site inspections of a potential vendor's facilities to observe factors such as work methods, cleanliness, and general organization. The condition of transport equipment is also important. For example, highly perishable fresh produce, meat and seafood, and dairy products must be delivered at the proper temperature.

While visiting vendors' sites, buyers may want to review the most recent inspection reports. These can be from the U.S. Department of Agriculture (USDA), the Food and Drug Administration (FDA), or a third-party inspector. They should be based on Good Manufacturing Practices (GMP) or Good Agricultural Practices (GAP).

GMPs are the FDA's minimum sanitation and processing requirements for producing safe food. They describe the methods, equipment, facilities, and controls used to process food. Both suppliers and their sources are subject to GMP inspections.

Manager's Memo

The financial stability of the operation is of concern to vendors, since they want to ensure they will be paid on a timely basis. Purchasers must also be concerned that vendors pay their own bills on time so they can continue to obtain the products they will sell to the organization.

Purchasers want vendors whose financial stability results from the same practices used by the establishment. The benefits of improved work methods, reduced costs, and better products with fewer defects can then be shared with the buyer's organization.

Make sure any inspection reports review several areas of the vendor's operation:

- Receiving and storage
- Processing
- Shipping
- Cleaning and sanitation
- Personal hygiene
- Employee training
- Recall program
- HACCP program or other food safety system

HACCP is based on identifying significant biological, chemical, or physical hazards at specific points in a product's flow through an operation. Once identified, the hazards can be prevented, eliminated, or reduced to safe levels.

GAP audits measure critical areas in which produce safety could be compromised. These audits typically focus on several concerns:

- Workers' health and hygiene
- Field sanitation and animal control
- Fertilizer and pesticide usage
- Irrigation water
- Harvest practices

Increasingly, a potential vendor's e-commerce capabilities are important to some buyers. E-commerce refers to activities related to buying and selling products and services through online sources. Some examples are electronic communication including RFPs, purchase orders, bids, and payment statements.

Determining Preferred Vendors

Reputation, information from the vendor and other sources, and visits to facilities will help the buyer make vendor selection decisions. All of these factors will have an impact on the final decision.

Exhibit 4.3 shows a sample vendor sourcing form that can be used to assess the potential benefits of using a specific vendor. It presents an overview of the information useful for making this important decision.

Exhibit 4.3

VENDOR SOURCING FORM

Vendor name: <u>McMillen Brothers Produce</u>   Representative: <u>   Ed McMillen   </u>
Products provided:<u>   Produce   </u>   Telephone: <u>   000-000-0000   </u>
                                                     Email: <u>   </u>
                                                     Address: <u>   102 Broadway   </u>
                                                     <u>   Sometown, HI   </u>
                                                     <u>   </u>

Sources of information about vendor (check all that apply):

☐ Interviews with vendor references   ☐ On-site visit
☐ Distributor sales representative   ☐ Trade publications
☐ Sales manager   ☐ Electronic marketing information
☐ Other interviews: ☐ Other:

<u>   </u>   <u>   </u>
<u>   </u>   <u>   </u>

Evaluation Factors	Unaccepable	Acceptable	Comments
Consistent quality (follows standards)	☐	☐	
Service procedures	☐	☐	
Service philosophy (cooperation)	☐	☐	
Management systems	☐	☐	
Facilities/delivery equipment	☐	☐	
E-commerce applications	☐	☐	
Financial stability	☐	☐	
Reputation	☐	☐	
Information (technical support)	☐	☐	
Input from others	☐	☐	
Sanitation/food safety (if applicable)	☐	☐	
Current customer recommendations	☐	☐	
Experience (years in business): _____	☐	☐	
Product availability	☐	☐	
Terms	☐	☐	
Delivery schedules	☐	☐	
Prices	☐	☐	
Breadth/depth of inventory	☐	☐	

Total Checks   _____   _____

Other information:

<u>   </u>

Vendor selection decision:

<u>   </u>

Evaluator: <u>   </u>   Date: <u>   </u>

Manager's Memo

Purchasers may approve some vendors that have not been used previously. They might begin using these vendors as a secondary supply source. Small orders that meet the vendor's minimum delivery requirements might be placed during a trial period. The results of these orders will provide purchasers with additional insights about their decisions.

Unfortunately, vendor selection decisions for one-time or infrequent purchases, such as a new dish-washing machine, do not provide opportunities for trial-and-error selection. These decisions are typically made on the basis of the buyer's experience with equipment manufacturers and the local distributors who sell and service the equipment, along with their reputations.

The Vendor Sourcing Form shown in *Exhibit 4.3* is completed for each potential vendor being considered. At this point it may be helpful for the general manager, buyer, and department heads to meet, review the vendor-specific information, discuss the information presented, and make the decision about whether the vendor should be added to the approved vendor list. They will need to work together as the relationship with the vendor evolves, so a team selection is a good idea.

When managers review a vendor sourcing form like *Exhibit 4.3*, they ensure that it provides contact information and a list of the sources used to learn about the vendor. The form contains numerous evaluation factors on which the buyer is asked to rate the potential vendor. No points are granted for factors judged unacceptable. The acceptable factors checked can be added to arrive at the total points for the assessment.

The vendor sourcing process is subjective. The buyer merely indicates his or her view about whether potential suppliers will be acceptable relative to each factor.

Managers must determine how many vendors should be approved for each category of food products and other items purchased. While there is no industry standard, a range of three to five vendors might be in order. The advantages of competitive bidding increase when more than two vendors are asked to submit prices. On the other hand, the purchasing process becomes difficult when more than several vendors are asked to respond.

A purchasing team might decide that four vendors should be approved as suppliers of specific products. They would be chosen by determining which vendors received the greatest number of points on the vendor sourcing form. Some establishments take the rating system to the next step and select preferred vendors, which are the approved vendors that have the highest ratings. The operation will then implement a policy that only approved vendors can be used. The policy might also indicate that prices should first be obtained from the preferred vendors, with other approved vendors being secondary sources.

Experienced buyers know that new vendors start businesses and other vendors go out of business over time. Effective vendor sourcing decisions provide several benefits for buyers:

- They can confirm that some of the vendors currently being used remain among the best and should continue to be used.

- They can learn about other vendors whose products and services can benefit the operation.

- They can use the input provided by vendors to improve their purchasing system and their relationships with the vendors.

ALTERNATIVE PURCHASING SOURCES

Buyers increasingly have purchasing alternatives. These options can impact the sources from which they obtain needed products.

Broad-Line and Specialty-Line Vendors

Broad-line vendors offer a wide variety of products, perhaps hundreds or even thousands. They are also referred to as "one-stop-shopping" vendors. For example, a broad-line vendor might sell everything from cocktail napkins to commercial dishwashers. In contrast, specialty-line vendors offer a deep selection of relatively few products. For example, a specialty cheese vendor may sell only numerous varieties of difficult-to-find cheese.

Which type of vendor is best? The question can be answered only by considering the specific situation. For example, one purchaser might buy frozen bread dough from a broad-line vendor that has just a few varieties of this product. The types offered are those that would be acceptable to the majority of product users. Another purchase may require products from a specialty frozen food vendor, who may offer buyers the choice of many additional varieties of frozen bread dough. In addition, if purchase quantities warrant it, the specialty-line vendor might even be able to produce or obtain special products to meet an operation's exact requirements. This vendor would likely offer few, if any, items outside this specialty line.

Advantages of broad-line vendors are related to reducing the number of vendors to select and interact with, including these factors:

- Reduced per-unit costs often available with increased purchase volumes
- Decreased costs of purchasing and accounting aspects of order placement
- Less time required for purchasing tasks
- Less time required for product-receiving activities
- Reduced time needed to evaluate, select, and interact with specialty-line vendors

Many buyers use broad-line vendors, and they are becoming more popular as distribution channels evolve. Some of these vendors are becoming even larger as they merge with other distributors, including those with specialty lines.

There are potential disadvantages to relying on one-stop-shopping vendors. These can include a lack of detailed product knowledge from the vendor's representatives. This is not always a problem, however, because the vendor likely has access to someone who represents the grower, processor, or manufacturer. This expert can provide information to the vendor, who can then assist the buyer.

Advantages to specialty-line vendors include access to products that might not otherwise be available and to detailed technical assistance applicable to the specialty products. Potential disadvantages were mentioned earlier as advantages of broad-line vendors. Per-unit purchase costs are likely to be higher, and time and costs will increase as more specialty-line vendors are used. More time will be needed for product purchasing and receiving, as well.

Buyer's Clubs

Buyers can also purchase products at regular retail stores and at buyer's clubs. When they purchase from buyer's clubs, buyers are making supply source decisions.

Buyer's clubs offer alternative supply sources for some operations, especially small ones. Buyers may find many of the products they commonly use, and purchases can be made frequently, even daily if there are cash flow or other concerns. Buyers may be able to call in their orders, which can then be ready for pickup when they arrive. Charge accounts for delayed payment plans may also be available.

Some buyer's clubs deliver products to the purchaser's property if minimum quantity requirements are met. As these services evolve and increase, buyer's clubs may become more similar to traditional vendors. As they do so, they become more attractive supply sources to buyers representing organizations of all sizes.

Increasingly, traditional grocery stores likewise offer a variety of products in large purchase-unit sizes. Local merchants may become the vendors of choice for some small-volume buyers who use "cash and carry" vendor sources.

Cooperative Purchasing

Some purchasers use a cooperative purchasing system, and this affects their vendor sourcing decisions. Cooperative purchasing involves multiple establishments combining orders for products of the same quality. One combined order is then submitted to the vendor with the lowest price, and the products are delivered to each participant's location.

State hospitality associations and for-profit co-ops may offer these services. An advantage is lower prices resulting from the higher volume ordered when purchase quantities are combined.

Local Sourcing

Managers, purchasers, and customers are increasingly knowledgeable and concerned about the food they buy. There is a trend toward concerns about the environment, freshness, and quality. Many customers want to support establishments that address these concerns. Restaurant and foodservice operations, in turn, can emphasize that they offer farm-to-fork or farm-to-table food in response to this trend.

Fresher ingredients, when properly prepared, produce superior menu items. Managers and chefs recognize several advantages of locally grown food products:

- They are often fresher and may be of better quality than those processed and shipped from distant locations.
- They can often be purchased cost-effectively.
- They support family farming and the local economy.
- They are appreciated by many customers.
- They can reduce transportation costs, pollution, and excess packaging.

Multiple Methods Are Used

Several purchasing methods have been discussed, and the selection of vendors depends, in part, on the purchasing method. However, it is incorrect to think that an operation uses only one purchasing method for all of the products it requires.

In fact, a buyer for a large-volume establishment may use several purchasing methods and vendor selection procedures at the same time:

- Buy produce in quantities needed for several days from approved vendors based on prices quoted in competitive bidding.
- Select vendors for fresh seafood purchases from specialty-line vendors based on current prices for required quality each time an order is placed.
- Use a long-term agreement to purchase paper products from a broad-line vendor (*Exhibit 4.4*).
- Purchase some products from a local buyer's club.
- Use a nearby grocery store for emergency or very small quantity petty cash purchases.

WHAT'S THE FOOTPRINT?

Of the numerous purchasing methods and vendor selection alternatives, local sourcing is among the few that recognizes environmental concerns. Local vendors are often used as sources for organic food items, which are also of increasing interest to many customers. Organic food products are grown in ways that encourage soil and water conservation and reduce pollution. Those who grow organic products do not use conventional methods to fertilize products or to control weeds.

Some establishments emphasize locally grown and organic food products and cater to a group of customers that are very concerned about these issues. Many other operations offer some menu items of interest to this market segment. They may, for example, continue to purchase large volumes of produce from vendors in their normal source of supply. At the same time they may also purchase smaller quantities of organic products to feature in specialty salads.

Exhibit 4.4

VENDORS FOR MULTIUNIT ORGANIZATIONS

Multiunit organizations can be composed of company or franchisee-operated units. A franchisee is a person or company that purchases the right to use the brand name and operating procedures of a franchisor for a fixed period of time in return for agreed-upon sales royalties and other fees. A franchisor owns and manages a brand and sells the rights to use its name, trademarks, and operating systems. Franchisees may own or lease their properties. Managers and purchasers in these organizations typically have less opportunity to select vendors than those who work in independently operated single-unit properties. For example, they may be required to use specific vendors that are owned and operated by the company. Purchasers in franchise operations frequently use franchisor-approved vendors or at least vendors that meet quality standards.

Within these broad limitations, purchasers in multiunit organizations may or may not use local supply sources, and they may or may not use the organization's approved vendors. They may or may not participate in buying groups operated by other franchisees or the franchisor. In other words, it is difficult to make broad statements about supply sources for specific units in multiunit organizations. However, whatever the process used to select vendors, product consistency between properties is typically necessary. This occurs by using purchase specifications developed for use in the entire organization.

Exhibit 4.5

Most customers ordering a sandwich or a salad at the drive-through window or counter of a quick-service restaurant have no idea how the ingredients for their order arrived at the establishment (*Exhibit 4.5*). Many employees and even their supervisors and managers think little about the purchasing process until the items reach their unit's receiving area.

Many employees in the restaurant and foodservice industry work for multiunit operations. They need to know how purchasing and distribution systems work in these organizations. There are jobs available all along the distribution chain for those interested in this important industry segment.

Many large restaurant chains in the United States operate food distribution systems. Their goal is to enable their company or franchisee-operated properties to obtain menu items and ingredients of the correct quality at a reasonable price. There are many differences in how these systems work, but there are also some similarities.

Exhibit 4.6 shows how a distribution system that moves products into the units of a multiunit organization might work. It provides a background for discussing how products needed by individual units flow through the system.

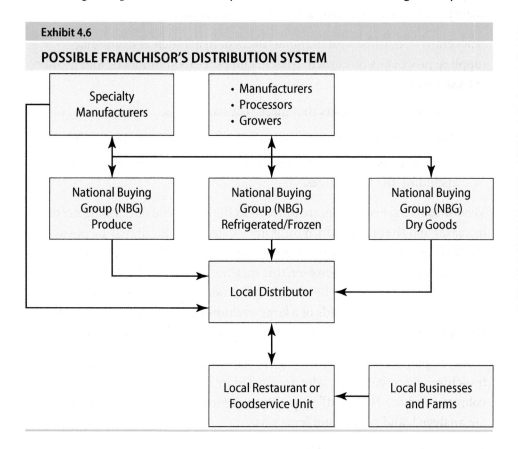

Exhibit 4.6

POSSIBLE FRANCHISOR'S DISTRIBUTION SYSTEM

Manager's Memo

A franchisor's contracts with soft drink companies represent significant dollars to the soft drink bottlers, or distributors, and the franchise. The campaigns of major soft drink manufacturers to win the business of multiunit organizations are well known by unit operators.

The stakes are even higher because the length of contracts for exclusive distribution to a franchisor may be five to eight years. This is much longer than normal contract lengths of one year or less for many products purchased by franchisors.

This sample distribution system involves several groups. A brief overview of each will explain how the system works.

National Buying Group (NBG)

The basic purpose of the national buying group (NBG) is to purchase products needed by the units. Product quality, price, and service—including delivery according to strict schedules—are very important, just as in independent operations. *Exhibit 4.6* shows three separate NBGs. One is used to purchase fresh produce, another purchases refrigerated and frozen items, and a third group buys dry and canned goods and disposable supplies. In some organizations, one NBG may be responsible for all categories of products. In others, NBGs may be responsible for regional or other buying needs.

Multiunit operators are very concerned about the products they use. They know their total purchase needs represent a very large amount of money. When purchasing needs of units are combined, the resulting large volumes can yield big price concessions. These savings benefit franchisees, and franchisors can use this advantage to help justify franchise fees. The savings realized should allow units to offer lower selling prices and optimize profits.

THINK ABOUT IT . . .

You visit somewhere new and eat at a regional chain you have never heard of. You have a very poor meal.

Will that experience influence your decision to visit that chain again? Explain your answer.

This may increase the revenue of both parties because the franchisor typically receives a percentage of the franchisee's revenues. Franchisors also benefit from the purchasing programs because there is better assurance that the product quality in all units will meet the franchisor's standards.

NBG employees work with manufacturers of items such as disposable supplies; processors of canned, frozen, and other food products; and growers of fresh produce:

- They identify products that meet NBG standards.
- They negotiate prices for the products that meet these standards.
- They address many contract details that favor their organization, including the franchisees.

Vendor sourcing becomes more difficult as the volume of purchasing needs increases and the area in which units are located expands. It may be possible for the NBG to contract all meat items required for a specified time for all units from one manufacturer. However, this may not be possible for fresh produce or other products. There may be many small producers but few very large ones that can meet all of the needs of a large multiunit organization. Then NBGs must negotiate with regional sources for the needs of the units in that region.

NBGs employ full-time purchasing specialists. They may receive advice from franchisee representatives, who are elected by all franchisees. These volunteers advise NBG staff as quality standards are established, price quotes are analyzed, and supply problems arise.

The price negotiated by the NBG may or may not be the product's final cost at the distributor's facility or when it is delivered to the unit. Transportation costs vary because of many factors, including distance. Manufacturers and processors bidding on NBG products must identify and conduct their own negotiations with those who will move products between locations. Large franchise organizations can have hundreds and even thousands of properties throughout the country.

NBGs may be physically located at the franchisor's national or regional headquarters, or they may operate out of other locations. They may be organized as purchasing divisions of the franchisor, or they may be separate organizations. Costs of operating NBGs may be paid by unit owners if the costs are included in the prices franchisees pay for products. Alternatively, franchisees may pay their share of the NBGs' operating costs indirectly as part of their franchise fee.

The discussion about NBGs to this point has considered the assistance they provide as food products are procured. However, some NBGs have expanded their services and negotiate for business insurance programs, large equipment, cooking utensils, and even **payment card discounts**: reductions in processing fees that credit and debit card issuers charge to those accepting payment cards.

Manager's Memo

Franchisors are concerned about the products used by their franchisees. Quality is especially important because of the need for consistency in each unit. A sandwich or salad cannot look, smell, or taste the same in every unit unless the same ingredients in the same quantity and of the same quality are used.

Franchisees cannot own profitable establishments if they charge the same basic menu selling prices as other units but have to spend more for ingredients. For these and other reasons, franchisors work very hard to help ensure that the ingredients used in their properties are of consistent quality and are available at a similar price to all unit owners.

Manufacturers, Processors, and Growers

Exhibit 4.6 shows that NBGs interact with the manufacturers, processors, and growers that supply products to be purchased by unit owners. Large companies that can meet product quality and quantity requirements may have relationships with local distributors for all areas in which products must be shipped.

For example, produce growers and those with seafood-related businesses may work together to provide the quantity of products needed. At other times, NBGs may contract with several sources to provide products meeting quality requirements for units in specific areas of the country that are served by specific distributors.

Manufacturers may employ some salespeople specifically to work with their national accounts: organizations with very large volume purchase requirements that are spread across the manufacturer's sales regions. They typically offer exclusive sales territories to manufacturer's representatives who sell the equipment in those sales territories. These more locally based representatives may be used to address the purchasing concerns of the buyers.

Specialty Manufacturers

Most of an NBG's work is done with organizations that can provide at least several of the ingredients and menu items needed by unit owners. However, units may require other items, such as toys for children's meals, which are produced by specialty manufacturers. These organizations provide only one or very few products not readily available from other sources at acceptable quality levels.

The role of the NBG with specialty manufacturers is the same as with other manufacturers. NBG employees must ensure quality, negotiate and award contracts, and resolve distribution and other challenges.

Local Distributors

Local distributors are identified in *Exhibit 4.6*. They order and receive products shipped from the manufacturer's location. Then they store and transport products in necessary quantities to the operation's units. They also bill the owners for products received and collect payments. The interactions that a unit's employees have with a distributor's delivery and accounting staff are typically more extensive than those with other organizations in the distribution system.

Some of the same distributors who deliver products from NBG sources may deliver other items purchased directly by a unit owner. For example, they may deliver canned goods and condiments arranged by the NBG and sell paper goods directly to the unit.

Manager's Memo

Some manufacturers selected by NBGs provide value-added services for franchisees. They may provide marketing materials or displays advertising their company's products. They may also provide samples of food products to individual units.

For example, a franchisee's agreement with the franchisor may allow multiple soups from a number of choices to be on the unit's menu. Product samples may be provided to franchisees to offer on a limited basis to allow the franchisee to learn about customer preferences.

Manufacturers' representatives may also provide indirect assistance to franchisees as they work with local distributors to address product quality concerns and distribution-related problems. They may also go with distributor representatives to units to assist owners with problems involving the manufacturer's products.

THINK ABOUT IT . . .

There is often a reverse correlation between quality and price of produce. When lettuce is in short supply, available lettuce is usually of low quality but high price.

Why do you think this is so?

Sometimes, one local distributor may provide all products purchased by the NBG for the units. If refrigerated and dry products are delivered by the same distributor, specially designed trucks that can transport both types of items at proper temperatures may be used. Alternatively, dry food products may be transported at refrigerated temperatures.

Local Businesses and Farms

Exhibit 4.6 indicates that local businesses may be another vendor source for unit operators. Items including fresh dairy products, eggs, and sometimes baked goods may be purchased from local sources. There are few, if any, organizations that can provide these products on a national or even regional basis. Also, perishable products that meet a specified quality level at an early point in the distribution channel may lose quality during transportation and storage. Several additional advantages to the use of local businesses and farms were presented in the earlier discussion of buying from local sources.

There are some potential concerns about purchases from local businesses and farms. One concern is that it may be difficult to recognize required quality standards at the owner's unit. For example, there will be no brand purchases. Additional problems may include frequent and unexpected product shortages and resulting price changes.

Franchisors work hard to minimize the need for products that must be purchased locally. This effort begins when menus are planned. If, for example, no menu items require fresh eggs, these products do not need to be purchased. If a recipe requiring eggs can be standardized to permit the use of a frozen or liquid egg product, numerous large-volume vendors become possible sources because of their ability to provide this market form (*Exhibit 4.7*). Fresh fruit and vegetables are among the greatest purchasing challenges for many franchisors. Typically, some or all of these products may be provided by local businesses.

Exhibit 4.7

VENDOR EVALUATION

The quality of each approved vendor's products, services, and information must be regularly evaluated. A primary reason is to determine whether the operation is receiving the anticipated value for the purchase dollars being spent. If so, the vendor will probably remain on the approved list. If not, corrective actions up to replacement of the vendor will become important.

Some vendor evaluation is ongoing and occurs in the routine day-to-day interactions between the buyer, other employees, and the vendor. It is not reasonable to say that a vendor is only as good as the last interaction. However, it is also true that these routine interactions affect the long-term relationship (see *Exhibit 4.8*).

Factors such as those used in *Exhibit 4.3* to initially approve vendors impact the ongoing relationship between the two parties. Therefore, these factors can also be used to determine whether vendors should continue to be used. In addition to these informal and ongoing evaluations, purchasers in some operations also conduct more formal assessments. This is especially important for new vendors and vendors of high-cost or high-volume products.

Exhibit 4.8

In high-volume organizations, the vendor evaluation process may begin as purchasing staff meet with those who use the purchased products and services. They can discuss vendor performance using the factors in the rating form. Information from other people, including the accounting and purchasing staffs, is also useful. So are discussions with vendor representatives, including sales managers. In smaller organizations, the manager may perform all or most assessment tasks.

Experienced purchasers know that their vendors may have suggestions about how the relationship can be improved. Some purchasers create awkward situations for their vendors in much the same way that the operation's customers can create problems. Every restaurant or foodservice manager can tell stories about customers who try to take advantage of the buyer–seller relationship. Examples include customers who do not "enjoy" their meal and request a refund after the meal is almost completely consumed. Think about customers at a large table during a very busy time who want to wait on a missing member of the party before ordering, and the person arrives 45 minutes later. Consider the customer who brings in an expired coupon and presents it at the end of the meal claiming the end date was not noticed.

The timing of vendor evaluation activities is important. Assessment should at least be done as vendor sourcing decisions for future purchasing cycles are made. If, for example, sourcing decisions are made for six-month periods, the evaluation process for currently approved vendors might begin six to eight weeks earlier. This will allow time for evaluation and consideration of other vendors, if necessary.

Exhibit 4.9 shows a sample approved vendor rating form. It would be used to evaluate the vendors currently supplying the establishment with one category of products. In this example, assume it is produce.

Notice that part 2 in *Exhibit 4.9* uses the same general rating factors that were considered in the vendor sourcing form in *Exhibit 4.3*. The buyer and his or her team approved the vendor based on those factors. Therefore, it is reasonable that these factors should also be considered when the vendor's performance is evaluated. One difference in the rating is the addition of *No Opinion* if the evaluator, for example, has no experience regarding a specific factor.

Part 3 in *Exhibit 4.9* allows evaluators to note their views about specific information. These items differ from those in part 2 because observations can be based on actual experience with the buyer's operation.

Those using the form should multiply the number of checks in each column by the points at the bottom of the columns. For example, there are 12 checks in the "acceptable" column (2 points), so the rater entered 24 points (12 checks × 2 points = 24 points) at the bottom of that column. After the points for each column are determined, the rater can add across the row and, in the example, this vendor received a 51-point score on the evaluation.

Part 4 of the approved vendor rating form provides a space for other information. For example, the rater could mention some positive or negative critical incidents that support the overall evaluation. Finally, in part 5, the evaluator can make a recommendation about whether the operation should continue or discontinue use of the vendor.

Manager's Memo

Purchasers sometimes put vendors in awkward situations. Consider the common receiving policy that incoming deliveries should be carefully checked to verify accuracy. Almost every vendor has stories about requests for policy exceptions when after-delivery quality concerns are noted. For products of relatively low value, most vendors will allow a purchase credit so their relationship with the purchaser is not affected. However, what about purchasers who state that many cases of products signed for were never received. Equipment vendors likely have similar stories about very expensive equipment received and later found to be damaged in a way that would have been easily noticed at delivery.

What is a vendor's proper response to these payment reduction requests? The answer, in part, probably relates to the volume of business the purchaser gives to the vendor. However, buyers at these operations should be alerted to the need to improve their receiving practices.

Exhibit 4.9

APPROVED VENDOR RATING FORM

Part 1: About Vendor

Vendor name: <u>McMillen Brothers Produce</u>   Telephone: <u>000-000-0000</u>

Representative: <u>Ed McMillen</u>   Email: _____

Part 2: General Rating Factors (check applicable box)

Rating Factors	Unacceptable	Acceptable	Excellent	No Opinion
Consistent quality (follows standards)	☐	☐	☑	☐
Service procedures	☐	☑	☐	☐
Service philosophy (cooperation)	☐	☑	☐	☐
Management systems	☐	☑	☐	☐
Facilities/delivery equipment	☐	☑	☐	☐
E-commerce applications	☑	☐	☐	☐
Financial stability	☐	☐	☐	☑
Reputation	☐	☑	☐	☐
Information (technical support)	☐	☑	☐	☐
Input from others	☐	☐	☑	☐
Sanitation/food safety (if applicable)	☐	☑	☐	☐
Current customer recommendations	☐	☑	☐	☐
Experience (years in business): _____	☐	☐	☑	☐
Product availability	☐	☐	☑	☐
Terms	☐	☐	☑	☐
Delivery schedule	☑	☐	☐	☐
Prices	☐	☐	☑	☐
Breadth/depth of inventory	☐	☑	☐	☐

Part 3: Specific Information (check applicable box)

	Unacceptable	Acceptable	Excellent	No Opinion
Accurate orders	☐	☐	☑	☐
On-time deliveries	☐	☑	☐	☐
Emergency requests	☐	☐	☐	☑
Purchase costs	☐	☑	☐	☐
Total acquisition costs	☐	☐	☑	☐
Payment policies/procedures	☐	☑	☐	☐
Discounts	☑	☐	☐	☐
Total Checks	3	12	8	
Rating (points)	1	2	3	
Score (points)	3	24	24	**51**

Part 4: Other Information

_____

Part 5: General Recommendation

☑ Continue use of vendor   ☐ Discontinue use of vendor

Comments: Our experience has been good to date; we will try to address e-commerce and delivery schedule issues.

J.S.B.	1/17
Director of Purchasing	Date

Exhibit 4.10 shows a Vendor Sourcing Summary Form. Information from the Approved Vendor Rating Forms shown in *Exhibit 4.9* can be carried forward to the summary form. Then the evaluation team can use all of this information to determine which vendors should continue to be approved to receive RFPs for produce and whether the services of any vendors should be discontinued.

Exhibit 4.10

VENDOR SOURCING SUMMARY FORM

Date:

Vendor Name	Comments and Other Information	No. of Points	Check (✓) Three Approved Vendors

Approved By: _____   Product Category: _____

If all persons evaluating a vendor agree that services should be continued, the buyer should inform the vendor of the decision. This would be a good time to discuss any general changes that should be made, such as delivery or payment times, minor problems that either party has observed, or suggestions about how to further improve the relationship.

If a decision is made to discontinue the services of a vendor, the buyer will need to begin the vendor sourcing process again. The goal will be to find another approved vendor in the specific product category.

The process just described can be used to determine the approved vendor list for each category of food, beverages, and supplies that are purchased. It can also be used for initial vendor selection. However, the process is cyclical: The evaluation process should be repeated on a predetermined basis, such as every six months. In addition, critical events that occur between evaluation periods may warrant reconsideration of a specific vendor.

The results of the rating process may suggest one other alternative: working with the vendor for a specified amount of time to determine whether improvements can be made. Ongoing feedback should have already suggested that the operation is not totally satisfied with the vendor's performance. A vendor wanting to continue the relationship should have been implementing revised procedures before the formal rating process took place. A schedule for making improvements with a follow-up evaluation is very important because the buyer will need to find a replacement vendor if the improvements are not satisfactory.

THINK ABOUT IT . . .

Vendor evaluation is similar to teachers evaluating students. Students must know what to do to earn a good grade, and teachers should provide feedback to help students.

In what other ways are the two similar?

SUMMARY

1. **Explain the importance of selecting the right vendors.**

   A vendor is a business that sells products or services to an operation. Restaurant and foodservice operations select vendors that will consistently provide products meeting quality standards at the best price. Vendors must meet requirements so customers will not be disappointed, nor production disrupted. In the most successful relationships, the operation and the vendor work together for mutual benefit.

2. **List the characteristics of the best vendors.**

   Factors used by purchasers to select approved vendors include consistent availability of the proper quality of products at the right price, delivered on time. Also important is availability of support services and willingness to resolve problems and respond to the purchaser's needs. The best vendors are stable financially, want to provide value, share similar ethics with the purchasing organization, and have a motivated workforce. They have a genuine interest in helping the buying operation and use ongoing communication. Food safety factors are also extremely important.

3. **Explain how to make vendor selection decisions.**

   Most buyers use several vendors for each food category. They request prices and make purchase decisions for specific orders based on prices provided.

   Buyers must learn about vendors, and reputation is an important concern. Information is available in trade and electronic marketing publications, from other vendors, and from trade shows and other meetings. Employees with experience at other properties may also know about vendors. Inspection reports detail safety compliance.

   A vendor sourcing form can be used to judge factors important to the operation and identify approved vendors. Approved vendors will submit prices for products for a specified time period.

4. **List and describe alternative purchasing sources.**

   Broad-line vendors offer a wide variety of many products. Specialty-line vendors offer deep selections of few products. Advantages of broad-line vendors include reduced per-unit costs and decreased costs of purchasing and accounting. Potential disadvantages include a lack of detailed product knowledge.

   Specialty-line vendors provide access to products that may not be available elsewhere. As more specialty-line vendors are used, additional purchasing time and costs will be incurred.

   Buyer's clubs allow buyers to shop as frequently as they like. Some clubs assemble orders in advance of arrival and may provide delivery.

   Cooperative purchasing occurs when multiple buyers agree on quality specifications, combine orders, and submit them to approved vendors. The vendor delivers products to each location.

   Locally sourced products provide a purchasing alternative that may result in fresher products or better quality. Locally sourced products can often be purchased cost-effectively, and they support the local economy. Many customers appreciate locally sourced products, and purchasing locally sourced products can reduce transportation costs, pollution, and excess packaging.

5. **Explain the flow of products that are purchased for use in multiunit organizations.**

   Unit owners and managers in many multiunit organizations have less buying authority than their peers in other operations. One reason is the need to have products of consistent quality in all units.

   One model uses national buying groups (NBGs) to interact with manufacturers, processors, and growers. NBGs purchase products of various types, such as produce, refrigerated and frozen products, and dry goods.

   Specialty manufacturers work with NBGs to provide products, such as toys, that are not available from other sources.

   Local distributors order and receive products from the manufacturer. They then store and transport them to units.

   Unit owners may purchase some products such as dairy, eggs, and baked goods directly from local businesses. Menus in many large, multiunit organizations are developed to minimize this need.

6. **Describe the procedures for evaluating vendors.**

   Buyers evaluate vendors to determine if they are receiving the anticipated value for purchase dollars. If buyers determine that they are receiving the anticipated value, vendors will likely remain on the approved list. If there are problems, corrective actions, which may include replacement of the vendor, will be needed.

   The same factors used to determine whether vendors should be approved can be used to determine whether expectations are being met. However, buyers can evaluate vendors based on actual specific performance, rather than potential.

APPLICATION EXERCISE

Identify two or three restaurant or foodservice operations and arrange a meeting or a telephone call with a manager of each one. Ask for the names of the vendors that provide the following products to the operation:

- Meat and seafood
- Fresh produce
- Canned goods and dry products
- Dairy products
- Baked goods

Access the Web site for each vendor and answer the following questions:

1. Based on the Web site, what advantages do buyers enjoy when they do business with the vendor?

2. What, if any, kinds of general product information, recipes, and buying suggestions does the vendor provide to readers?

3. How effective is the Web site message at convincing buyers to consider the vendor? Rank the Web site using the scale shown. Explain your response.

No Interest				Great Interest
1	2	3	4	5

REVIEW YOUR LEARNING

Select the best answer for each question.

1. **Vendor sourcing involves activities in which the buyer**
   A. determines who generally sells at the lowest prices.
   B. evaluates vendors' prices for specific orders.
   C. determines which vendors will be approved.
   D. questions manufacturers about vendors.

2. **What happens in the best relationships between buyers and vendors?**
   A. Vendors always offer lower prices than other vendors.
   B. Vendors are located very close to the buyer's operation.
   C. Buyers are consistently able to take advantage of vendors.
   D. Vendors and buyers maximize benefits from their relationship.

3. **What is the approximate number of vendors that should be approved for each category of food products?**
   A. 1
   B. 4
   C. 6
   D. 9

4. **Which is the best information on which to base selection of a vendor?**
   A. The vendor has a good reputation.
   B. The vendor offers the lowest prices.
   C. The vendor is close to the establishment.
   D. The vendor successfully filled a test order.

5. **What is a request for proposal (RFP)?**

    A. An inquiry to a vendor about prices for products of a specified quality

    B. A document from storeroom staff asking for more products to be ordered

    C. A letter to a vendor asking for marketing information about the company

    D. A form to vendors asking for noncompeting vendor recommendations

6. **Which type of vendor offers a large selection of relatively few products?**

    A. Buyer's club

    B. Broad-line vendor

    C. Specialty-line vendor

    D. Cooperative purchasing vendor

7. **Who purchases most of the products needed by the units in very large organizations?**

    A. Local managers

    B. National buying groups

    C. Franchisee representatives

    D. Cooperative purchasing groups

8. **Who typically bills the franchisees for products received through the purchasing system established by a large multiunit franchisor?**

    A. The franchisor

    B. The manufacturer

    C. The distributor

    D. The processor

9. **What type of product is most difficult to purchase and distribute in a large multiunit organization?**

    A. Dry goods

    B. Frozen food products

    C. Canned goods

    D. Fresh produce

10. **Information helpful in evaluating the performance of local vendors can come from**

    A. customers.

    B. employees.

    C. franchisors.

    D. manufacturers.

FIELD PROJECT

The purpose of this exercise is to develop a comprehensive list of factors used to evaluate which vendors should be approved to sell products to a restaurant or foodservice operation.

The questionnaires you completed for the Chapter 1 field project can be used to help develop these lists. Use the responses from both the restaurant or foodservice operation questionnaire and the vendor questionnaire, as well as information you gathered from the text, to create a list of factors used to approve vendors.

	Suggested Factors to Approve Vendors
Part A: Responses from restaurant or foodservice operation questionnaire (question 4)	
Part B: Responses from vendor questionnaire (question 4)	
Part C: Additional factors from Exhibit 4.3 in text	

5 Ordering Products: Pricing Decisions

INSIDE THIS CHAPTER

- Understanding Pricing
- Negotiating Prices
- Pricing Discounts

CHAPTER LEARNING OBJECTIVES

After completing this chapter, you should be able to:

- Explain the factors that affect product pricing.

- Summarize the importance of and the steps useful in effective negotiation.

- Describe several types of pricing discounts and explain rebates.

KEY TERMS

cash on delivery (COD), p. 126

cherry picker, p. 125

demand, p. 119

differential pricing, p. 123

discount, p. 138

fall-back position (negotiation), p. 132

free market, p. 124

going-in position (negotiation), p. 132

negotiation, p. 127

net price, p. 138

purchase unit (PU), p. 120

rebate, p. 140

value perception, p. 122

CASE STUDY

"It's really tough to get lower prices from vendors, isn't it?" asked Jake, the chef and food buyer at Carmel Straits Restaurant.

"Yes," replied Ilze, the restaurant's manager. "I think we've tried lots of things to reduce our prices. Maybe we should reduce our quality standards and then just shop around with different vendors to get the lowest price."

"Well," Jake said, "you might be right. But quality is important, and I think we need to determine the *quality* of products that we need and then look for vendors that will give us the best price."

1. Who do you think has better ideas about reducing prices: Ilze or Jake? Why?

2. What are some things that the chef and manager can do to reduce the cost of food products without sacrificing quality?

Exhibit 5.1

UNDERSTANDING PRICING

The objective of effective purchasing is to obtain the right quality of products at the right price from the right source in the right quantity at the right time. The right price is not always the lowest price.

Few restaurant or foodservice managers think that the best meals are the least expensive meals. In fact, a focus on lowest price alone often indicates a lack of understanding about the economics of pricing on the part of buyers.

Buyers must know how to obtain the right price when they purchase food and beverage products (*Exhibit 5.1*). A good way to begin is learning how vendors establish their product selling prices.

Factors Affecting Selling Price

Vendors set prices by using specific information. Four primary factors influence the prices vendors charge their customers:

- Prices reflect costs
- Prices reflect consumer demand
- Prices reflect service features
- Prices reflect vendor quality

A buyer's understanding of these four factors is important. They suggest the complexity of vendor pricing and illustrate the need to consider all aspects of price when products are purchased.

PRICES REFLECT COSTS

Few people are in business "just for fun," and even those who are probably do not want to lose money. A vendor sells a product for which it paid $10 including all allocated expenses. To recover that cost, make a profit, and maintain the business, the product will typically need to be sold for more than $10. If the $10 paid was fair and reasonable and customers do not value the product enough to even pay $10 for it, the business will fail.

Professional buyers understand that vendors must make a fair profit on what they sell. If they go out of business, this reduces competition and can place the buyer at risk of paying even higher prices. This text has emphasized a "win–win" partnership between buyers and vendors. A fair price that includes a profit in return for products, services, and information is part of that relationship.

PRICES REFLECT CONSUMER DEMAND

In many cases, prices are influenced by consumer demand: the total amount of a product or service that buyers want to purchase at a specific price. When products are in limited supply and are highly desired, the prices buyers must pay for those products will generally be high. In some cases, such as rare wines, the prices charged will reflect the limited supply. In some other cases, such as gasoline, it is not scarcity but simply the consumers' willingness to pay that most influences price.

Restaurant and foodservice buyers are just like other consumers. The price they pay for a product will be affected by the supply of and demand for that product. The best buyers know when they are paying for scarcity and when they may be paying a premium price for something like organic food items or bottled water that many people seem to want. This understanding is important because what other consumers are willing to pay for a specific product can vary widely based on factors beyond the buyer's control, including a greater perceived need for the product and lower profit requirements.

PRICES REFLECT SERVICE FEATURES

This factor can be easily understood by considering two buyers. One pays $100 for a case of fresh sirloin steaks but must drive to the vendor's location several miles away to pick it up. The other buyer pays $105 for a case of the same quality steaks, but the product is delivered to the buyer's establishment. Which buyer received the best price? Despite the fact that the price was higher, the second buyer received a service feature, the delivery, which would easily justify the slightly higher price.

When present, the importance of these added features cannot be overlooked. Timely delivery, the condition of the vendor's facility and delivery vehicle, and the quality of a vendor's service are important. Accurate invoicing and payment processing, order accuracy, payment and credit terms, and ease of order placement are likewise crucial. These are examples of service features that will be reflected in a vendor's prices.

PRICES REFLECT VENDOR QUALITY

Operations with a reputation for quality food and outstanding service can charge more for their products. Likewise, vendors that have excellent reputations can realize an important benefit: increased prices that deliver higher profits. Buyers who place a high value on vendors with a reputation for quality may pay more for the products they purchase from those vendors. However, the extra costs will be justified because of the peace of mind that comes from having confidence in the vendor.

WHAT'S THE FOOTPRINT?

Understanding what a product is really worth can be difficult because the demand for food and beverage products is not constant. As recently as a decade ago, significant sales of bottled water in restaurant and foodservice operations were virtually unheard of. The 2000s, however, saw an explosion in the sale of still and carbonated bottled waters, and profits were good.

Beginning in the late 2000s, environmental concerns caused many consumers to ask questions such as, "Does shipping bottles of water from Europe make environmental sense?", "How much energy is spent to bottle and ship it?", and "Is it really superior to filtered water from local water supplies?"

The consumers' view of value and, therefore, what they were willing to pay for bottled water was changing. A move away from bottled water reflects concerns about the "going green" movement to reduce the environmental costs of bottling and transporting water, energy spent recycling bottling material, and keeping plastic out of landfills.

If buyers focus only on a product's selling price per purchase unit without considering reputation, they may end up purchasing from vendors that provide neither quality nor value. **Purchase unit (PU)** refers to the weight, volume, or container size in which a food is normally purchased. For example, ground beef may be purchased by the pound, syrup by the gallon, and lettuce by the case. Vendors that do not operate ethically and do not stand behind their products and services often end up costing buyers more, sometimes much more, than what the buyers originally paid for the products.

Pricing: The Buyer's View

Some of the factors vendors consider when developing their prices have just been discussed. Buyers must also recognize that their own views affect buying decisions when alternative prices are evaluated.

Much has been written about how buyers react to selling prices. One way to examine prices from the buyers' view is to think of these views as being either traditional or nontraditional.

TRADITIONAL VIEWS OF PRICING

One traditional way that buyers view pricing assumes that vendors have carefully evaluated their own costs. Buyers assume vendors have determined a selling price that is low enough to attract customers and high enough to cover costs and provide a reasonable profit. When they think this way, buyers make one or more of the following assumptions:

- Increased price = Increased quality. This is often an attractive and reasonable assumption that can help buyers make informed decisions. For example, bar tops made from solid wood are generally perceived to be of higher quality than similar products made from pressed board. The quality of the better bar tops will be reflected in their higher prices. Similarly, a 20-year-old Scotch whiskey will likely taste better, and cost more, than a 5-year-old Scotch produced by the same distillery.

  To avoid purchasing errors, however, buyers must ensure that they are comparing similar products. Pressed-board bar top prices from two vendors should not be compared directly to the solid wood bar top prices of a third vendor.

  Likewise, 20-year-old Scotch prices should not be compared to those of 5-year-old products. The assumption that increased quality equals increased price should be used only when products that are truly identical in nature, such as two brands of solid wood bar tops, are compared.

- Increased price = Scarcity and value. Purchasers often think that if something is rare, a higher price is charged. Buyers who purchase Russian caviar, steaks of the very highest quality, or rare French wines understand the importance and often the truth of this belief. In many cases when demand for a product is significantly strong, the product's availability is limited, and this will be reflected in the selling price.

  However, scarcity alone is not a reason for increased value that justifies a higher price. If it were, the drawings young children make—rare and unique and likely highly valued by their families—would be worth a lot of money. In fact, scarcity of a product frequently reflects widespread lack of consumer interest and often justifies a lower, not higher, price.

- Increased price = Increased image. Customers of restaurant and foodservice operations have the same peer pressure and self-image concerns as other consumers. For example, consider customers dining at an operation that places ketchup bottles on the tables. They will likely view the establishment more favorably if a well-known brand is displayed rather than an unknown, generic product.

Exhibit 5.2

  Buyers should understand that paying for image makes sense only when the image is truly appreciated or demanded by customers. If it is not, the price paid for image is wasted. Consider the fact that buyers can spend hundreds of dollars per place setting, which includes glasses, plates, knives, forks, spoons, and other items (*Exhibit 5.2*). If they do so, buyers must ensure that the image, as well as the products they are purchasing, is worth the often much higher prices.

Traditional views about pricing most often relate the selling price of an item to the costs incurred by the item's vendor. This is also a typical way of setting menu item selling prices. It is common for a manager to determine a product's cost and then increase it by a multiplier to reflect non-food costs and profit in order to achieve a desired product cost percentage.

For example, assume a manager is working with an approved operating budget that requires a 25 percent food cost. This means that 25 percent of all revenue should be spent on food and that yields a multiplier of 4.

$$100 \div 25 = 4$$

| **Percent of revenue** | **Percent of revenue** | **Multiplier** |

This manager can then multiply a hamburger with a food cost of $2 by 4 to arrive at an $8 selling price, or a 25 percent food cost:

$$\$2 \div \$8 = 25\%$$

| **Product cost** | **Selling price** | **Food cost** |

LESS TRADITIONAL VIEWS OF PRICING

There are also less traditional views of pricing that might seem strange at first. However, they reveal some of the most useful thoughts about pricing:

• Price and costs are unrelated. This less traditional view of pricing recognizes that a vendor's cost and selling price may be unrelated. This situation occurs more often than some buyers suspect. For example, vendors may sell specific brands of bottled water at very high prices. They are able to charge high prices because extensive advertising campaigns sponsored by the manufacturer have convinced some buyers that the water is special and is worth the higher cost.

Buyers who encounter situations in which vendors sell below their true costs can significantly offset one of the basic foundations of vendor pricing. These situations arise when, for example, vendors change product lines or even go out of business. Buyers should be alert to take advantage of them when they benefit the operation.

• Cost plus value = Price. Many accounting textbooks discuss a common and traditional view of how businesses should establish prices:

Cost + Desired profit = Selling price

A less commonly taught view restates how prices might be established:

Cost + Value to buyer = Selling price

This less traditional view shows that the buyer, not the vendor, ultimately determines selling price. Buyer value is the idea that a product's value relates to the purchaser's need for or interest in the product. Value is not inherent in the product itself. In this view, value is in the eye of the beholder. Value perception is the customer's opinion of a product's value to him or her. In the long run only buyers—not growers, manufacturers, distributors, or brokers—determine the prices that buyers are willing to pay.

Purchasers should understand that value perception is more important than vendor cost because buyers are not interested in the vendor's cost. It is easy to disprove the idea that cost plus desired profit equals selling price. Just think about restaurant and foodservice operations that go out of business. If all managers had to do was determine their costs and add their desired profits, even the least skilled operators could remain in business.

Rather, customers choose to visit some establishments based on whether their experiences have provided a value to them. Again, customers do not care about the owner's operating costs or desired profits. They care only about whether the operation provides value to them. If it does, they will gladly pay the posted prices. If not, they will not pay the price even if the owner accurately computed all costs and the desired profits.

The important point for buyers to remember relates to the value they place on an item to be purchased. The value they place on a less-than-essential item should be low. Then, the price they pay should also be low *regardless* of the vendor's price or costs. Alternatively, the value placed on some services will likely be very high. Consider, for example, the hourly rate for a plumber hired to fix restroom toilets at an establishment on a busy Saturday night. Excessive time should never be wasted over relatively small differences in vendor prices in situations like this one.

- Different prices are normal. Differential pricing involves charging different customers different prices for the same product. For example, a buyer who purchases 100 cases of a specific product will likely pay less per case than another buyer who purchases 10 cases of the same product because of a quantity discount.

  No business should charge higher or lower prices based on a buyer's race or ethnic background. However, many operations have historically practiced differential pricing based on gender and age. Consider "ladies' nights" at clubs, senior citizen meal discounts, and reduced menu prices for children. Experienced buyers understand that differential pricing decisions are often made without considering the vendor's actual cost of providing the product.

  Purchasers who can receive preferred prices because of differential pricing methods used by their vendors will pay lower prices, and they should do so. Those buyers whose operations do not receive a differential price should talk with their vendors to learn about the requirements to receive lower prices. There are often a number of reasons for being included in a special pricing group.

Here are three common reasons vendors sell the same products to different buyers at different prices:

- **Frequency of delivery:** Vendors incur a great expense when they deliver products to an operation (*Exhibit 5.3*). When they do so less frequently, their costs are lowered. Then, some of these savings can be passed on to their customers. In some cases, purchasers can reduce their costs significantly if they eliminate vendor delivery entirely and pick up their products at the vendor's place of business. This is not a widespread practice. However, it may be practical if the establishment is located close to a vendor or if someone from the operation routinely travels near the vendor's location. For example, the owner or manager might pass the vendor on the way to the bank or on the way to work.

Exhibit 5.3

- **Dollar volume of purchase:** Many vendors offer lower per-purchase-unit prices when items are purchased in large volumes. Buyers influence the amount of product delivered when they determine how frequently they want delivery, noted above as a factor. Buyers may also enjoy reduced costs when they combine orders and purchase a larger variety of items from the same vendor.

- **Payment terms:** Vendors typically provide reduced prices to buyers who pay more frequently, such as once weekly rather than once monthly. Vendors are concerned about cash flow just as restaurant and foodservice managers are. Vendors requiring cash quickly to pay their own bills may offer lower prices based on payment terms.

Other Pricing Concerns

Buyers will encounter several additional factors that affect the prices they pay for products. While their impact can vary, several of these factors affect all industry segments.

GOVERNMENTAL CONTROLS

The pricing discussion to this point has focused on willing vendors and willing buyers. Sometimes, however, local, state, or federal government plays a role in price determination. For example, the prices charged for utilities such as electricity, gas, water, and sewage are, to some degree, governmentally regulated and are not subject to normal pricing decisions. Alcoholic beverage prices are another example of governmental price controls.

Government agencies can directly affect the prices buyers must pay. Consider what businesses pay for water. This utility is generally owned by the community and is sold to commercial accounts. Water prices differ based on scarcity in an area and the total quantity purchased per month by the business. In some places, larger-volume users receive a reduced price for quantity purchases. In other communities, high-volume users pay higher per-gallon prices as their water usage increases.

CONTRACT TERMS

In a free market situation, the prices paid for products and services are determined by the vendor and the buyer who voluntarily enter into a contract. Their agreement addresses numerous issues including selling price.

Pricing based on contractual agreements is very common in the restaurant and foodservice industry for many purchases. For example, products are often purchased after a discussion about quantity, quality, pricing, and other issues that are summarized in a contract. Services such as cleaning of exhaust hoods, windows, carpet, and upholstery are also performed according to a contract. A price is agreed on for a specific period of time, and it is not generally subject to revision until the contract period expires. Sometimes the agreed-upon price is the vendor's actual costs plus an additional amount for profit.

NUMBER OF VENDORS

Many buyers must decide whether to buy specific products from one or more vendors. They recognize that as the number of vendors increases, more time must be spent in ordering, receiving, and invoice payment activities. However, they may fear that if they award all or most business to one vendor, prices will increase due to lack of competition. As a result, many buyers routinely split their business among several vendors on principle. That is the approach suggested in chapter 4 when addressing vendor sourcing decisions.

Experienced buyers in high-volume operations recognize that vendors are not likely to increase prices unless there is a real need to do so. Restaurant and foodservice operators share the same view. They are unlikely to take advantage of their best customers. In fact, restaurant and foodservice managers would likely offer additional service features, such as preferred tables to these customers. In the same way, many vendors offer preferred pricing to operations that do most of their buying from them. It is in the vendor's best interest to give a better price to a high-volume customer to retain that buyer's business.

The impact on price when a buyer decides to use single or multiple vendors can be complex. Professional buyers understand that the cost of delivering a $1,000 order is not very different from the cost of delivering a $100 order. Each delivery will require one truck and one driver. When the vendor's cost of delivery must be spread across fewer items, the likely result is an increase in purchase unit price.

Purchasers who concentrate their business with one or a very few vendors will generally pay lower purchase unit prices. This is why buyers employed by multiunit operations are able to obtain such attractive product pricing. For a vendor, the possibility of securing a very big order allows significantly reduced pricing because the cost of service can be spread across all of the products that are being sold.

Considering the prices charged by a few vendors for each order and selecting the one with the lowest prices for the same quality tends to increase average delivery size and reduce per-item prices. Alternately, giving one vendor all of an operation's business can be costly if the products vary widely in quality and price, or if they are often difficult to obtain.

For many buyers the logic of using multiple vendors appears sound. Often it is, but not always. For example, consider purchasers who continually compare prices among competing vendors. When quality is equivalent, they buy from the vendor offering the lowest price. They appear to be maximizing effort and minimizing cost. These buyers should, however, recognize that cherry pickers who purchase only a vendor's lowest-priced goods will be serviced last. **Cherry pickers** is a term commonly used by vendors to describe buyers who request bids from several vendors and then buy only those items each

REAL MANAGER

MULTIPLE VENDORS

As you probably know, there are two major soft drink suppliers in the world. Company B had used the same soft drink supplier since its founding, 25 years earlier. The contract came up for renewal, and it was a huge multiyear contract. I was asked to negotiate, but was told "we really don't want to change suppliers."

I noted that if we wanted the best decision, it had to be an equal playing field. If both companies submit a proposal, then both have to have a shot at the contract. The result was a long, complex negotiation. The company that had *not* had the contract previously made such a strong proposal, it would have been fiscally irresponsible to turn it down. We had formed a team of franchisees and company employees, and they made the recommendation to the president.

Moral: It took some convincing, but he could see that the playing field had been fair and equal. And this was the best decision for the company and the shareholders.

vendor has "on sale" or for the lowest price. If a buyer purchases only a vendor's low-priced items, that vendor will usually respond by providing limited service. This is a natural reaction to the buyer's failure to consider varying service levels, long-term relationships, dependability, or any other vendor characteristic besides lowest price.

PAYMENT HISTORY

Buyers for operations that do not pay their bills on time might be surprised to know what their competitors are paying for similar products. In many cases, managers of establishments that are slow to pay will find that their vendors have added the extra cost of carrying slow-pay accounts to the price. They do so because the slow-pay buyers are really purchasing products with the vendors' money, rather than their own.

Vendors are very concerned about when they are paid, and they carefully keep track of when they receive payments. When a buyer's payments lag behind due dates, notices are sent, and some costs for late fees and finance charges may be incurred. When payments are not made after the first or second notice, the prices quoted for products typically become less competitive. At some point, vendors will require cash on delivery, if they will make deliveries at all. **Cash on delivery (COD)** refers to a requirement that a buyer pay the full amount owed in cash or other acceptable payment form at the time products are delivered.

Lowest Price Is Not Always the Best Price

Buyers must be concerned about many things as purchasing decisions are made. Not surprisingly, the challenge of determining the best price will always be important. The importance increases along with the amount of money involved.

The recognition that the best price is not always the lowest is one factor that separates an experienced buyer from someone who is just learning the basics. The best purchasers know they are buying a product, such as fresh seafood or canned vegetables. However, they also understand that the price they are paying covers several additional factors.

First, they must consider the quality of the product being purchased, which will be reflected in the product cost. Larger-sized shrimp cost more than smaller shrimp. A can of green beans containing beans of different sizes and colors and with stems should cost less than a can of trimmed, similarly sized green beans. When buyers say they want the lowest price, they should be saying they want the lowest price for a product of proper quality.

Service is also an important part of price. Why would a buyer make a purchase agreement for a lower-priced product required for the Sunday buffet if it will not be delivered until Monday? On-time delivery is a valuable service, and a purchaser should be willing to pay for it.

THINK ABOUT IT . . .

What should a buyer or manager do if a payment is due but must be delayed for a few days? What are the advantages and disadvantages of alerting the vendor immediately? What would you do?

The selling price of a product also includes information. The value of information can range from almost nothing, when a vendor does not know about the products, to almost invaluable when a vendor provides critical information that can save a manager a lot of money. For example, a knowledgeable vendor could provide information about how to keep products safe and enjoyable for customers. It is acceptable and preferable to want the best price for products being purchased. However, the best price is not typically the lowest. Instead, the best price is the lowest price for a product of desired quality provided by a vendor that offers excellent service and the information needed to best use the product.

NEGOTIATING PRICES

Effective purchasers know how to negotiate as they buy the products and services required by their organizations. Negotiation is a process by which parties with mutual interests try to reach an agreement about something. Sometimes, negotiation involves only one issue, such as product price. Frequently, however, several concerns such as service, delivery schedules, and payment terms are important issues as the purchaser attempts to receive value.

Negotiation sessions with a vendor can involve only a single representative of the operation, such as the purchaser, or multiple representatives. Negotiations can be face-to-face or undertaken electronically. The time needed for negotiation can range from a few minutes to several months, or longer.

Overview of Negotiation

The desired outcome for negotiation is for the persons who are negotiating to reach an agreement that benefits each of them. Not surprisingly, that can be a challenging objective. Compromise is typically necessary, and it is common because negotiating parties usually have incentives to overcome each other's concerns.

There are three possible outcomes from any negotiation process:

- The parties can reach a mutually acceptable agreement, or compromise.
- The parties can fail to compromise; they can, in effect, "agree to disagree."
- The negotiation can be unsuccessful with an understanding that there will be more negotiation in the future.

"Win–Win" Negotiation Is Important

Some buyers think that one party must "win" and the other party must "lose" when they negotiate. This can occur when the parties are negotiating about the cost of a product for a single order, an equipment purchase on a one-time basis, or a nonrecurring service such as a construction project. For example, a buyer might be purchasing equipment from an exhibitor at a trade show. Another buyer might negotiate for the construction of a storage shed.

THINK ABOUT IT ...

Negotiators must "think on their feet." Even with preparation, they cannot predict all points that might arise. What are two strengths negotiators can use? What are two weaknesses they must avoid?

If both parties believe it is unlikely there will be a future business relationship, the issue of price is likely to be very important. As the purchase price is negotiated, the vendor "wins" as the price goes up, or the purchaser "wins" as the price goes down.

However, there are even instances in these examples where issues other than cost can be negotiated. Perhaps, for example, the buyer purchasing equipment will transport it to the establishment at no expense to the vendor. The price of the shed construction may be influenced by payment terms.

More commonly, successful negotiation allows both parties to "win." This is the desired outcome when a long-term relationship is desired. For example, a vendor offering a price concession might be interested in a long-term relationship with the purchaser. In the previous situations, the equipment exhibitor might be interested in selling a new item because its presence in the community makes it convenient for other operators to see and learn about the equipment. The contractor building the storage shed may want a hospitality-specific reference to expand his or her business.

Purchasers representing their operation may sometimes be confronted with persons whose views about negotiation do emphasize the "I win, you lose" approach. Differences between the "win–win" and "I win, you lose" viewpoints are noted in *Exhibit 5.4*.

Manager's Memo

Why is the negotiation process necessary? After all, chapter 4 stressed the importance of identifying approved vendors to quote prices for needed products. Why is there a need to negotiate prices when competitive bids will be obtained?

Wise buyers know that there are other factors besides price for which agreements are needed. For example, one vendor might quote a very competitive price for a product of the required quality. However, perhaps the preferred delivery time is not convenient for the operation. Or, perhaps a buyer has a good price and the quality is excellent but payment is required before the buyer's establishment wants to pay it. These are examples of issues for which negotiation can be helpful.

Exhibit 5.4

DIFFERENCES BETWEEN TWO NEGOTIATING APPROACHES

Win–Win Approach	Win–Lose Approach
• Participants solve problems.	• Negotiators are adversaries.
• Goal is for all parties to win.	• Goal is for other parties to lose.
• Remove people from the problem.	• Focus on the problem and the people.
• Both parties trust each other.	• Do not trust the other party.
• Focus on and explore common interests.	• Do not compromise a position.
• Do not have a "bottom line."	• Focus on the "bottom line."
• Develop options that allow both parties to win.	• Search for one-sided gains.
• Develop multiple options; make decisions later.	• Insist that one position is correct.
• Use objective factors to evaluate compromises.	• Win a "contest of wills."
• Yield to principle rather than to pressure.	• Apply pressure.

The notion that vendors should provide value has been emphasized throughout this book, and it is also important in win–win negotiating. When possible, it is important that both parties gain lasting benefits from the negotiation process.

Negotiation and Value

Experienced buyers agree that the price of a product is important. However, value, which is the relationship between price and quality, is even more important. They also understand that the service and information they require is part of a product's cost. Three things—product, service, and information—are components of what is being purchased from the vendor. Wise purchasers realize that the vendor's information and service is bundled with the purchase price and, like the price, can be negotiated.

Most buyers recognize that it is worth something to consistently receive the correct quality of products, in the right quantities, at the agreed-upon price. They also know there are costs if these purchasing goals are not consistently attained. They are willing to pay for vendors' information about products and the possibility of price changes in terms of a slightly higher product cost. They also recognize the value of specialized expertise to address product-related problems (*Exhibit 5.5*).

It is also valuable for the purchaser to consider price negotiation issues from the vendor's perspective. Vendors are not likely to want to do business with a purchaser who paid a very high price when the chances for payment were risky and payments likely to be slow. They do not like to do business with buyers who consistently allege product defects that may not exist, or who have all-too-frequent stockouts with the need for additional deliveries.

While oversimplified, buyers want to purchase from good vendors, and vendors want to do business with good buyers. Strategies used during negotiation and the results of the process are likely impacted by the relationship between these two parties. The better that relationship, the greater the benefits to both will be.

Successful Negotiation Traits

Two types of concerns must be addressed as the negotiation process evolves. These relate to the interests of the operation and human concerns about those involved in the negotiation session. These concerns are interrelated, and several factors impact the success or failure of negotiation:

• The personality and skill levels of the negotiators

• The extent to which the personalities of the negotiators are compatible

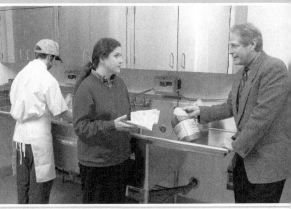

Exhibit 5.5

Manager's Memo

Negotiation is only one way for non-agreeing parties to interact, and there are others:

• **Giving in:** One party may just accept the other party's offer. This may be the only alternative when there are few vendors or limited product availability. Conceding to a price for rare wines is an example of this "take it or leave it" situation. Conversely, multiunit organizations that purchase in large volumes may be able to dictate prices. Vendors can accept the price or risk loss of business.

• **Eliminating the issue:** A purchaser may experience difficulty obtaining an ingredient for a specialty menu item and must pay a high price. A menu change may eliminate the need for the ingredient.

• **Persuading:** Frequent and reasonable defense of a position may be helpful. For example, information sharing and explaining the circumstances of a purchase need are strategies that may encourage a vendor to accept a lower price.

RESTAURANT TECHNOLOGY

One traditional model of negotiation involves the vendor attempting to obtain the highest price for products. A relatively new approach uses technology. Potential vendors compete electronically to sell products at the *lowest* price.

To prepare for a reverse auction, buyers may contract with an outside company to manage the process. That company identifies and alerts potential vendors, organizes and manages the event, and provides information helpful in decision making.

The buyer issues a request for proposal (RFP) to purchase one or more items. Then, interested vendors input their proposed prices into an Internet auction site over a relatively short time period. Quotes indicate the price for which vendors are willing to sell the product meeting the requirements in the RFP. Buyers typically reserve the right to purchase from any vendor. This might be a vendor that did not submit the lowest price or even one that did not participate in the auction.

- Each negotiator's expectations about the other party's strengths and weaknesses, intentions and goals, and commitments to positions
- The ability of each negotiator to use persuasion and other strategies to modify the other party's position and to move both sides toward a mutually beneficial outcome

Many skills used by effective negotiators are the same as those necessary for success in any management position. For example, effective negotiators are excellent communicators. They use general communication skills, including effective speaking, listening, and organizing thoughts before expressing them. They can also use facts to defend their decision, and they recognize the importance of cross-cultural communication skills.

Buyers who are creative thinkers and who are dedicated to their establishment and concerned about the interests of the other party will likely be better negotiators. Each of these characteristics can be learned, or at least improved on. The saying "experience is the best teacher" applies to becoming a better negotiator.

Successful negotiators know that the process involves more than just making mutual compromises. People skills, especially listening ability, are critical.

The best negotiators are good problem solvers and decision makers, and they can spot shortcomings in the logic used by the other party. For example, an equipment vendor might say that his or her equipment is widely used and is therefore the "best." A wise buyer knows that what is best is that which is most suitable for its intended use. This will create a need for the vendor to discuss the equipment's features relative to the buyer's specific organization.

Incorrect information can be misleading and help one party gain an advantage. A negotiator might, for example, indicate the utility consumption rate for a specific equipment item. That rate might be correct for one but not all phases of equipment operation. Actual consumption might be significantly different from what was suggested. Skilled negotiators are able to consider statements, analyze them objectively, and quickly discover what statements should be questioned and what questions should be asked.

All of the successful negotiation traits discussed in this section can be summed up in being professional. The need for the purchaser to be courteous, respectful, and show concern should be obvious.

Negotiation Procedures

Exhibit 5.6 provides an overview of the steps in the negotiation process.

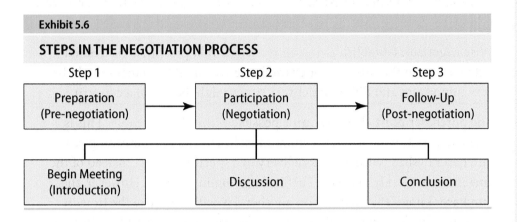

Exhibit 5.6

STEPS IN THE NEGOTIATION PROCESS

Step 1 → Step 2 → Step 3

Preparation (Pre-negotiation) → Participation (Negotiation) → Follow-Up (Post-negotiation)

Begin Meeting (Introduction) — Discussion — Conclusion

As seen in *Exhibit 5.6*, the negotiation process can be divided into parts. There are three steps: preparation, participation, and follow-up.

STEP 1: NEGOTIATION PREPARATION

There is no rule of thumb about the amount of time or effort required for negotiation preparation. The complexity of the negotiation and its importance to the operation will likely impact the amount of preparation time needed.

There are several tactics that are important when preparing for a negotiation session:

- Identify the objectives of the negotiation.
- Identify negotiation strategies.
- Establish going-in positions.
- Consider fall-back positions.
- Collect information and input from product users.

Purchasers preparing for negotiation have several primary concerns. First, they must know exactly what they want. Often, answering the following question can help: "If the negotiation process is ideal, what will happen?" Related questions include "How will we know?" "What benefits will we receive?" "What will be our relationship with this vendor?" and "How will our customers benefit?"

Some objectives of a negotiation activity may be relatively easy to quantify. Examples include a lower price, a different payment arrangement, and faster or different delivery times. By contrast, other objectives may be more difficult to quantify. Desired changes in product quality and ways to improve value in the products, services, and information provided by the vendor are examples.

In addition to considering the objectives of the negotiation session, buyers should consider strategies designed to achieve those objectives. If more than one person from the operation will be involved in the negotiation, it is important to consider the basic responsibilities of each party. In other words, who will say what and when?

Wise negotiators establish going-in positions that prioritize the desired outcomes from the session. For example, desired quality changes might be very important, and different delivery times might be less of a concern.

The purchaser must also determine possible fall-back positions. This is where negotiation on a specific point must be concluded. For example, a purchaser desires twice-a-week delivery of a specific product instead of the current once-weekly delivery. That is the going-in position. However, the purchaser knows that delivery on another day will minimize the time in inventory for the majority of products. Therefore, a once-weekly delivery is acceptable if it is on a specific day. This becomes the purchaser's fall-back position.

Careful preparation can usually identify the best going-in and fall-back positions for a negotiator's most important concerns. However, during the negotiation process one party may change fall-back positions if the other makes a sufficient concession on a different issue.

In the example above, the vendor is concerned about delivery cost and will not likely want to provide twice-weekly delivery. The vendor also recognizes the buyer's concerns: two deliveries each week reduces inventory quantities as well as quality, theft, and storage concerns. The delivery schedule can be revised to bring products in on Friday because most of the buyer's business is on the weekend. There will be little or no additional cost for the vendor to do so, and the operation will benefit. In the process, the purchaser will realize greater value for the purchasing dollars being spent.

The vendor that has made this concession has gained an "edge" when the next point is discussed. As this process evolves, the relationship between the two parties will be improved. The purchaser should consider these compromises when preparing for the negotiation.

Often, the actual negotiation process will be much more complicated than these examples, and both parties must prepare accordingly. Remember also that the existing relationship of the two parties will impact their interests in moving away from their desired positions. For example, most buyers would rather pay $2.21 per pound for a product if they believe they would receive the right quality than pay $2.19 per pound to a vendor with a reputation for inconsistent quality.

Purchasers should use "common ground" agreements as a foundation for negotiation. For example, both parties may agree about the need for quality and appreciate their lengthy and mutually rewarding relationship. They both also likely share an interest in better serving customers to enable their business relationship to grow.

The purchaser may require significant information and input from product users while planning for the negotiation. What are the best estimates of business volumes? This will drive quantity needs. How, if at all, will changing customer preferences affect what is purchased? For example, changes in menu preferences impact the quantity of ingredients that will be needed. Are competitors doing anything now that may influence what the operation will need to purchase in the near or long-term future?

The list of possible questions could continue. The goal is to obtain the best estimates of what is needed during the period to be addressed during the negotiation. Knowledge of these facts will help the buyer stay on track during the negotiation.

Exhibit 5.7 shows examples of factors that may impact the negotiating abilities of buyers and vendors. Preparation includes considering these factors.

> **THINK ABOUT IT ...**
>
> Do you think the factors listed in *Exhibit 5.7* would be important to you as a purchaser? If you were a vendor?
>
> What other factors might be important for both parties?

Exhibit 5.7

FACTORS IMPACTING NEGOTIATION ABILITIES OF BUYERS AND VENDORS

Buyers Have a Better Negotiating Position When:	**Vendors Have a Better Negotiating Position When:**
• They are professionals.	• Company representatives are professionals.
• They pay their bills on time.	• Payment processing problems are minimal.
• Large quantities are purchased.	• The buyer's service expectations are met.
• Their quality standards are reasonable.	• There are few errors in product delivery.
• Commonly used (not specialty) products are purchased.	• The quality of their delivered products consistently meets the buyer's standards.
• They practice ethical purchasing procedures.	• They are ethical in all interactions with buyers.
• They provide value in the vendor–purchaser relationship. The vendors have an ongoing interest in continuing the relationship.	• They provide value in the buyer–vendor relationship. The buyers have an ongoing interest in continuing the relationship.
• Their organization has a reputation of being a good "community citizen."	• They help the buyer resolve problems.
• They desire a win–win relationship with the vendor.	• They desire a win–win relationship with the buyer.
• They have a long-term relationship with the vendor.	• They have a long-term relationship with the buyer.
	• They provide important information to the purchaser.

A final concern when preparing for the negotiation is to determine details such as the session's location, time, and related concerns. With these issues addressed, the buyer will be prepared to represent the establishment during the negotiation session.

STEP 2: NEGOTIATION PARTICIPATION

Exhibit 5.6 indicates that there are three parts to the actual participation in negotiations. Participants must begin the meeting, undertake discussion, and reach a conclusion.

MEETING INTRODUCTION   Being on time and ready for the negotiation session is important (*Exhibit 5.8*). The purchaser should help maintain an environment that is professional and positive. Emphasizing the benefits of the historical relationship between the two parties is a good start. This can be followed by noting a sincere interest in reaching a mutually successful conclusion.

Exhibit 5.8

The beginning of the meeting is a good time to recall the importance of making careful, not necessarily quick, decisions. The buyer should also remember to use the three most important skills of negotiation: questioning, listening, and observing.

Someone should agree to take notes about the meeting's agreements. The notes can then be used as a summary of the session.

MEETING DISCUSSION   As the negotiation process evolves, several strategies will likely be useful:

- Remember that arguments are never helpful. When problems are noted, the proposal of a constructive solution is better than assigning blame or becoming offensive.

- Provide summaries of important points as they are agreed on. This can help reduce later communication problems.

- Be aware that body language can help in understanding what the other party thinks. Body language involves nonverbal actions such as gestures, positions, movements, and expressions that a person uses to communicate. People often "say" a lot about their thoughts and feelings even when they do not use words. Knowledge of nonverbal communication can be a helpful tool as the buyer interacts with another party.

Exhibit 5.9 shows some examples of body language. The actions listed frequently have certain significance. Experienced negotiators often can determine whether the body language does communicate messages or whether the actions are meaningless.

Exhibit 5.9

EXAMPLES OF BODY LANGUAGE

Body Language	What Action May Mean
• Tapping fingers; drifting eye contact; moving body away from the other person	• Being untruthful or unwilling to compromise
• Hands and arms open; good eye contact; sitting on edge of seat	• Readiness to take action or to compromise
• Broad gestures; chin raised; leaning forward in seat	• Dominance
• Arms close to body; head down	• Submissiveness or unwilling to compromise
• Rubbing back of neck; increased eye blinking; crossing/uncrossing legs	• Nervous, tired, not feeling well, or bored
• Tapping fingers or pencil; yawning; angling body away from speaker	• Information overload
• Arms crossed over chest; frown or superficial smile; positioning body toward exit	• Closed mind or disagreement
• Looking away or at watch	• Desire to avoid further discussion or end negotiation session

Exhibit 5.10

Successful buyers consider several important issues as they negotiate. First, they remember that in one way or another, everything is negotiable. They do not necessarily accept the other party's going-in position. Buyers recognize that a vendor typically has fall-back positions, just as they do.

Buyers also ensure that they are negotiating with the person or persons with the authority to make a decision (*Exhibit 5.10*). For example, the purchaser might most frequently be in contact with a distributor's sales representative. However, it may be that person's supervisor, the sales manager, or even someone at a higher organizational level who has the final authority to make negotiating concessions.

Successful negotiators have several characteristics:

- They know the advantages of listening much more than they speak and of "reading between the lines."
- They ask open-ended questions that cannot be answered with yes or no.
- They are patient and do not appear to be in a hurry.
- They do not accept the first offer unless it is a very good one.
- They do not make one-sided concessions. For example, if purchasers receive something (e.g., frequent deliveries), they give up something (e.g., less frequent payments).
- They wait to learn the vendor's position before stating their own.
- They know it is not possible to negotiate without options, and one option should always be the ability to "walk away" from the negotiation.

Effective negotiators do not pretend to know everything about the vendor's situation. Instead, they ask questions, make simple points, and avoid getting involved with technical details unless it is necessary. They also take the time to consider responses before answering.

The use of several additional principles can help negotiators:

- They know the limits of their authority.

- While they have gathered all important information, they do not need to refer to it frequently.

- They think in "real money" terms. For example, a vendor indicates that an unnecessary processing step in a convenience food will cost only an additional fraction of a cent per serving. However, this can represent thousands of dollars or more during the life of the contract.

- They remain focused on the issues. Purchasers may or may not have control over the sequence in which concerns are discussed. However, they will understand their importance and know their priority.

- They end the meeting by congratulating the other party. An ideal negotiation session yields a win–win outcome. In contrast, imagine the impact on the long-term relationship if, after negotiation is concluded, the vendor is informed about numerous critical concessions he or she made.

MEETING CONCLUSION   The final part of the negotiation session should include a review of major points and agreement about what both parties expect. Details should be recorded, and these notes can serve as session summary points that are circulated to review the results of the negotiation session. Any differences of opinion on the notes should be cleared up before the meeting ends. Then the agreed-upon summary will help provide the mutual understanding necessary to implement the agreement.

STEP 3: NEGOTIATION FOLLOW-UP

Negotiated agreements must be implemented. As a result of the meeting, both parties should know who will do what and when. What occurs after the negotiation will impact the relationship between the buyer and the vendor.

Final steps in negotiation follow-up include these actions:

- Ensure that persons in the purchaser's organization will act according to the negotiated agreement. A negotiation is not successful until this occurs.

- Prepare the written contracts, if any, which address the agreement.

- Evaluate the buyer's effectiveness in the negotiation process: preparation, participation, and follow-up. This evaluation process is important because lessons from one negotiation can be helpful in future sessions.

Manager's Memo

Vendors routinely negotiate with purchasers, so the best vendors are effective negotiators. They know and practice the same basic negotiation principles used by effective purchasers.

Many vendors would likely make two important suggestions to buyers to help maintain a long-term mutually beneficial relationship:

- Do not use one vendor's price quotation against another vendor. This occurs when a purchaser tells a vendor the price quoted by a competitor so the second vendor might sell the product at a lower price. Ethical vendors like a "best price first" policy in which all vendors are evaluated on the first price they submit.

- Ensure that all vendors know quality requirements, and confirm that the desired quality is received. Some vendors may submit a lower price based on a lower quality product. Vendors may also ship lower quality products if quality is not confirmed at time of delivery.

PRICING DISCOUNTS

This chapter has discussed many factors that impact vendors' selling prices and what buyers might do to reduce prices without sacrificing quality. However, wise buyers also know that many vendors offer **discounts**, which are deductions from the normal price that is paid for something.

Buyers must understand the difference between a lowered price and a discount. To qualify as a discount, the price reduction must be offered only to select buyers based on some definable characteristic or action. If the reduction is offered to all potential buyers, it is not a discount; it is a simple price reduction.

The technique of discounting should be very familiar to managers and customers of the restaurant and foodservice industry. To clarify the difference between a discount and a reduced price, consider the manager who offers this promotion: "Buy one meal and receive 50 percent off the second meal." A customer pays the regular menu price for the first meal, but he or she must only pay 50 percent of the menu selling price for a dining companion. Notice that to qualify for the 50 percent discount, there is a required action: paying full price for the first meal.

Successful vendors are very creative, and there can be any number of reasons for which they might offer discounts. As a result, experienced buyers ask about all discounts offered by those with whom they do business. Doing so allows the buyer the potential of paying the very lowest possible net price. A **net price** is the total or per-unit amount paid for something after all discounts have been applied to the original purchase price. While an exhaustive list of all possible types of discounts would not be practical, buyers should routinely inquire about discounts in several broad categories, such as those discussed next.

Prompt Payment Discount

A buyer's payment history is a factor in establishing the price that vendors will charge the buyer. Discounts for prompt payment are granted because vendors want to reward customers who do not keep them waiting for their money. Buyers typically qualify for this type of discount for one of two reasons.

First, they may pay the entire amount they owe within a predetermined number of days. Second, they may pay COD for the entire cost of the products they buy at the time they are delivered.

While sometimes difficult to qualify for, typical vendor discounts related to prompt payment can range from 1 to 5 percent of the normal price. For professional buyers, they are very much worth pursuing.

Quantity Discount

Many vendors use quantity discounts as incentives to encourage customers to buy more of their products. This type of discount is popular with both vendors and buyers. Vendors benefit from them because the cost of producing or delivering additional products is generally marginal after the initial costs of production and delivery have been recovered. Buyers like quantity discounts because they yield lower net prices.

In some cases, quantity discounts are offered for just the additional quantity. Other vendors consider the total amount ordered at one time and apply the quantity discount to all products ordered. In still other cases, vendors offer quantity discounts for a large volume of products purchased over several order periods.

While quantity discounts can be significant, buyers must be cautious about them. Purchasing more product than needed can be risky and result in waste. This is especially true with products whose quality deteriorates rapidly in storage. In addition, there may be short-term additional costs incurred to finance and store excess products.

Customer Status Count

Preferred customer status is another reason vendors may offer discounts to certain buyers. Establishments typically maintain selling prices between menu reprints and generally charge the same nondiscounted price to all customers. In comparison, vendors may offer a variety of customer status–based discounts depending on their business objectives.

Reasons for customer status discounts include length of relationship, annual purchase volume, and membership in a specific company, brand, or chain. Location discounts may also be offered when, for example, a vendor desires to expand into a new sales area. Some vendors offer discounts based on an operation's nonprofit status.

Special and Promotional Discounts

There are many types of special discounts that are offered by many vendors. For example, they may be associated with holidays, seasons, or special local, state, or even national events. A desire to increase brand or product awareness is a motivating factor behind these types of discounts.

In some cases, significant discounts may be offered when a vendor is interested in clearing inventories of older or discontinued products. Savvy buyers should inquire about the reasons for any special discounts that are offered. If the vendor's reasoning is sound, the discount may be of real value. However, buyers should never accept defective, poor-quality, or beyond-expiration-date products just because they are heavily discounted.

Rebates

Rebates are similar to discounts, and they are also often promotional in nature. While discounts are deductions from normal selling prices, rebates are deductions offered *after* a purchase has been made at the normal selling price. Rebates are sometimes referred to as "cash back" offers. Manufacturers that sell products to others in the distribution chain often use rebate offers to introduce new products or to enhance awareness and sales volumes of existing products.

Effect of Price Reductions

Exhibit 5.11 shows how discounts and rebates can reduce net price. This example uses one case of sliced peaches containing six #10 cans.

Exhibit 5.11		
EXAMPLE OF EFFECTS OF DISCOUNTS AND REBATES		
		Case Price (6 #10 cans)
Normal price		$42.00
Less vendor's 2% "prompt payment" discount	$ 0.84	
Less manufacturer's rebate	$ 3.00	
Less total discounts and rebates	$ 3.84	$ 3.84
	Net price	**$38.16**

If six cans are purchased for $38.16, the cost of each can is $6.36:

$$\underset{\textbf{Case price}}{\textbf{\$38.16}} \quad \underset{\textbf{Cans per case}}{\div \quad \textbf{6}} \quad = \quad \underset{\textbf{Price per can}}{\textbf{\$6.36}}$$

This is a savings of $0.64 per can:

$$\underset{\textbf{Per case}}{\textbf{\$42.00}} \quad \underset{\textbf{Cans}}{\div \quad \textbf{6}} \quad = \quad \underset{\textbf{Per can}}{\textbf{\$7.00}}$$

$$\underset{\textbf{Original price}}{\textbf{\$7.00}} \quad \underset{}{\textbf{--}} \quad \underset{\textbf{Discount price}}{\textbf{\$6.36}} \quad = \quad \underset{\textbf{Discount}}{\textbf{\$0.64}}$$

The final price per can, $6.36, can be compared among different vendors when a buyer evaluates the cost of canned peaches. When making this evaluation, buyers must always ensure that the quality offered by different vendors is the same and meets the operation's purchase specifications.

SUMMARY

1. **Explain the factors that affect product pricing.**

   There are four primary factors that influence the prices vendors charge: costs, demand, service features, and quality.

   Traditional views of pricing assume that vendors determine their costs and set selling prices at a level to attract customers and generate a profit. This view may involve three assumptions: increased prices equal increased quality, increased prices equal scarcity and value, and increased prices equal increased image.

   Less traditional pricing views include the ideas that price and costs are unrelated, cost plus value equals price, and different prices are normal.

   Other factors that can influence prices include governmental controls, contract terms, number of vendors selling the products, and the buyer's payment history.

2. **Summarize the importance of and the steps useful in effective negotiation.**

   Negotiation is a process by which parties with mutual interests try to reach an agreement about something. The most effective negotiation is win–win, which involves compromise to reach a mutually acceptable agreement. This is the best approach if long-term vendor relationships are desired.

   The negotiation process must focus on more than just selling price. Other features that add value, such as services received, are also an important concern. Effective communication is an important negotiation skill, as is the ability to make compromises, solve problems, and make decisions.

   There are three steps to the negotiation process, beginning with preparation by considering objectives and strategies and obtaining needed information. Participation involves beginning the meeting, conducting the discussion, and concluding with a summary of important agreements. The third step relates to follow-up activities such as preparing contracts.

3. **Describe several types of pricing discounts and explain rebates.**

   Discounts are deductions from the normal price that a buyer pays to a vendor. There are several types of discounts. These include discounts for prompt payment, for increased quantities purchased, for customer status such as membership in a specific company, and special and promotional discounts. The latter may be offered when a seller is interested in reducing inventories of older or discontinued products.

   Rebates are reductions to price after a purchase has been made at the normal selling price. The results of discounts and rebates should be considered in the price used as a basis for comparison with other vendors.

APPLICATION EXERCISE

You are the buyer for a small seafood restaurant chain that purchases several thousand pounds of shrimp each month. This item is by far the most expensive item purchased by your chain, and the price has been going up for the last three months.

You have scheduled meetings with each of the three approved vendors, and they know your primary concern is price. They also know you will not accept a product of lower quality.

1. What is your negotiation objective?

2. What steps should you use as you prepare for the negotiation session?

3. What will be your going-in position for the desired outcomes from the negotiation session?

4. What are your possible fall-back positions during the negotiation?

5. Review *Exhibit 5.7* and explain how you might turn several of these factors into a negotiating advantage.

6. What are three strategies that you will use during the actual negotiating session?

7. What are some factors you will consider as you decide which vendor should supply the shrimp?

REVIEW YOUR LEARNING

Select the best answer for each question.

1. **Which is true about the prices charged by the most reputable vendors?**
   A. They normally charge lower prices than less reputable vendors.
   B. They normally charge higher prices than less reputable vendors.
   C. They normally allow payment according to the buyer's schedules.
   D. They normally require payment upon delivery to keep prices low.

2. **Buyers who focus primarily on a product's per-purchase-unit selling price**
   A. do not normally receive either quality or value.
   B. are best assured of receiving quality products.
   C. do not normally worry about their food costs.
   D. are best assured of receiving purchase value.

3. **Which concept is a traditional view of pricing?**
   A. Buyers cannot influence purchase price.
   B. Cost plus value equals selling price.
   C. Higher prices equal better image.
   D. Price and cost may be unrelated.

4. **What happens in a win–win negotiation?**
   A. The parties change their negotiation objectives.
   B. One party takes advantage of his or her position.
   C. The parties reach an agreement that benefits all concerned.
   D. Neither party is required to make concessions or change position.

5. **Which is an important characteristic for an effective negotiator?**
   A. Avoiding disagreements
   B. Sticking to one issue
   C. Listening carefully
   D. Being aggressive

6. What type of negotiation position reflects when negotiation on a specific point should be concluded?

   A. Fall-back

   B. End-of-line

   C. Termination

   D. Compromise

7. What type of negotiation position reflects a buyer's ideal outcome?

   A. Going-in

   B. Fall-back

   C. Bottom-line

   D. Common-ground

8. What can buyers do to establish a better negotiation position?

   A. Purchase specialty products

   B. Be tolerant of delivery defects

   C. Emphasize product cost as primary

   D. Establish reasonable quality standards

9. A vendor's price reduction is a discount when it is

   A. offered to all buyers.

   B. applied to the net price.

   C. given to selected buyers.

   D. taken after payment is made.

10. Which amount would be typical for a prompt payment discount?

    A. 4%

    B. 8%

    C. 12%

    D. 16%

6

Ordering Products: Effective Procedures

INSIDE THIS CHAPTER

- Overview of the Ordering Process
- Basic Steps in the Ordering Process
- Special Ordering Concerns
- Developing Vendor Contracts
- Expediting Ordering Procedures
- Technology and the Ordering Process

CHAPTER LEARNING OBJECTIVES

After completing this chapter, you should be able to:

- Summarize the ordering process.
- Explain the basic steps in the ordering process.
- Identify special ordering concerns involving bidding.
- Explain the types of purchase contracts, elements in contracts, and common terms and conditions used in contracts.
- Describe the procedures to hasten the delivery of products that have been ordered but not yet delivered.
- Explain how technology can impact the ordering process.

KEY TERMS

CASE STUDY

"I'm not excited about the changes in how we order products," said Nicole, the chef at Timeless Sands Restaurant.

Jake, the dining-room manager, replied, "We have a small restaurant. We've never had any problem with contacting our normal vendors and ordering what we want when we need it. I've looked at the Web sites of other vendors, and the prices we pay are in the same ballpark."

Nicole added, "Well, now we need to agree on three vendors and ask each of them for prices when we order. Then we need to compare prices and order from the vendor offering the lowest price. That's going to take some time, and I don't really think we will save any money!"

1. What steps are necessary to ensure that the new ordering plans will be successful?

2. What should the manager say to Nicole and Jake about the benefits of the new ordering system?

OVERVIEW OF THE ORDERING PROCESS

The **ordering** process occurs when a purchaser makes a commitment to a vendor relating to a specific purchase. Formally or informally, that commitment involves much more than just an agreement to purchase a specified quantity of products that meet quality requirements at prices that have been agreed on. These factors must, of course, be addressed. However, there are other issues about which the purchaser and vendor must agree.

Ordering products involves a series of activities that enables the purchaser to learn all necessary information about a potential purchase from the approved vendors. The efforts required for earlier purchasing steps, such as determining quality and quantity requirements, will be wasted if there is no careful follow-through when the vendor is selected and the order is placed. The results of the purchaser's ordering decisions represent legal and financial commitments that will either help or hinder the operation's employees as they produce products and serve customers.

No single step in the purchasing process is more important than any other. To some, the task of selecting vendors for a specific order and ordering the products is the most important. However, this step really benefits from the careful decisions made before vendors are contacted. Other managers and purchasers think that decision-making ends when the order is ready to be placed. After all, the purchaser just has to pick up the phone and call in the order or wait until the distributor sales representative stops by to receive it. In fact, ordering is more complex. Procedures for ordering must be developed and followed consistently.

Internal Communication and Ordering

Managers in small-volume operations may undertake purchasing activities as one among many responsibilities. Large-volume and multiunit organizations may employ one or more staff members with full-time purchasing responsibilities. Regardless of how purchasing tasks are organized, purchasers must determine several things:

- Exactly what products must be purchased
- Proper quality requirements for the products to be purchased
- Which products should be produced by the employees and which should be purchased from approved vendors
- The quantity of products needed, which is impacted by the length of time for which products should be purchased

Purchasers in small-volume operations may make these decisions by themselves or in cooperation with their staff members. Managers in large-volume operations may use the services of purchasing staff to help make these decisions. In both instances, those who purchase must have the information necessary to determine which of the approved vendors should be used to fulfill specific product orders.

Each of these activities may involve no more than oral communication in small-volume properties. Extensive written or electronic communication may be used in larger organizations. Examples include purchase specifications, purchase orders, and other purchasing tools discussed in this chapter.

One major theme of this book has been that the basic principles of purchasing are the same regardless of an operation's size. It is always the purchaser's responsibility to know and to tell vendors exactly what is required. This cannot be done unless the purchaser is the user or has communicated with others in the operation to determine exact product needs.

External Communication and Ordering

This book has also emphasized a continuing relationship between the purchaser and approved vendors that benefits both organizations. The ordering process helps ensure that the operation's purchase requirements are met, an important aspect of this ongoing relationship.

Purchasers must communicate with all approved vendors to request prices. They must have additional communication with the specific vendor that will supply the required products (*Exhibit 6.1*). These activities must be undertaken according to consistently used policies and procedures. Then there is better assurance that all parties understand each other and that the right products are delivered at the right price in the right quantity and at the right time.

Sometimes communication or other problems can occur when orders are placed. If this happens infrequently, the purchaser and the vendor will likely cooperate to resolve the problem. As they do, the satisfaction that results helps encourage a continuing relationship. However, if there are frequent problems that, from the purchaser's perspective, are caused by the vendor, this works against the purchaser's interest in continuing to place orders. In the same way, vendors are less likely to want to provide value-added services for their "problem" accounts.

Common Ordering Challenges

There is a saying, "You can't solve a problem unless you are aware of it." Sometimes employees who receive and use the products purchased are aware of problems but do not share their concerns with purchasers. Then purchasers cannot address these concerns when orders are placed. Here are

Exhibit 6.1

Manager's Memo

There are times when market-related problems affect the supply sources of all vendors normally carrying an item. A common example is fresh produce. Bad weather conditions can destroy or damage crops for an entire growing season. The resulting disruption in availability then creates product shortages and unexpectedly high prices.

Another example is large-scale outbreaks of foodborne illness traced to many products. These problems create an interesting challenge. During times of product shortages, purchasers must pay more for products that are typically of lower quality. Wise purchasers consider how they can substitute other products, or discontinue offering some items until the market recovers.

some common challenges that might be resolved with more effective communication between purchasers and receiving, production, or service staff:

- **Quality problems:** Purchasers who are unaware of inconsistent product quality cannot reemphasize the need for specified quality when orders are placed. Discussions with the vendor's representative or sales manager can be undertaken only if purchasers know about quality issues.

- **Frequent backorders:** Backorders occur when a vendor does not have the products required to fill a purchaser's order. When necessary products are on backorder, they must be purchased from another vendor. Purchasers should learn about these problems quickly so that an additional source for immediate needs can be found. Also, if they occur frequently, a different approved vendor for the problem products may be needed.

- **Problems with quantities or purchase unit sizes:** Some vendors freely substitute different packaging sizes for those ordered. Consider an order for one 50-pound bag of all-purpose flour that is met with five 10-pound bags. How does this create a problem, since 50 pounds of flour are still delivered? First, the price per pound is likely to be lower when it is ordered in a larger unit. The vendor should make a price adjustment if the problem was noticed at the time of delivery. However, the employees using the flour will still need to spend excessive time opening numerous bags as they fill flour bins.

- **Problems with on-site shortages:** Purchasers must always be careful when determining the quantities of products to order. Numerous examples of potential problems were noted in chapter 3. Product theft, pilferage, spoilage, and accidental spills can create unexplained decreases in inventories. These, in turn, create the need for ordering additional products sooner than purchasers normally expect. Communication is critical to alert purchasers about these problems. If they occur frequently, procedures used to manage inventory should be reexamined.

- **On-site storage capacities:** Storage equipment and space is always expensive, and the best kitchen designers work hard to plan ideal storage requirements. Unfortunately, the "ideal" capacities for a new operation being planned may be overstated or understated for operations that use the space in the future. Purchasers for high-volume operations with inadequate storage space have ongoing ordering challenges that often involve more frequent and expensive deliveries. They may also need to create additional storage space when most often there is none available without converting other space.

- **Coordination between receiving and production employees, purchasers, and vendors:** Purchasers and managers should observe ongoing operations as they walk around in the establishment. They should also be present at random times when products are received, stored, and prepared. Then they can look at products in storage and production areas and review the procedures in use to handle them. They can also participate in conversations and meetings with receiving and production employees to learn about any challenges they may be having.

All of these examples emphasize the need for close cooperation and communication between purchasers and receiving and production employees. As this occurs, there will likely be fewer challenges during the ordering process.

BASIC STEPS IN THE ORDERING PROCESS

This section discusses basic ordering procedures. Small-volume operations use decentralized purchasing procedures, and larger-volume operations use more centralized purchasing systems.

Ordering in Small-Volume Operations

Small-volume operations do not normally employ full-time purchasing staff. Instead, a decentralized purchasing process is used. A representative of each department orders the products needed for the department.

While specific ordering procedures vary widely in small-volume operations, an important concern relates to who will be responsible for ordering products. In a very small operation, the owner or manager may assume responsibility for ordering all required products. In establishments with designated department heads such as chef, dining-room manager, and bar manager, these employees may order products for their department. For example, the chef may order food products, the dining-room manager may order service-related items, and the bar manager may order alcoholic beverages.

If persons other than the owner or manager order products, they are frequently given purchasing authority up to a preestablished limit. If orders valued at more than the limit are to be placed, preapproval by the owner or manager is required.

Purchasers in decentralized purchasing operations should have a list of approved vendors for each product type. This list was developed as a result of earlier vendor sourcing decisions (see chapter 4). For example, purchasers may have approved several vendors for produce, dairy products, grocery items, and so on. When these products are needed, the approved vendors for each type of product will then be asked to submit their current prices.

The list of approved vendors and the products they can supply is often assembled into a product order guide. This guide is an easy reference for purchasers when orders must be placed. If the order guide was developed by each purchaser, it should be submitted to the owner or manager for approval. If it was developed by the owner or manager, it should be provided to each employee that will be requesting prices from vendors. The purchasers should be informed that these vendors must be used to supply products needed by their department.

Purchasers in operations with decentralized purchasing systems should also organize product specifications by approved vendor. Vendors should have copies of the applicable specification, and prices they quote should be for products meeting the specification requirements. Then vendors will not need to be given the specifications each time prices are requested.

The purchasers should be trained in all procedures that will be used to request prices and order products. For example, they must know how frequently orders should be placed and how the quantities for each order are determined. They must also know the procedures for requesting prices and be able to answer vendors' questions about specifications or other details. They must know the vendors' requirements for minimum order quantities as well as delivery schedules and frequency.

Exhibit 6.2

In larger operations, effective coordination between departments is required because orders may need to be combined. For example, food-production staff will require fresh fruits and vegetables for salads, and the bar manager may need some of these items for beverage garnishes (*Exhibit 6.2*). The bar manager will need cocktail napkins, and the dining-room manager may need disposable napkins. A procedure should be in place to combine orders for these products with responsibility for ordering always assigned to one specific purchaser.

This purchaser should use an order guide that spells out requirements for orders. Examples include the specifications, approved vendors and their delivery schedules and lead times, and acceptable product substitutions, if any.

Procedures used by small-volume operations to request prices and order products vary from informal to almost the same as those used by large-volume purchasers. Purchasers in some small establishments may call vendors to request current prices. Alternatively, sales representatives may routinely visit the operation to provide prices and take orders. Purchasers in other small-volume operations may use requests for proposals and purchase orders like their large-volume counterparts. These ordering documents are discussed in detail later in this chapter.

The vendors' prices, whether obtained informally or with formal purchase documents, must be carefully analyzed to determine which vendor should be awarded the order. The best ordering systems involve a two-step procedure for requesting prices from approved vendors followed by awarding the order.

All products of one type such as produce can be listed on a master order form which serves as an internal "shopping list" to indicate which products are needed. If more than one vendor will be used, for example, to supply all of the establishment's needs for produce for a specific order period, information from the master order can be transferred to separate purchase orders for each vendor when orders are placed. If a request for proposal (RFP) will be sent to different vendors to determine the supply source, then items will be transferred to the RFP.

All ordering procedures should be consistently followed. These include ordering deadlines, minimum orders, agreed-upon pricing, and methods used to select vendors.

It is always important to have a copy of the purchase order available when the products are received. This enables receiving employees to check products, quantities, and agreed-upon prices that are specified in the delivery invoice. They should confirm this information as products are received, before signing the delivery invoice.

The vendors often provide purchasing contracts. If purchasers have concerns about the language of the contracts, they should discuss their concerns with the owner or manager, who may wish to seek legal advice about specific clauses. Once developed, vendors and purchasers should always adhere to the terms of purchasing contracts. Some small operations and many large establishments have special concerns about purchasing contracts. This topic is discussed later in this chapter.

In many small-volume operations, departmental purchasers keep order documents until the products are delivered. They or the receiving employee sign the delivery invoice after confirming that the order is complete and correct. Then it and the original documentation are given to the manager, who may process them or send them to another person with accounting and payment responsibilities. In other properties, order documents are routed immediately to the manager or accounting employee, who holds it until the signed delivery invoice is received.

THINK ABOUT IT . . .

Purchasers in some small establishments have an understanding with vendors that the last price will be the current price unless the purchaser is contacted.

What do you think about this method of obtaining vendors' prices?

The basic procedures just described suggest how the product ordering process might be undertaken in a small-volume operation. Whatever the method used, small-volume operations must share at least one characteristic with larger organizations. The proper ordering documentation is always required because it will be used to help authorize payment.

Ordering in Large-Volume Operations

The purchasing process becomes more formalized in a large operation. *Exhibit 6.3* shows the basic steps first presented in chapter 1. The discussion that follows provides more detailed information about the process by focusing on the purchasing department (box C).

Exhibit 6.3

PURCHASING IN LARGE OPERATIONS

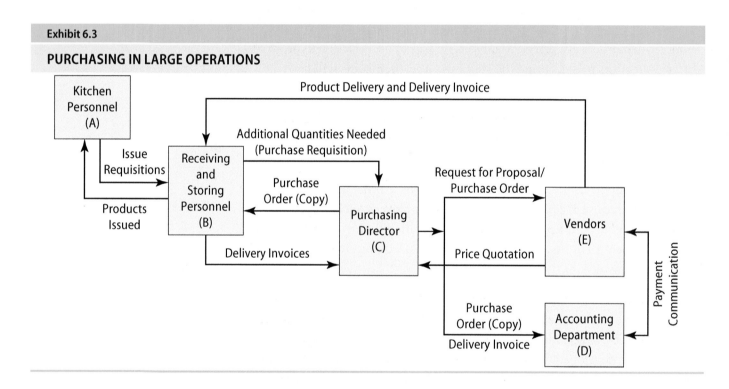

Purchasers learn about the need to purchase additional products when they are alerted by someone with receiving and storeroom responsibilities (box B). The "need to buy" decision results when quantities of products available reach order points or must be purchased to reestablish par levels, as previously discuss in chapter 3.

Information about the products that must be purchased is routed to the purchasing department on a purchase requisition. *Exhibit 6.4* shows an example of a purchase requisition. This document can be a hard copy or an electronic form.

Exhibit 6.4

SAMPLE PURCHASE REQUISITION

Requesting department: _____   Requisition number: _____

Date needed: _____

Item	Purchase Unit	Number of Needed Units	Specification Number

Authorized by: _____   Date: _____

On receiving the purchase requisition, the purchasing department issues an RFP to approved vendors. *Exhibit 6.5* on the next page shows a sample RFP that can be used to request current prices for the items listed on a purchase requisition.

Purchasers can be assured that vendors will submit current prices for items of the required quality for two reasons:

- The purchaser has given the approved vendors copies of the specifications with the requirement that prices must always be quoted for that specified quality.

- Someone from the purchasing department will check incoming deliveries to confirm that products of the required quality are received. If incorrect quality is noted, the products will be returned, and a credit memo will be issued. Also, if the problem continues, the vendor will likely not be considered for future orders.

Manager's Memo

Issuing RFPs to approved vendors cannot ensure that purchasers will receive the best price. Vendors interact with each other just as many restaurant and foodservice managers do. They may share information about "slow-pay" and "high-maintenance" purchasers. Vendors are not likely to quote the lowest possible prices for less-than-optimal business. While several price quotations may be received, each may be higher than those quoted to more preferred purchasers.

This can also occur when one vendor is commonly asked to submit a price quotation but seldom receives a purchase order. This vendor may submit a high price because an order is not likely. If the order is received, the higher price becomes a return for wasted time in the past.

Purchasers should know that their experience with vendors will affect prices. They must interact with vendors in ways that help ensure that they receive the best prices, not just the lowest of high prices.

Exhibit 6.5

SAMPLE REQUEST FOR PROPOSAL (RFP)

Date: 12/10/12   RFP number: 13547

To: Bill's Provisions   Please quote your price and delivery.
     112 Garden St.   Return by: 12/12/12
     Bloomville, IL 60457
          (vendor address)

| Product | Quantity | | Vendor Price | |
	Unit	Total	Per Unit	Total
Canned peaches	Case/6 #10	3		
Sugar	Bag (50 lb)	1		

Date of delivery: _____   Lakeman's Restaurant _____
Price valid for: _____   (name of company)
                    (number of days)   1234 Brown Ave. _____
Signed: _____   Chicago, IL 60613 _____
                    (vendor)
                                                              (address)
_____   James Zellie
_____   (purchaser)
                    (address)
_____
        (vendor representative)

After approved vendors submit their prices, the purchaser can determine from which vendor the products will be ordered. He or she can then submit a purchase order to confirm order details.

PURCHASE ORDERS

A sample purchase order is shown in *Exhibit 6.6*. It can be used to inform the vendor that the price quotation was accepted and the purchaser wants to order.

When reviewing *Exhibit 6.6*, consider that the purchaser for Townee Café sent RFPs to several vendors and selected Riverside Grocers to provide all products on the RFP. Specifications were sent previously and are on file at Riverside Grocers. Therefore, both the purchaser and vendor are aware that the RFP

Exhibit 6.6

SAMPLE PURCHASE ORDER

Purchase Order

From/Ship to:

Townee Café
1717 W. 17th Ave.
Townville, IL 00000
Telephone: 000-000-0000

Purchase from:

Riverside Grocers
2451 Riverside Rd.
Riverside, IL 00000

PO no. _____ 21t678

PO date: _____ 12/18/12

Delivery date: _____ 12/22/12

Contact: _____ Sherri Wisozki

Terms: _____ Net 30

Item	Quantity	Purchase Unit	Purchase Unit Price	Total Price	RFP #
Canned Peaches	3	Case (#10 cans)	$29.75	$89.25	23456
Sugar	1	Bag (50 lb)	32.17	32.17	23456
			Total	$121.42	

Purchaser: Sherri Wisozki   Date: 12/18/12

Terms and Conditions:
This purchase order expressly limits acceptance to the terms and conditions stated above and included on the following page. Any additional terms and conditions are rejected.

Page __1__ of __3__ pages

prices supplied by the vendor and the purchase order prices agreed on are based on products meeting these quality requirements.

Note in the upper right-hand corner that the purchase order (PO) number and date are included, along with the preferred delivery date and the property contact, Sherri Wisozki, in case the vendor has questions. The purchase order also indicates that the terms are "net 30." This means that the purchaser will pay the total invoice amount of $121.42 within 30 days of the delivery date.

Manager's Memo

Some operations have a policy that vendors' discount offers should routinely be accepted. These policies then guide purchasers' decisions. In the absence of a policy, purchasers should discuss the purchase of large quantities of products with their managers to take advantage of significant discounts. There may be ongoing or temporary cash flow problems that make the discount less attractive. Cash flow relates to the receipts and disbursements of cash and their impact on the establishment's ability to pay bills when due.

If there are any cash flow concerns then managers, perhaps after receiving advice from accounting staff, might consider short-term borrowing to pay invoices before they are due. Their analysis can focus on the invoice savings compared to the costs of the short-term loan required.

Exhibit 6.7

RESTAURANT TECHNOLOGY

Like many other purchasing activities, the ordering process has undergone significant change. In the past, salespersons visited their purchasers on a regularly scheduled basis. They explained current specials and worked with purchasers to resolve any problems. They also wrote down the order on a hard copy document often preprinted with the vendor's most popular items. A copy of this document was provided to the purchaser for use as an in-house record of the purchase order.

Other ordering variations existed as when, for example, purchasers used the telephone or a fax machine to place orders. More recently, orders are placed by email and directly on the vendor's Web site. Today, even relatively small vendors may prefer, or require, that orders be placed over the Internet on the company's Web site.

Sometimes purchasers negotiate a discounted price for faster payment. For example, payment terms might be 2/10; net 30. In this instance, the purchaser will receive a 2 percent discount if the total invoice is paid within 10 days. Otherwise the total is due within 30 days of the invoice date.

MANAGING PURCHASE ORDERS

Procedures for managing purchase orders are straightforward. In large properties, all orders except small purchases for which a petty cash fund will be used should be authorized with a formal purchase order.

Purchasers in centralized operations should send a copy of the purchase order to the vendor that is awarded the order and to the operation's receiving staff. They will need it to check incoming products against the ordering information sent to the vendor (*Exhibit 6.7*). Depending on the operation's procedures, additional copies may be retained by the purchasing department, and another copy may be routed to accounting staff. It will be held there until the applicable delivery invoice and the copy of the purchase order sent earlier to receiving staff are returned to the accounting department. In some operations, a manager or purchaser may need to countersign the delivery invoice that has been signed by the person receiving the delivery. Then all of these documents can be matched up in the process used to pay the vendor.

In small establishments with decentralized purchasing, the purchaser may keep a copy of the purchase order in his or her work area. Alternatively, copies of all purchase orders may be kept in the receiving area. In addition, the ordering procedure may require that a copy be sent to the property's bookkeeper or accountant.

SPECIAL ORDERING CONCERNS

There are advantages to using competitive bidding. It is also important to effectively analyze vendors' price quotations when they are received.

Using Competitive Bidding

Many operations have a policy that requires the use of a competitive bidding process. As explained in chapter 2, competitive bidding involves sending RFPs to more than one approved vendor. Its goal is to best ensure that the purchaser is paying a reasonable price that is similar among competitive vendors. For example, policy might require the purchaser to send RFPs to at least three approved vendors.

A vendor offering a much lower price might be offering a great deal. Perhaps, for example, the vendor desires to break into the market by initially offering low prices. However, it may also mean that the vendor is offering a product of a different quality or excluding some services overlooked in the RFP. This is why vendor sourcing and purchase specifications are so important.

Some may question whether a requirement for competitive bidding, with its emphasis on lowest cost, is contrary to the need for purchasers to be value-conscious. In fact, purchasers requiring competitive bidding are not just emphasizing cost when they have completed the activities described in previous chapters:

- They have developed and given to vendors purchase specifications that define quality requirements. They require that prices be quoted for the quality of products detailed in the specifications.
- They know the quantity of products to be purchased and have clearly communicated this information to vendors asked to respond to RFPs. They do this because many vendors reduce the price per purchase unit when quantity commitments increase.
- They have made good vendor sourcing decisions by considering quality, value-added services, and information. These approved vendors will be able to contribute to the professional relationship that enables both purchaser and vendor to be successful.
- They undertake negotiations, if necessary, to best ensure that they understand details about the products to be ordered. Remember that negotiation is not needed before every order. Instead, it is most useful for one-of-a-kind orders, expensive orders, or a new vendor relationship.

When these activities have been undertaken, purchasers can be reasonably assured that the prices quoted by all vendors are for the same quality and quantity of product. They will also know that the services and information offered by each vendor will be acceptable. With these assurances, only price differences should affect the purchaser's decision.

Wise purchasers know that vendors operate their business in much the same way managers run the operation. Vendors work hard to reduce costs without sacrificing quality of products or services. They innovate, use technology when applicable, and practice leadership skills to help ensure that their labor force is productive and treated fairly. These and related strategies allow vendors to operate more efficiently. They can then pass savings on to purchasers while still generating a fair financial return.

Analyzing RFP Responses

What concerns should purchasers have as they review RFP responses? A first review should ensure that the vendor is submitting a **bid** for the same products in the quantity specified. A bid is another term for price quotation.

If there are no discrepancies, the purchaser's next concern relates to each vendor's proposed prices. If the vendor does not submit a price for one or more items on the RFP, the purchaser may exclude that vendor's response from consideration for that particular RFP. Whether or not the purchaser chooses to do this depends on how the purchaser intends to select a vendor:

- The purchaser may select the vendor quoting the lowest total price for all items. In this case, a vendor quoting a price for only some products would be excluded. An advantage to this method is eliminating the need for multiple purchase orders, deliveries, paperwork, and payments. While the costs of documentation are difficult to quantify, some analysts believe it is in excess of $10 per purchase order. These costs must be considered when vendors are selected on a by-item rather than a total-order basis. A disadvantage to selecting a single vendor is the concern that the purchaser may be paying a higher price for some products.

- The purchaser may select the vendor based on the prices quoted for each product. For example, vendor A may have submitted the lowest price for several products, and he or she will receive a purchase order for these products. Vendor B may have submitted the lowest price for other products, and they will be purchased from vendor B. An advantage to this method is that the lowest price of all will be paid for every item. A disadvantage exists as noted earlier: the time and expense of interacting with more than one vendor.

Exhibit 6.8 shows a sample competitive bid analysis for three items. Note that vendor A submitted the lowest price for chicken, and vendor B will be awarded the ground beef and tenderloin steak purchases. Purchasers who want the right to accept only specific products should indicate this on the RFP. Additionally, many purchasers specify that they reserve the right not to award a bid to any vendor submitting a price quotation in response to a specific RFP.

Exhibit 6.8

SAMPLE COMPETITIVE BID ANALYSIS

Analysis of RFP no. 5736

Product	Purchase Unit	Vendor A	Vendor B	Vendor C
Ground beef	1 lb	$ 4.29	$ 4.24	$ 4.31
Tenderloin steak	1 lb	13.87	13.59	14.03
Chicken	2½-lb bird	6.29	6.47	6.54

DEVELOPING VENDOR CONTRACTS

When purchasers and vendors agree to do business, they create a special legal relationship. The agreements made between two or more parties are called contracts, and they can be enforced in a court of law. Professional purchasers should know about the different types of contracts they will likely encounter.

It is also important to understand that not every agreement made between two parties is a contract. Contracts contain very specific and identifiable elements. Contracts related to the purchase of foodservice products must be clearly understood by both the purchaser and the vendor. To help reduce the possibility of misunderstandings or disagreements about the specifics of a contract, key contract terms should be directly and clearly addressed.

Types of Contracts

The term *contract* can mean two different things. As a verb, it is frequently used in sentences such as "Let's contract with Miller's Gourmet Blend to provide our coffee next year." The term can also be used as a noun that describes a legally enforceable agreement or promise. For example, a manager might say, "Please review the contract with the vendor."

Exhibit 6.9

Contracts and the laws that relate to them allow both parties to understand exactly what they have agreed or promised to do. Professional purchasers often make many agreements every day, so they must have a thorough understanding of contracts and how they are enforced.

Contracts may be established in writing or orally. In most cases, written contracts are preferred because if they are clearly written, they identify the responsibilities of each party. In addition, time can cause memories to fade and staff may be replaced. Recollections, even among the most well intentioned parties, can differ. These factors can create differences of opinion about the content of oral contracts.

Even though written contracts have advantages, many transactions in the restaurant and foodservice industry are established orally (*Exhibit 6.9*). Oral transactions can be enforced by the courts. Therefore, when a purchaser calls a vendor and orders three cases of lettuce, a contract has been established. The purchaser has agreed to pay for the lettuce that is delivered. The vendor has agreed to deliver the product that meets the purchase specification at the agreed-upon price.

In a similar manner, a manager may be required by local law to have the operation's fire suppression system inspected twice a year. The agreement with the service provider that does this inspection may not be committed to writing each time. In fact, if the same company has been performing the inspection for several years, the inspection company rather than the manager may, within reason, determine the best day to conduct the inspection. Then the arrival of the inspector, access to the property, an invoice for services performed, and a written inspection report all indicate that a contract existed, even if there was no oral or written agreement for that specific inspection on that day.

Elements in Contracts

Regardless of whether a contract is oral or written, it must include specific elements to be enforceable. A contract is considered enforceable if it is recognized as valid by the courts and is, therefore, subject to the court's ability to require compliance with its terms. If any of the required elements are missing, the courts will consider the contract unenforceable.

To be enforceable, a contract must be legally valid, and it must contain several elements:

- It must have an offer, which is a proposal to perform an act or to pay an amount that, if accepted, becomes a legally valid contract.
- Consideration is needed. This refers to the payment to be made in exchange for the promise(s) contained in the contract.
- There must be acceptance, an agreement to the exact details of the offer.

Not all agreements between two or more parties are legally valid. Consider, for example, a purchaser who agrees in writing to purchase an endangered species of animal for a menu item. That purchaser will not be able to sue the vendor if he or she does not deliver the product. The courts will not enforce a contract that requires breaking a law.

To be considered enforceable, a contract must not specify activities that violate the law. A contract must also be made by parties who are legally old enough to make the contract.

If two parties are of legal age and the contract involves a legal activity, the first element required is an offer. It states exactly what the party making the offer is willing to do and what he or she expects in return. The offer may include very specific instructions for how, where, when, and to whom the offer is made. It may include deadlines for acceptance. In addition, it will include the price or terms of the offer.

For example, when a purchaser places a seafood order with a vendor, an offer is made. The purchaser offers to buy the seafood for a price quoted by the vendor. The reason that an offer is a required part of a contract is clear, as it sets the terms and the responsibilities of both parties. The offer essentially states, "I will promise to do this, if you will promise to do that."

There are many lawsuits that involve plaintiffs who file the lawsuit, and defendants who want the court's help to define what is "fair" in regard to a specific offer. This is necessary because the offer was not clearly spelled out in a contract. Purchasers should understand that the courts will enforce contracts with clearly identifiable terms, even if the terms are heavily weighted in favor of one of the parties. Therefore, purchasers must understand all of the terms of an offer before making or accepting it.

Consideration is the second essential element in an enforceable contract. It is the part of the contract that identifies the value, payment, or cost. Each party must receive consideration for the contract to be valid. In the case of the purchaser buying seafood, the consideration to the purchaser is the seafood. The consideration to the vendor is the price paid for the seafood.

Consideration does not have to be money. For example, a manager agrees to host a holiday party for the employees of a local newspaper in exchange for the newspaper running some ads for the establishment (*Exhibit 6.10*). The consideration by the operation is the employee party. The consideration by the newspaper is the advertisements. Trade-outs, or agreements between two businesses in which the contract's consideration is not in the form of money, are common in the restaurant and foodservice industry.

Exhibit 6.10

Courts are concerned that contract considerations exist, but they are not concerned about their size. A seafood vendor can sell a pound of shrimp for $1, $10, or $100. The purchaser can agree or not agree to purchase the shrimp at the vendor's price. As long as both parties to a legitimate contract are in agreement, the amount of the consideration is not generally disputable in court.

Purchasers should recognize that the courts will not usually declare a contract unenforceable based on the amount of the consideration. It is the agreement

Manager's Memo

Legal acceptance of a contract is commonly established in three ways:

- **Verbal or nonverbal agreement:** Contract acceptance can be made orally, with a handshake, or even with an up and down nod of the head.

- **Acceptance of full or partial payment:** Full or partial payment of a contract amount is viewed as accepting the contract's terms. If, for example, a vendor agrees to replace a water heater with "half the price down upon acceptance," the purchaser's deposit would indicate acceptance of the price and terms.

- **Agreement in writing:** The best way to indicate acceptance of an offer is generally an agreement in writing. While many purchase contracts in the restaurant and foodservice industry are made orally, when there is a large sum of money involved, contracts should be confirmed in writing if possible.

to exchange value that establishes consideration and therefore enforceability. Purchasers who willingly agree to pay more than they should for something will not typically obtain relief from the courts if the vendor provides the product the purchaser agreed to purchase.

A legal offer and its consideration made by one party must be clearly accepted by a second party before the contract comes into existence. The acceptance must duplicate the terms of the offer if the contract is to be valid. If the acceptance does not mirror the offer, it is a counteroffer and a new contract rather than an acceptance of the original contract. A counteroffer is an offer made in response to another offer that was not acceptable.

When acceptance is the same as the offer, an express contract has been created. An express contract is one in which the components of the agreement are clearly understood and are stated orally or in writing.

An offer may be accepted orally or in writing, but it must be clear that the terms were accepted. For example, consider a contractor who offers to change the light bulbs on an outdoor sign for an operation. It would not be reasonable or ethical for the contractor to quote a price and then complete the job without the manager's acceptance.

TERMS AND CONDITIONS

Vendors and purchasers may have terms and conditions included in their contracts. These are general provisions that apply to a vendor's responses to RFPs and a purchaser's purchase orders regardless of the specific products being sold or purchased. For example, vendors typically specify a minimum dollar amount of purchases before deliveries are made. They may deliver only on specified days when their delivery vehicles are near the purchaser's location.

Purchasers may have some general concerns that they want to address in their agreements. They may include boilerplate language in their purchase orders that addresses these concerns. Boilerplate language refers to contract clauses that do not change even though the contracts are developed for use with different vendors selling different products.

There are numerous boilerplate clauses for purchase orders that will apply unless separate written agreements are negotiated. Here are some examples:

- **Exclusive agreement:** The purchase order indicates all of the purchaser's and vendor's responsibilities.

- **Services and deliverables:** The vendor agrees to perform the services or to provide the products described, including following all terms and conditions.

- **Delivery schedules:** Deliveries are to be made within a reasonable time to the purchaser's location.

- **Risk of loss:** Unless otherwise specified, the vendor assumes the risk of loss until the delivery invoice is signed by the purchaser.

- **Packaging and crating charges:** All packaging and crating charges are included in the product price or stated clearly as a separate charge on the vendor's response to the RFP.

- **Guarantees and warranties:** Vendors agree that products will be free from defects and conform to specifications.

- **Insurance:** Vendors must maintain the types of insurance required by law.

- **Indemnification:** Vendors will hold the operation harmless from claims, liabilities, damages, and other costs related to the products that are purchased.

- **Rejected products:** Vendors will take back any items refused at the time of delivery with no product charge to the purchaser.

- **Confidentiality:** Information related to the sale of any product to the operation will not be shared with anyone.

- **Termination:** The purchaser can terminate the purchase order if the vendor fails to perform according to it. Also, the vendor can terminate the agreement if the purchaser does not pay for products delivered within a specified time period.

- **Legal remedies:** The purchaser specifies how it will recover damages incurred if the vendor fails to perform.

- **Failure to perform:** Neither the purchaser nor the vendor will be penalized for failing to perform for reasons beyond his or her control. Examples include fire, flood, acts of war, and labor difficulties.

Some very large multiunit operations provide their terms and conditions on their Web sites. Many purchasers in establishments of all sizes include terms and conditions in the purchasing handbooks given to their approved vendors.

EXPEDITING ORDERING PROCEDURES

Purchasers will, at some point, likely need to expedite deliveries. Expediting refers to a purchaser's activities to hasten the delivery of products that have been ordered but not yet been received.

Approved vendors will have been preselected based on the purchaser's experience and the vendors' reputations. The consistent delivery of purchased products according to a predetermined delivery schedule will likely have been a significant factor impacting the vendor sourcing decision. Likewise, the purchaser should be using inventory and ordering procedures that best ensure that desired product quality and quantity concerns are considered when orders are placed. Also, the timing of RFPs, the analysis of price quotations, and the issuing of purchase orders should be planned to minimize the need to expedite deliveries.

Manager's Memo

Some less-than-reputable vendors may submit a very low price for one product that is not in stock and that the vendor does not intend to carry in the future. This low price may allow the vendor to receive the order if the purchaser awards it based on the total price for all products. When the delivery is made, the product that was "low-balled" will not be delivered. A low-ball selling price is one that is significantly below current market price and is quoted for a product the vendor does not intend to sell at that price.

Wise purchasers recognize that this strategy can be used. They address it with a boilerplate remedy: "The purchaser reserves the right to purchase, at current market prices, any missing products in the quantity specified in the purchase order with that amount deducted from the amount due to the vendor."

Even with the best planning, however, problems within the operation can occur that affect orders. Perhaps the needs of production employees were misunderstood and purchase requisition problems occurred. Unexpected business volumes can affect purchasing lead times, and inventory management issues can misstate the quantities of products available. Weather conditions, labor strikes, equipment breakdowns, and problems creating errors when delivery vehicles are loaded are examples of reasons for product shortages. In all of these and numerous other instances, expediting may become necessary.

A passive reaction such as simply waiting until the product is delivered should be among the last approaches to resolving problems. Useful strategies vary according to the situation. Several alternatives are noted in *Exhibit 6.11*.

Exhibit 6.11

EXAMPLES OF EXPEDITING STRATEGIES

Problem	Possible Expediting Strategy
1. Inadequate quantity at time of delivery.	1. Purchase product from another supply source.*
2. Improper product quality.	2. Purchase product from another supply source.
3. Purchaser error; product needed quickly.	3. Pick up product at vendor's location; buy product from another supply source.
4. Product shortage (multiunit property).	4. "Borrow" product from another unit; complete property transfer form.
5. Product on backorder but available at the vendor's location before time of need.	5. Request that vendor make special delivery; request that product be delivered by a sales representative.

*Recall the earlier Manager's Memo discussion of purchasing the missing product in the marketplace and obtaining a credit to the amount owed to the vendor.

The coordination of delivery schedules with times that are convenient to receive products can do much to minimize problems creating the need for expediting. Purchasers should know when vendors can make deliveries. If these times are not convenient, purchasers have two options:

- They can negotiate with vendors about delivery schedules. Vendors know that delivery times are important concerns, and they may adjust schedules, especially if the operation is a desired account.

- Purchasers can replace vendors with unacceptable delivery schedules with other approved vendors.

Potential problems with delivery schedules should be addressed as vendor sourcing decisions are made. For example, the acceptable receiving schedules for the operation can be given to the vendor.

If there are potential conflicts in times, determine whether they can be resolved before making vendor sourcing decisions. Vendors' delivery schedules can likely be coordinated so that the times will be convenient to the operation.

Delivery schedules for each approved vendor should be posted in the receiving area. They can also be used to have vendors confirm approximate delivery times when a response to RFP is submitted. When this is done, a delivery schedule can be developed and posted on a work sheet or calendar.

Purchasers should establish a system to check with those who receive whether deliveries occur at scheduled times. This approach is much better than waiting until production or service employees complain about the operating issues caused by vendor delivery problems.

Vendors that do not meet delivery requirements should be contacted and the problems addressed if possible (*Exhibit 6.12*). Follow-up evaluations will be important because corrective actions will be required if the problem is not resolved.

Exhibit 6.12

Purchasers should consider the need to expedite as an opportunity to implement actions to minimize problems. They should also work with vendors to anticipate and resolve vendor-related causes of product shortages and quality issues. They must correct any problems caused by the operation that occur more than very infrequently. Problems caused by the vendor may create the need to examine the benefits of a continued relationship.

TECHNOLOGY AND THE ORDERING PROCESS

Purchasers can use technology in numerous ways at almost every step in the purchasing process. This section will provide an overview of how technology enables earlier steps to provide information required at the time of ordering. It will also review automated ordering alternatives.

Determining Inventory Levels

Traditional ordering systems including the par level and minimum–maximum systems discussed in chapter 3 consider existing levels of inventory and are implemented when order points are reached. Alternatively, orders can be placed on a regularly scheduled basis. For example, orders can be placed on

RESTAURANT TECHNOLOGY

Purchasers interested in using a vendor's online ordering system will likely have to meet with a salesperson or other representative to learn how to use it. A very important part of that discussion will be sharing the establishment's purchase specifications and learning which products meet the specifications.

For example, a vendor may offer several types of canned green beans or fresh-cut sirloin steaks. The purchaser should learn the vendor's product number or other identification for the product meeting specifications. This information can then be used when orders are placed.

Wise purchasers know that automated ordering will not ensure that purchase specifications are met in the products delivered. There is a continuing necessity to check incoming products.

Tuesday for delivery on Thursday. Then existing inventory levels are reviewed and orders are placed to return storage quantities to their par levels. Both strategies require knowledge about the quantity of products in inventory before orders are placed.

Automated systems are available to maintain an ongoing count of products in inventory. Systems can track the quantity of products entering inventory, which increase balances, and record the quantities leaving inventory, which reduce levels. This information can be reviewed at any time by managers and purchasers. It provides an instant answer to the question, "How much product should we order?"

COMMUNICATING WITH VENDORS

There are several times during the routine ordering process when communication between purchasers and vendors is important:

- The purchaser uses an RFP to request prices from vendors for specific products.
- Vendors provide a price quotation (bid) in response to the RFP.
- The purchaser uses a purchase order to notify a vendor that the proposal response was approved.

Each of these activities can be, and increasingly is, automated. The use of technology streamlines the ordering process, reduces time-consuming paperwork, and enables easier information tracking and storing.

Many vendors allow and actually encourage purchasers to place their orders online. This process is often easier and faster than relying on salespersons to take orders in person or by telephone or email.

Purchasers must typically do several things as they use an online ordering system:

- They visit the vendor's Web site and use a protected identification code to reach their account information.
- They enter the products along with order quantities into an order template on the screen.
- They can review previous orders and note current prices for products as ordering information is entered.
- They provide other information and complete the ordering process.

SUMMARY

1. **Summarize the ordering process.**

   Ordering involves activities required when a purchaser makes commitments to a vendor about a specific purchase. Effective communication between product users and purchasers is important so purchasers will know exactly what products, quantity, and quality are needed. Effective communication is also required with approved vendors and the vendor that will receive the order.

   When procedures are followed, quality problems, backorders, and issues with quantity or purchase unit sizes can be minimized. Product availability and quantity delivered are always of special concern. Careful coordination is required between receiving and production employees and between purchasers and vendors to ensure needs are met.

2. **Explain the basic steps in the ordering process.**

   Small establishments typically use a decentralized purchasing process in which the owner, manager, or specific production, service, and bar employees order products required for their department. Policies and procedures indicate when and how product orders are placed and from whom products are purchased.

   Large-volume operations often use a centralized purchasing system in which a single purchaser orders for all departments. A purchase requisition indicating the need for additional products is received by the purchaser. He or she then issues a request for proposal (RFP) asking approved vendors to submit bids according to purchase specifications. RFP responses are analyzed, and a purchase order is issued to the chosen vendor.

3. **Identify special ordering concerns involving bidding.**

   Some establishments have a policy that requires competitive bidding, where purchasers send requests for proposals (RFPs) to more than one approved vendor. It is important to ensure that all vendors quote prices on the same quality of products. Product specifications help purchasers to do this. RFP responses may be analyzed by lowest price for all products or lowest price for individual items. Selecting one vendor is easiest and will save the processing costs for multiple orders, but some purchasers select vendors on the basis of prices quoted for each product.

4. **Explain the types of purchase contracts, elements in contracts, and common terms and conditions used in contracts.**

   Agreements between purchasers and vendors are called contracts, and they are enforceable in court. Contracts may be established in writing or orally, but written contracts are normally preferred.

   Contracts must be legally valid and contain an offer: a proposal to perform an act or pay an amount that, if accepted, becomes a legally valid contract. There must also be acceptance, an agreement to the exact terms and conditions of the offer, and consideration, the payment made in exchange for the contract promise. If the acceptance is not the same as the offer, this becomes a counteroffer and a new contract. When acceptance is the same as the offer, an express contract is created.

Terms and conditions refer to general provisions that apply regardless of the specific products being sold or purchased. Examples of these boilerplate clauses include exclusiveness of the purchase order, services and deliverables, delivery schedules, and risks of loss. Other terms and conditions can concern packaging and crating charges, guarantees and warrantees, insurance, indemnification, and procedures for handling rejected products. Still other concerns can relate to confidentiality, termination, legal remedies, and failure to perform.

5. **Describe the procedures to hasten the delivery of products that have been ordered but not yet delivered.**

Expediting refers to activities to obtain products ordered but not yet received. Deliveries may be late, product quality may be incorrect, or too few products may be delivered. These and related problems affect production and must be effectively managed. If they occur frequently, purchasers should reconsider the vendor's status.

6. **Explain how technology can impact the ordering process.**

Electronic systems can track products entering and leaving inventory and maintain inventory counts. This technology is useful to help make purchase quantity decisions. Technology can also be used to communicate with vendors when RFPs are sent, bids are returned, and purchase orders are placed. Increasingly, purchasers place orders using an online system at the vendor's Web site.

APPLICATION EXERCISE

You are the manager in a small-volume operation that uses decentralized purchasing. Within the last several weeks, the food-production, foodservice, and bar operations staff members who buy products for these areas have discussed several problems. What should you do in each situation?

1. The chef told you that one vendor indicated prices could probably be reduced if food such as produce used for garnishes and dairy products used as drink ingredients were combined with bar orders. When she discussed this with the bar manager, he was not interested because he liked a specific vendor's product.

2. The dining-room manager told you that salespersons for a local restaurant supply company have a good deal on serviceware (plates, bowls, etc.) that the establishment uses. The pattern is being discontinued and the vendor will sell the remaining inventory at a 40 percent price reduction. However, the purchase quantity would have to equal about what the operation uses in two years.

3. When checking the bar storage area, the head bartender noticed that some brands of spirits were in inventory that had never been used previously. The establishment has a policy that all new brands of spirits must be approved by the manager before purchase.

REVIEW YOUR LEARNING

Select the best answer for each question.

1. **What must a purchaser do before contacting vendors about a potential purchase?**
   A. Learn if the purchases can be delayed a while to save money
   B. Determine quality and quantity requirements for items needed
   C. Determine if quality requirements can be reduced to save money
   D. Learn if there is a new vendor that might be willing to make deals

2. **What happens when a backorder occurs?**
   A. The vendor supplies more than the quantity ordered.
   B. The purchaser orders more products from the vendor.
   C. The purchaser returns a product to the vendor.
   D. The vendor cannot fill the purchaser's order.

3. **What typically happens in decentralized purchasing if an order exceeds a preestablished cost limit?**
   A. The purchaser orders if the quality is acceptable.
   B. The vendor is removed from the approved vendor list.
   C. The order must be approved by the owner or manager.
   D. Production staff members are asked to use lower-quality products.

4. **Which characteristic of the ordering process is the same in large- and small-volume operations?**
   A. The manager must approve all purchase orders.
   B. Department heads order products for their department.
   C. Approved documentation must authorize the purchase.
   D. A purchase requisition is needed before orders are placed.

5. **In centralized purchasing, what document is used to inform purchasing staff that more products are needed?**
   A. Purchase requisition
   B. Request for proposal
   C. Express contract
   D. Purchase order

6. **To which approved vendors should RFPs be sent?**
   A. To those that will negotiate each price in the order
   B. To those with low prices on all items required
   C. To those selling the products being ordered
   D. To those used within the last three months

7. **What is the meaning of the expression "3/15; net 30" in a purchase order?**
   A. Products will be delivered in 3 to 15 days and must be paid for within 30 days.
   B. A 3% discount is given for payment within 15 days; full payment is due within 30 days.
   C. Three deliveries will arrive within 15 days; all products will be delivered within 30 days.
   D. Three vendors will supply orders within 15 days; payment is due within 30 days.

8. **Who should receive a copy of the purchase order in a centralized operation?**
   A. Executive chef
   B. Dining-room manager
   C. Head bartender
   D. Receiving staff

9. The payment to be made in exchange for the promise(s) contained in a contract is called the
   A. offer.
   B. consideration.
   C. acceptance.
   D. guarantee.

10. Expediting may be necessary when
   A. products in an order being received are improperly priced.
   B. products are received a day earlier than expected.
   C. products have been ordered but not yet delivered.
   D. a vendor does not respond to a request for proposal.

FIELD PROJECT

The product ordering system used by a restaurant or foodservice operation can have a significant impact on purchasing effectiveness and costs.

A. Summarize the responses from the chapter 1 restaurant or foodservice operation questionnaire (questions 5–7).
    Note: *The responses to question 8 in the questionnaire will be used for the chapter 8 field project.*

_____

_____

_____

_____

_____

_____

B. Draw a flow chart that documents the purchasing process in the operation you interviewed.

C. What are your ideas about how the ordering process in the restaurant or foodservice operation can be improved?

_____

_____

_____

_____

_____

_____

7 Purchasing Ethics and Vendor Relations

INSIDE THIS CHAPTER

- Purchasing Ethics
- Vendor Relations

CHAPTER LEARNING OBJECTIVES

After completing this chapter, you should be able to:

- Explain the importance of ethical concerns in purchase decision making.

- Explain how codes of ethics and purchasing policies provide guidelines to purchasers as they interact with vendors.

- Describe the importance of professional vendor relationships.

- Summarize the basics of vendor's handbooks.

KEY TERMS

code of purchasing ethics, p. 174

ethical, p. 174

kickbacks, p. 183

legal, p. 174

moral, p. 174

reciprocity, p. 183

statement of business conduct, p. 183

steward sales, p. 183

supply chain, p. 186

vendor relations, p. 185

vendor's handbook, p. 187

CASE STUDY

"I'm trying to save when I purchase, and my latest ideas are even better," said Edgar, the kitchen manager at Gesiorski's Southside Café.

"There probably aren't any secrets about reducing food cost, and we are already doing fine. What are your ideas?" asked Rene, a cook.

Edgar said, "I am going to ask vendors to quote prices. Then I'll call the vendor with the second-lowest prices. I'll tell him that we will buy products from him if he lowers his prices below the lowest bid. I will know we are receiving the best price because it is lower than the lowest bid."

Rene replied, "I think you are really onto something. Let me know how it works."

1. What do you think about Edgar's plan to reduce food cost?

2. What would you do if you were the vendor submitting the lowest price and found out what Edgar was doing?

PURCHASING ETHICS

THINK ABOUT IT . . .

• Legal = permitted by law
• Ethical = complying with standards for conduct
• Moral = based on principles about right and wrong

Why should managers consider actions from all three points of view?

Some people believe any activity that is not illegal must be legal. In other words, it is lawful and acceptable to do it. They would be technically correct because a legal activity is permitted by law. A person cannot be prosecuted for doing it.

However, professional managers and purchasers know that not every activity that is legal is acceptable or professional. They understand that some legal activities should still not be done because of ethical concerns. These concerns relate to following the standards and practices of an establishment or a profession. Purchasers also have morals that are based on principles about what is right and wrong. These morals can influence how purchasers interact with vendors.

In many operations, ethical behavior is explained using a policy and a set of guidelines, procedures, or even a code of purchasing ethics. These codes state guidelines that should be followed as purchasers implement purchasing procedures and make purchasing decisions.

Ethical Behavior

Ethical behavior refers to behavior that society in general or the culture of the establishment or the industry considers "the right thing to do." For professional purchasers, choosing ethical behavior can be an important strategy for avoiding legal difficulty. The reason is that a purchaser may not always know exactly what the law requires. If purchasers' actions are ever questioned by their manager, or even in a court of law, decisions will likely be made about whether actions were intentionally ethical or unethical.

It is sometimes difficult to determine precisely what ethical behavior is and what it is not. However, seven guidelines can help purchasers evaluate a possible course of action:

1. Is it legally permitted?

2. Does it follow company policy or code of ethics?

3. Does it harm anyone?

4. Is it fair and truthful?

5. Would I care if it happened to me?

6. Would I tell others about it?

7. What if every person did the same?

How a person evaluates behavior that is potentially unethical is likely affected by cultural background, religious views, professional training, and personal moral code. Each person can, however, apply these ethical conduct guidelines. Consider the following situation:

> Tasha purchases food and beverage products for a large establishment. She is working with the food and beverage manager and others to plan the property's annual New Year's Eve party. The event will require a large amount of wine and brandy. She uses a competitive bidding process with her approved vendors for these products. Based on quality and price, she places an order in excess of $10,000 with a single vendor. One week later, a case of very expensive brandy is delivered to Tasha's home with a note from the vendor's representative. It begins "Happy Holidays" and continues with a thank-you for the order and statements about being eager to do a lot of business with the operation in the future. What should Tasha do with the brandy?

To answer this question, Tasha asks herself the seven questions:

1. Is it legally permitted?

It is probably not illegal for Tasha to accept the case of brandy. However, there could be liquor laws in her state that prohibit vendors from making a gift of alcoholic beverages. She must find out about any laws that affect her decision. Assuming that it does not violate a law or operation policy for Tasha to accept the gift, she should consider the second question.

2. Does it follow company policy or code of ethics?

Tasha must consider whether keeping the gift is allowed by the purchasing policy or code of purchasing ethics established by her operation. Many establishments have gift acceptance policies that limit the value of or types of gifts that employees are allowed to accept. Violation of a stated or written company policy may lead to disciplinary action or even termination. If this is the case, acceptance of the gift might be considered incorrect from her employer's perspective.

3. Does it harm anyone?

It probably would not hurt Tasha to drink the brandy in moderation. However, is it likely that she could be fair and objective when evaluating future vendor bids? When she is interacting with vendors, will she think about the free case of brandy? If influenced by the gift, she might award a purchase order to a vendor that would not otherwise have received the order. If the products would not have otherwise been purchased because of quality, cost, or other concerns, some persons will be hurt. These include the owner and managers, who receive a bonus for the financial or other goals they achieve. Even customers might be affected if the purchase yielded inferior products. Assuming Tasha does not think her decision to accept the brandy causes any harm, including to her own judgment, she should proceed to question 4.

THINK ABOUT IT . . .

Purchasers for government establishments such as universities often are bound by a long list of prohibited behaviors.

Do you think purchasers for private establishments should have similar or more relaxed guidelines? Why or why not?

---

4. Is it fair and truthful?

This question requires Tasha to think about who will be affected by her decision. For example, how might others in the establishment feel about the gift? Since keeping the gift is a benefit, fairness requires that she assess whether the benefit is to the restaurant or to her. When she thinks about honesty, Tasha will have the opportunity to reconsider her earlier answers. Does she really think that she can remain objective when she makes beverage purchasing decisions? Will she continue to search for the best quality of products at the best price? Will she expect the vendor to reward her again? Assuming Tasha has decided that it is fair and honest for her to keep the brandy, she should proceed to question 5.

5. Would I care if it happened to me?

What would Tasha do if she owned the establishment and learned that her purchaser had accepted a case of expensive brandy? Would Tasha question the future ability of the purchaser to always make decisions based on what was best for the establishment? Would she wonder if the purchaser had accepted other gifts? Would she like it if some or all of her managers received gifts of this type, or would she likely be concerned? By this point, Tasha is beginning to form her decision, but she continues by asking the next question.

6. Would I tell others about it?

If Tasha honestly answers "It's OK" to all of the preceding questions, this question becomes very important. In many cases, it will be the most important question. Would Tasha accept the gift if she knew that the next issue of the employee newsletter would begin with the following statement: "Tasha, our food and beverage purchaser, received a free case of expensive brandy after placing a large order for our holiday party." What if a notice were placed on the employee bulletin board? Would Tasha care? The operation's manager would know about the gift, as would the owner and Tasha's fellow employees. It is likely that other vendors would also learn about the gift. If she knew that these things would happen, would Tasha be concerned?

7. What if every person did the same?

If Tasha can still justify her choice, she might consider the question "Where would we draw the line?" What would happen if the executive chef received a carton of steaks every time steaks were ordered? Would the dining-room manager receive tickets to athletic events when she ordered new table linens?

By this time, most readers would likely agree that it is unethical, even if it is legal, for Tasha to accept the brandy. Therefore, what are her alternatives? There are several things she can do:

- Return the case of brandy with a professionally written note stating how much the gift was appreciated, but that company policy, or her personal policy, will not allow her to accept it.

- Ask the manager what she should do with the brandy.

- Bring the brandy to the establishment and place it in the operation's normal beverage inventory, if local liquor laws will allow this action.

- Donate it to the employee holiday party.

Codes of Purchasing Ethics

The best operations have a highly developed sense of professional ethics to protect and enhance their reputation. They can strengthen their purchasers' and vendors' awareness of ethical concerns and provide guidelines for purchasers by implementing a code of purchasing ethics. The best codes are formal written documents that are well known by purchasers and provided to approved vendors in vendor's handbooks. These are discussed later in this chapter.

Exhibit 7.1 on the next page shows a sample code of purchasing ethics. It covers a variety of situations that purchasers may encounter.

Notice that item 8 of the sample code of purchasing ethics mentions the importance of following all applicable laws. Laws do not exist to cover every situation that purchasers encounter, however. Also, specific laws change. Society's view of acceptable behavior can also evolve. Codes help purchasers achieve consistency in ethical behavior, which is important to the long-term success of their establishments.

Managers take an important first step by developing carefully thought-out codes of purchasing ethics to guide purchasers' decisions. However, a code, even if it is written, will not be effective unless there is ongoing enforcement and consequences for failure to follow it.

Disciplinary actions for failure to comply with the code should be planned, written, and communicated to purchasers. Purchasers should know the actions that will be taken, up to and including termination, when the guidelines are not followed. The establishment's discipline policy that may include oral and written warnings and, perhaps, probation should apply to purchasing policies as well as to any other type of policies.

Written penalties are important because they minimize problems that arise when judgments are made on a case-by-case basis that may seem to show favoritism. Enforcement is also important. If an employee does something wrong and a disciplinary action exists, it must be implemented.

THINK ABOUT IT . . .

Use the seven questions to assess what you would do.

What would be your decision? Which question most influenced your decision? How helpful was answering each question to your decision?

Manager's Memo

Experienced purchasers have probably been confronted by less-than-professional vendors that have offered gifts or other incentives to accept their bid. However, purchasers who accept these incentives are actually accepting profits that would otherwise have benefited their employer.

Some purchasers claim that their acceptance of incentives does not actually influence their choice of vendor. While this might be true for some purchasers, it is much less likely for many others. In the most serious cases, an incentive influences the purchaser to accept a less favorable offer. In some cases, this can lead to illegal activities such as "buying" products that are never delivered. If found guilty by a court of law, the purchaser could be imprisoned. It is temptations of this type that codes of purchasing ethics attempt to address.

Exhibit 7.1

SAMPLE CODE OF PURCHASING ETHICS

Code of Purchasing Ethics

The objective of _____*(insert company name)*_____ Code of Purchasing Ethics is to ensure that purchasing staff never use their authority for personal gain and shall seek to uphold, at all times, the reputation of the Company.

To achieve the objective, purchasers will:

1. Always give first priority and consideration to the financial objectives and operating policies of the company.
2. Seek to obtain the maximum value for each dollar spent.
3. Decline all personal gifts or gratuities.
4. Reject any business practice that might reasonably be considered improper.
5. Never use their authority or position for personal gain.
6. Ensure the information provided in the course of their work is correct.
7. Grant all competitive vendors equal consideration based solely on their ability to supply the company with the correct quality of products and services at a fair value.
8. Conduct business with potential and current vendors in an atmosphere of good faith, without intentional misrepresentation, and in keeping with all applicable laws.
9. Demand honesty in sales representations whether offered through oral statements, advertisements, or product samples.
10. Make every reasonable effort to negotiate an equitable and mutually agreeable settlement of any problem with a vendor.
11. When conditions permit, provide a prompt and courteous reception for all vendor representatives who call on the company for legitimate business purposes.
12. Encourage support for socially diverse and acceptable purchasing practices.
13. Develop and maintain professional purchasing competencies.
14. Cooperate with trade and professional associations for the purposes of promoting and developing ethical business practices.
15. Counsel and guide other purchasers within the organization in upholding this code of purchasing ethics.

Presented by: *Read and understood by:*

_____   _____
          (Company official)   (Purchaser)

_____   _____
                  Date   Date

Codes of purchasing ethics should be fully explained to purchasers (*Exhibit 7.2*). Managers in some establishments make a brief attempt to help purchasers understand the code when they ask the purchaser to read and sign it. However, it would not be unusual for a purchaser to scan through the document quickly and sign it. When this occurs, the purchaser will not really understand the guidelines. Also, this brief communication gives purchasers the impression that the guidelines are not important. They may think that the company was required to do this for some external reason and, to comply, the manager had to prove that purchasers were given copies.

Common Ethical Policies

Purchasers, working with top-level managers, typically develop policies related to ethical concerns that can guide them as they make decisions and take actions. These policies provide guidance about what actions are proper when purchasers are confronted with a specific situation. Purchasing policies help provide consistency because issues will always be addressed and problems resolved in the same way; that is, according to the applicable policy.

In a legal sense, purchasers act as agents as they represent their operation and make decisions involving vendors. In other words, purchasers have the legal authority to make decisions for the operation within the limitations established. Therefore, purchasers must do what is best for the employer, not what is best for themselves personally.

There are several common situations among many that have ethical implications for purchasers. What should they do in these situations? Here are some guidelines, but it is important that every operation develops its own policies addressing its own concerns. When these policies are in place, fewer problems are likely to arise.

ACCEPTING GIFTS

Concerns about accepting gifts were mentioned earlier in the chapter. Some operations establish maximum values for gifts, while others state flatly that no gifts of any type should be given to purchasers.

The definition of gifts may also be important. Many persons would agree that an inexpensive ballpoint pen with a vendor's logo may not be considered a gift. Few people would say the same of a weekend hunting trip costing thousands of dollars.

What about free items that vendors give to managers, production staff, and purchasers at trade shows or free samples purchasers receive as they are considering future purchases? Whether they will influence the purchaser is a priority concern. An analysis, as in the brandy example earlier, can help determine whether specific gifts can be accepted.

Exhibit 7.2

Manager's Memo

How should a manager train a purchaser about an operation's code of purchasing ethics? The best approach is to sit down with the purchaser and go through the code item by item. The discussion will be best if examples of "do's and don'ts" are provided. Then sample situations can be posed, and the purchaser can be asked what should be done. The manager can judge the purchaser's responses to ensure that each guideline was understood. As this occurs, the purchaser will become familiar with the code, the need to comply with it, and the recognition of its importance to the operation.

Manager's Memo

Policies related to favoritism and competitive bidding often help purchasers in more ways than they are probably aware of. For example, when these policies are in place, vendors are more likely to offer their best prices because every vendor knows that he or she has a fair opportunity to be awarded the purchase order. In contrast, purchasers who submit requests for proposals to multiple vendors, but generally award their orders to a single favored source, are not likely to obtain the best competitive prices from other vendors.

Concerns about preferred vendors should be addressed when decisions about approved vendors are made. Purchasers will then have confidence that all vendors being sent RFPs will be those with whom the operation wants to do business.

FAVORITISM

Ethical concerns about favoritism are similar to those related to accepting gifts. The purchaser should grant approved vendor status to those whose products, services, and information is judged best for the operation. Purchase orders should be awarded to the vendor whose bid most favors the establishment.

COMPETITIVE BIDDING

Many operations have policies relating to competitive bidding. These policies require that several approved vendors be invited to quote prices for products on purchase orders and the lowest price be accepted if all other requirements are met. By definition, approved vendors provide the information and service levels required by the purchaser.

A competitive bidding policy is intended to address two goals. The first is to ensure that the best price is received for products meeting quality requirements from among the approved vendors. A second goal relates to implementing a process that reduces the possibility of favoritism. This goal can be achieved because the order will be awarded on the basis of an objective factor: lowest price. This approach is much better than awarding the order on the basis of subjective factors such as "vendor A is easier to work with" or "vendor B has always been a good friend of our business."

Some managers require competitive bidding for all purchases; others require it only for purchases above a specified dollar value. The vendors' responses to RFPs should remain on file for a specified amount of time (*Exhibit 7.3*). Some establishments also require that the competitive bid analysis leading to the award be submitted with other documentation as vendor payments are processed.

Exhibit 7.3

BEST PRICE FIRST

This ethical challenge has a specific meaning but also broader implications. Purchasers use a best-price-first policy when they indicate that the first bid will be the only price that the vendor can offer.

The issue being addressed is the subject of the case study at the beginning of this chapter. Some purchasers tell vendors about the prices quoted by other vendors and ask, "Can you beat that price?" This strategy is not fair to the less-favored vendors that are not given a "second chance," and it also does a disservice to the purchasers. Why should a vendor submit the lowest price first if the vendor's representative can submit another price later?

Purchasers show their interest in the ongoing relationship with vendors emphasized throughout this book when they do not use one vendor's prices against another. They promote positive purchaser–vendor relationships by being courteous and impartial. They also show their professionalism in other ways. They do not allow vendors to submit proposal responses beyond specified deadlines, and they do not expect vendors to make changes in contract details after purchase orders have been agreed on.

CONFLICT OF INTEREST

Conflict-of-interest concerns can arise when a purchaser or any relatives or friends own or have an interest in a business that sells products to the operation. Managers normally feel very uneasy about purchase arrangements with these vendors. Also, family or friendship pressures can create unnecessary stresses for purchasers who want to maintain an "arm's length" relationship with their vendors. The best approach is normally to avoid potential problems by implementing a reasonable conflict-of-interest policy.

VENDOR ERRORS

What should an ethical purchaser do when, for example, a vendor's bid indicates a selling price of $1.10 per pound for high-quality steaks when it is obvious that the price is probably $11.10? One possible answer is apparent: "Vendors should be responsible for their errors." This is correct, but in a similar situation, such as when a customer is incorrectly charged $8 for an $80 bottle of wine, what would the manager want the customer to do?

Perhaps there are different responses to the question depending on whether these mistakes occur very frequently or almost never. One approach is to review all vendor documentation carefully and ask for verification prior to awarding the contract if something appears unusual. Taking advantage of a vendor, even when it is legal, is not in the best interest of a long-term relationship between the two parties.

THINK ABOUT IT ...

How do you think a well-developed, communicated, and enforced code of purchasing ethics helps purchasers? How, if at all, does it help the operation improve its reputation and set it apart from competitors?

WHAT'S THE FOOTPRINT?

An operation's policy about buying locally may consider issues such as purchasing some products from local growers at farmers' markets. Managers may want to do this for reasons other than saving money. For example, they may want to show support for their community while obtaining the freshest products and reducing environmental concerns about pollution from the transportation of products over long distances.

There may be other non-cost aspects of these ongoing purchases. The reputation of the establishment may be enhanced, and it may even develop advertising messages related to visiting these markets to obtain the freshest possible products. Also, it may obtain seasonal items such as fruit that can be used to prepare fresh desserts to be featured on the menu.

LOCAL BUYING

Purchasing products locally has already been discussed relative to the use of organic foods and other items by operations concerned about the environment. Another dimension focuses on whether preference should be given to vendors in the community to "keep the money at home." For-profit operations such as restaurants typically have financial concerns that are best met by approving the best vendors whether local or not.

Noncommercial operations include local facilities such as public schools and state facilities such as prisons and hospitals. Sometimes these institutions prefer local-buying policies to help the businesses that pay the taxes. Some of these operations have different policies that suggest that all taxpayers should be concerned about receiving the best prices for products of the required quality, so the vendors' locations are not important.

Just as with many situations that address ethics, there are sometimes no obvious good answers to issues that arise. This further supports the potential need for a policy about buying locally to be developed by high-level officials, in order to guide the decisions made by all of the organization's employees including purchasers.

BACK-DOOR SELLING

Back-door selling occurs when a vendor's representative attempts to contact or influence a production employee without approval of the purchaser. For example, a salesperson may talk to a chef about a new product or to a head bartender about a new wine promotion without first contacting the purchaser. One reason is to inform the production employee about the product. However, another purpose may be to request that the employee urge the purchaser to purchase the item.

Purchasers want input from the establishment's employees, and they can learn much from them. However, without preapproval of vendor's visits with production staff, there is little way to know whether recommendations are genuine. There is always the possibility that the employee was offered an incentive such as a percentage of the amount paid to the vendor for the item.

TRIAL ORDERS AND SAMPLES

Suppose a chef desires some samples of food products that are being considered for a new menu. Should these samples be purchased? If so, the purchaser will need to send a purchase order for the small quantity needed. There will be additional time spent on processing the order for payment. Alternatively, should a vendor be asked for free samples or a free trial order?

Many vendors would probably be pleased to provide small quantities of products at no cost to establishments considering their use. However, is the operation in any way obligated to purchase that product or any other product from the vendor? This question cannot be easily answered. Also, it is likely to be answered in different ways by, for example, the chef and the purchaser. Therefore, a policy stating the owner's or manager's position may be in order.

KICKBACKS

Kickbacks consist of money or other gifts received by an employee in return for purchasing from a specific vendor (*Exhibit 7.4*). Kickbacks are often viewed as the most serious ethical violations and they are also illegal.

RECIPROCITY

Reciprocity occurs when a purchaser agrees to buy something from a vendor in return for some kind of business from the vendor. For example, the vendor representative may hold his or her company's holiday party at the establishment if the purchaser agrees to purchase a certain amount from the vendor. Reciprocity typically complicates the purchaser–seller relationship and should normally be avoided.

PERSONAL PURCHASES

Some companies allow their employees to buy products purchased by the establishment. These are called steward sales. For example, an employee may want to purchase some high-quality steaks for a special personal party. Many establishments discourage steward sales because they can create accounting difficulties. Other operations allow the practice when there are inventory overages that should be reduced.

Statements of Business Conduct

Some restaurant and foodservice organizations combine concerns and policies about purchasing ethics into a statement of business conduct. The result is a broad code of behavior that addresses many aspects of the business and its employees who have a wide variety of functional responsibilities within it.

For example, Darden is the world's largest full-service restaurant company with brands that include Red Lobster, Olive Garden, LongHorn Steakhouse, and Capital Grille. Darden has a Code of Business Conduct and Ethics (RP-3, issued July 21, 2003; revised March 7, 2011) that addresses a wide range of business- and purchasing-related topics. For example, here is part of the company's statement about accepting gifts and gratuities:

> i. Meetings with vendors or suppliers may include an aspect of entertainment, provided the entertainment is of reasonable value and occasional frequency. The nature of meetings and entertainment should always be in good taste and not in conflict with Darden's values. The employee should maintain detailed records of these contacts and the business nature of the discussions on the appropriate expense reporting forms or other journals or business calendars.

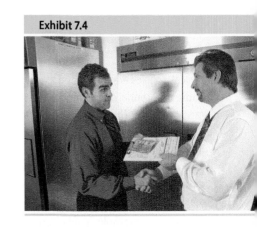

Exhibit 7.4

Manager's Memo

The spirit and intent of ethical guidelines can be a summary of the ethical concerns of the establishment's owners and managers. Their standards will address concerns about loyalty to the operation, fairness in vendor interactions, and professional decision making.

The best professional guidelines consider the legal, ethical, and moral concerns that should be addressed when purchasers interact with vendors. This means that the guidelines should help purchasers make decisions that are not illegal, that will be ethical, and that will be in line with the establishment's values.

Ethical policies are developed to address potential situations that raise concerns. Their purpose is to establish guidelines for purchasing decision makers. However, not all purchasing policies are developed because of ethical concerns.

Consider, for example, a policy on reciprocal purchases. These are transactions in which a vendor agrees to purchase something from the purchaser if the purchaser, in turn, agrees to purchase something from the vendor. An earlier example related to an operation offering a banquet for a newspaper's employees in return for free advertising. While this situation may be an example in which no ethical concerns are important, the offer for a reciprocal purchase should not be considered by the purchaser unless the purchaser is the manager or owner. The policy should direct the purchaser to contact the manager to make the decision. The purchaser may not have a "big picture" overview of the needs and costs and benefits associated with a reciprocal arrangement.

ii. No cash gift or gratuity or any kickback, free services or special favors from any vendor, supplier, contractor or agency may be solicited, requested or accepted. Gifts of a nominal value (defined as less than $100) may be accepted provided they have not been solicited and are not being made in return for a special consideration or decision.[1]

The Wendy's Company is the world's third largest quick-service hamburger company. The Wendy's system includes more than 6,500 franchise and company restaurants in the United States and 27 other countries and U.S. territories worldwide. It also has a Company Code of Business Conduct and Ethics. Here is a portion of its statement about the acceptance of gifts:

You may accept infrequent, nominal gifts valued at less than $100. Gifts of greater value may be accepted if protocol, courtesy or other special circumstances exist, as sometimes happens with international transactions; however, all such gifts must be reported to the Compliance Officer who will determine if you may keep the gift or must return it or whether it should more appropriately become Company property. Frequently, gifts of food are given by vendors at holiday time. If possible, these gifts should be shared with your team.

You may never accept cash or cash equivalents such as gift cards. You may not benefit personally from any purchase of goods or services for Wendy's or derive any personal gain from transactions made on behalf of Wendy's.[2]

As is evident from these code of business conduct statements, both companies are concerned about potential conflicts of interest that can arise as employees interact with representatives of other businesses. The two companies have expressed their concerns about these issues in statements that provide meaningful assistance to guide the actions of their employees.

In addition to creating guides for their employees, some of the world's largest foodservice organizations also develop guidelines for their vendors. These guidelines govern what those in the supply chain should and should not do if they are to be approved vendors.

For example, some of these organizations express concerns about the treatment of employees including minors who work in the processing plants and other businesses that produce the products these organizations purchase. Others address ecological issues such as seafood that can be harvested from the oceans or in seafood farming operations.

[1]www.darden.com/pdf/corporate/Code_of_Business_Conduct_and_Ethics.pdf (accessed February 16, 2012).
[2]http://ir.wendys.com/phoenix.zhtml?c=67548&p=irol-govconduct#5 (accessed February 16, 2012).

The humane treatment of animals is another significant concern of some large-volume purchasers. Size of cages, use of growth hormones, and slaughtering methods are among the issues that may be addressed. Farm-to-fork, buying locally produced food, and concerns about the transportation of products through the supply chain are still other concerns.

The world's largest restaurant and foodservice organizations have special opportunities to interact with and regulate their vendors' practices. Some of their concerns address societal issues that go beyond their financial needs.

VENDOR RELATIONS

The concept of vendor relations relates to the ways in which purchasers interact with their vendors. An appropriate professional relationship is important, and information provided in vendor handbooks can be helpful in maintaining this relationship.

Purchaser–Vendor Relationships

What is the appropriate relationship between a purchaser and vendors? *Exhibit 7.5* shows the range of possible purchaser–vendor relationships.

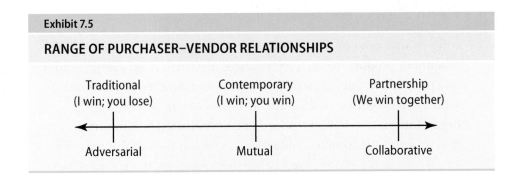

Exhibit 7.5

RANGE OF PURCHASER–VENDOR RELATIONSHIPS

When reviewing *Exhibit 7.5*, note that the traditional win–lose relationship anchors one side of the scale. The other extreme shows a partnership relationship. A middle point along the range is labeled contemporary, or win–win.

The traditional relationship is referred to as adversarial because the purchaser and vendor both want to win. The purchaser wants the product at the lowest possible price, which would reduce the vendor's profit. The vendor wants the highest possible price, which would reduce the operation's profit.

The middle position is called contemporary. It increasingly describes the type of purchaser–vendor relationships that exist today. It is labeled mutual because the purchaser and seller both attempt to win while maintaining their professional relationship. Both parties recognize the need for the other to make a reasonable profit to remain in business and to continue their buying and selling arrangements.

The third position on the scale is one of a partnership. It is collaborative because both parties work together to attain goals that could not be accomplished without their relationship. For example, the vendor might be the purchaser's only supplier for specific products. In exchange, the vendor will make very frequent deliveries to reduce the purchaser's need for storage space. The concept of just-in-time purchasing that involves frequent deliveries was discussed in chapter 3.

Purchasers and their organizations typically have differing relationships with each of their vendors. These may include each of the points along the range shown in *Exhibit 7.5*. This is to be expected because many purchasers do not attempt to develop a "one size fits all" relationship with vendors. Their vendor-specific relationships are based on numerous factors including those used to determine approved vendor status. These factors are listed in chapter 4.

In addition, there are several other general factors that often influence the relationship between purchaser and seller:

- **Relative size or business volume of both organizations:** A very large operation is not likely to commit significant resources to developing a collaborative relationship with a vendor that provides only a small amount of product needs. The reverse is also true. A very large vendor will probably not devote significant time and effort to its relationship with a small-volume establishment. This is one reason multiunit organizations develop centralized and coordinated purchasing systems that gain the attention of vendors and others in the supply chain. The supply chain is a coordinated system of businesses, people, activities, information, and resources that move products from the manufacturer, processor, or grower to an operation. Supply chain activities change raw materials such as wheat into finished products such as bread.

- **Reliance on the vendor:** This can occur when, for example, one vendor is the only source of an item because it has exclusive distribution rights to specific products in the purchaser's location.

- **Compatibility:** This is the extent to which the purchaser and vendor share cultural, moral, ethical, and other beliefs that help shape their businesses. If there is not a good fit, one or both parties may wish to limit the relationship to a position on the more traditional end of the scale.

- **Extent that resources are committed:** Manufacturers that extend product lines and increase production capacities to better serve large-volume operations desire a long-term commitment from purchasers.

Importance of Professional Relationships

Purchasers want their vendors to treat them fairly. They should recognize that vendors will likely treat them in a manner similar to how the vendors are treated. Long-term relationships allow for collaborative efforts that emphasize trust, flexibility, and innovation. Both parties can benefit from the improved communication and increased levels of trust that result.

The best vendor relations begin when vendor sourcing decisions are made. Vendors that are approved are the ones that managers and purchasers think will work best with their establishment. Ongoing activities are then implemented to best ensure that the desired relationship begins and is continued. Any problems that arise between the purchaser and the vendor should be identified, discussed, and resolved quickly, and communication between the purchaser and the vendor should be ongoing.

What factors typically impact the positive relationship from the purchaser's point of view? These are the same concerns that should have been considered as the decision to approve the vendor was made. The purchaser's experience with vendors will be based on several factors:

Exhibit 7.6

- Consistency of product quality and availability
- On-time and accurate deliveries (*Exhibit 7.6*)
- Effectiveness of communication
- Value pricing
- Interest in addressing the purchaser's concerns
- Level of service provided
- Quality of information supplied
- Problem-free payment processing and reasonable payment terms

The extent to which these and related factors are satisfactorily addressed by the vendor directly impacts the purchaser–vendor relationship. The relationship is likely to become stronger when few, if any, problems related to these concerns arise over time. Then purchasers have a greater incentive to continue and expand on the business relationship.

Vendor's Handbooks

Many operations, especially large ones, provide a vendor's handbook to approved suppliers. A **vendor's handbook** is developed by the establishment to inform vendors about the organization's purchasing policies and procedures. These handbooks can be excellent communication tools to inform new vendors and remind existing vendors about details of the purchaser's purchasing process.

Topics that can be addressed in a vendor's handbook are varied. Many handbooks begin with an introduction that provides general information about the operation. This section may be in the form of a letter from the owner or manager of a single-unit establishment or from a higher-level official in a multiunit company. Alternatively, it may be the first section in the handbook. It may include a mission statement, a brief history of the operation, an organizational chart, and a description of customers.

The remainder of the handbook reviews basic policies and procedures that vendors must follow. Emphasis is placed on contacts and communication between the organization and its vendors. *Exhibit 7.7* suggests examples of topics that are commonly addressed in vendor's handbooks.

Exhibit 7.7
SAMPLE TABLE OF CONTENTS FOR VENDOR'S HANDBOOK

Overview of (Name of Organization)
Vendor Selection and Sourcing Procedures
Code of Purchasing Ethics
Purchasing Policy Statements
Role of Vendor's Representative
Requests for Proposal
Bidding Procedures
Bid Award Analysis Process
Purchase Orders
Procedures for Product Receiving, Including Inspection
Payment Policies and Procedures
Preferences for Sustainable Products
Vendor Performance Reviews
Appendix: Copies of Purchasing Documents

Once developed, the vendor's handbook should be provided to all vendors with whom the organization does business. Vendors wanting to conduct business with the operation can also be given copies. Copies should be provided to vendor representatives who make unannounced visits, or cold calls, to purchasing staff, and sent with RFPs to potential vendors for one-time equipment or other purchases.

Vendors can provide the best possible assistance to purchasers only when they know facts about the establishment, what purchasers want, and procedures that purchasers expect to be followed. A vendor's handbook provides this information. It can help minimize communication problems or misunderstandings about purchasing procedures and the policies that govern them.

As with all other materials developed by the operation, vendor's handbooks must be maintained and updated regularly. Most important, they must be used as a foundation for how the purchasing department operates. As with standard operating procedures for employees, there should be no difference between what the procedures say and how the process is actually conducted.

SUMMARY

1. **Explain the importance of ethical concerns in purchase decision making.**

   Activities that are legal may not be ethical. Purchasers can ask several questions to help them determine what to do when there are no specific policies in place: Is it legally permitted? Does it follow company policies? Does it harm anyone? Is it fair and truthful? Would I care if it happened to me? Would I tell others about it? What if every person did the same?

2. **Explain how codes of ethics and purchasing policies provide guidelines to purchasers as they interact with vendors.**

   Many operations develop codes of purchasing ethics that provide guidelines about what purchasers should and should not do. Common purchasing situations include those relating to gifts, vendor favoritism, competitive bidding, and "best price first." Other ethical policies can relate to conflict of interest, vendor errors, local buying, back-door selling, and trial orders and samples.

   Some organizations develop a statement of business conduct to address a broad code of required behavior that covers many aspects of the business. These statements include ethical issues and policies related to purchasing.

3. **Describe the importance of professional vendor relationships.**

   The concept of vendor relations deals with ways that purchasers interact with vendors. Relationships can range from "I win; you lose" to "We win together." There are numerous factors that influence these relationships. These include the relative size of both organizations, whether a purchaser must rely on a vendor, their compatibility, and the extent to which one party commits extensive resources.

4. **Summarize the basics of vendor's handbooks.**

   Some operations provide a vendor's handbook to approved suppliers. These handbooks provide general information about the operation. Most important, they cover purchasing policies and procedures. Handbooks must be maintained and distributed to all approved vendors to ensure the best possible results.

RESTAURANT TECHNOLOGY

Traditionally, vendor's handbooks were distributed through the mail and given to vendor representatives as orders were placed. Copies were even left on tables in purchasing offices of large organizations for review by representatives as they waited for appointments. Increasingly, however, vendor's handbooks are posted on the Internet for review by current and potential vendors or other parties.

An advantage to this practice is the wide circulation of the handbook. After all, there are few, if any, purchasing secrets that managers and purchasers do not want those outside the purchaser–vendor relationship to know.

All handbooks, including those that are electronically generated, must be kept current, and this is often easier to do when it is online. Whether the person in charge of updating the online handbook is a purchaser or an associate in the purchasing department, the necessity of keeping vendor's handbooks current is critical.

APPLICATION EXERCISE

Review the section about ethical policies and select four of the policies discussed.

You are the manager of an operation that has developed guidelines for each of the policies you selected. Describe a purchasing situation that would *not* be acceptable under your policy.

REVIEW YOUR LEARNING

Select the best answer for each question.

1. Guidelines that should be followed when purchasers make decisions are found in
   A. codes of purchasing ethics.
   B. printed job specifications.
   C. vendor's handbooks.
   D. purchase orders.

2. In smaller, independent operations, who is responsible for developing codes of purchasing ethics?
   A. Courts
   B. Purchasers
   C. Managers
   D. Vendors

3. Which question can help a professional purchaser evaluate possible courses of action in a purchasing situation?
   A. Would I care if it happened to me?
   B. What will happen if I get caught?
   C. Will it help me be successful?
   D. Is the reward worth the risk?

4. Disciplinary actions for failure to comply with codes of purchasing ethics
   A. apply differently to new and experienced purchasers.
   B. should be explained item by item to all purchasers.
   C. do not need to be written if they are well known.
   D. should not be shared with approved vendors.

5. The need to ask several vendors to submit prices for products being ordered would be covered in which type of policy?
   A. Competitive bidding
   B. Conflict of interest
   C. Best price first
   D. Vendor errors

6. Which type of purchaser–vendor relationship is the best to maintain an ongoing relationship between the two parties?
   A. Purchaser wins; vendor loses
   B. Both parties lose
   C. Vendor wins; purchaser loses
   D. Both parties win

7. Which topic is most likely to be included in a vendor's handbook?
   A. Procedures for product receiving
   B. Maximum prices to be paid for products
   C. Types of purchaser–vendor relationships
   D. Information about the operation's attorney

8. Which purchasing policy is generally an appropriate one for most restaurant and foodservice operations?
   A. Competitive bidding
   B. Personal purchases
   C. Steward sales
   D. Reciprocity

9. **Who develops a vendor's handbook?**
    A. Product manufacturers
    B. Food product vendors
    C. Restaurant and foodservice operations
    D. Local product distributors

10. **Which policy relates to a vendor contacting a production employee without the purchaser's approval?**
    A. Local buying
    B. Back-door selling
    C. Conflict of interest
    D. Favoritism

FIELD PROJECT

The purpose of this exercise is to determine procedures that should—and should not—be used to maintain an ongoing professional relationship with approved vendors.

Summarize the recommendations made in the chapter 1 restaurant or foodservice operation questionnaire and the vendor questionnaire.

Procedures to Maintain Positive Relationship	Summary of Responses
Part A: Responses from restaurant or foodservice operation questionnaire (questions 9 and 10)	
Part B: Responses from vendor questionnaire (question 5)	

Part C: Provide an example of a purchasing policy that addresses two of the recommendations made by the restaurant or foodservice operation or the vendor.

Procedures to Maintain Positive Relationship	Example of Policy to Implement Procedure

8 Purchasing Follow-Up

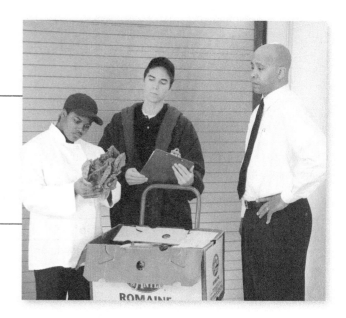

INSIDE THIS CHAPTER

- Receiving
- Payment for Purchases
- Purchasing Evaluation

CHAPTER LEARNING OBJECTIVES

After completing this chapter, you should be able to:

- Explain the basic procedures to monitor vendor compliance with quality standards at the time of receiving.

- Summarize the basic requirements for effective product receiving.

- Explain the necessary documentation and procedures that should be followed to pay vendors for product purchases.

- Describe the importance of and basic methods that can be used to evaluate the purchasing process.

KEY TERMS

CASE STUDY

"Checking all the delivery invoices is another thing we don't have time to do!" said Gracelynn, a cook at Snowy Pines Restaurant. "Most deliveries arrive during lunch when we are busy. We all know what products should be coming in. We almost always order the same amount. Cooks don't deal with prices, so what is the big deal?"

"I agree," replied Demarco. "So one time our salesperson said that even though the delivery invoice was signed, one box of steaks had not been delivered. There was no problem because he brought them over the next day."

"Yes," said Gracelynn. "And now we have to check our honest vendors by counting or weighing everything before we sign. Is all of this necessary?"

1. What can happen when the delivery invoice is signed even though one case of steaks is missing?

2. How would you emphasize the importance of consistently using procedures to check incoming products?

RECEIVING

Receiving is a series of activities that ends with the transfer of product ownership from a vendor to a restaurant or foodservice operation. It occurs when products are delivered and the delivery invoice is signed. The responsibility for receiving depends on several factors. Of these, business volume is one of the most important aspects. The procedures used to receive products often become more detailed in larger-volume establishments. *Exhibit 8.1* illustrates the concept that the control procedures for receiving tend to increase with property size.

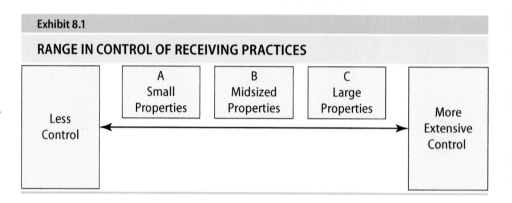

Exhibit 8.1

RANGE IN CONTROL OF RECEIVING PRACTICES

| Less Control | A Small Properties | B Midsized Properties | C Large Properties | More Extensive Control |

In a small operation (A), the manager or the person responsible for food production or beverage operations may receive incoming products and place them in storage. In many very small operations, storage locations may be shelving units in or close to production areas rather than in separate rooms.

Midsized operations (B) include many franchised and other multiunit establishments. Operating procedures, such as those for receiving, are part of the foundation of assistance that franchisors provide to franchisees in return for several types of fees. These units often have designated persons who, while not usually full-time in this function, have received specific training for receiving duties. Procedures to address quantity, quality, security, and record-keeping concerns during receiving and storing are likely to be used.

Large-volume properties (C) often employ persons with full-time receiving and storing responsibilities. In the largest of properties these duties are split, and different persons have specialized receiving and storing obligations.

Alcoholic beverages are expensive and theft-prone. Therefore, after they are received in operations of all sizes, they are moved into lockable storage areas (*Exhibit 8.2*).

Importance of Receiving

Every purchasing activity is important. However, without the use of effective receiving practices, the time, effort, and creativity expended to ensure that proper products will be available may be wasted.

Exhibit 8.2

Very few vendors, or their employees who handle products and deliver them, are dishonest. However, there are some that may take advantage of weaknesses in an establishment's receiving control system. In addition, honest vendor and operation employees can make mistakes that have a negative impact. Therefore, the goal of every manager should be to reduce the chances of these problems occurring by consistently using effective receiving procedures.

Manager's Responsibilities

In some establishments, especially small owner-operated ones, the owner or manager may be responsible for receiving activities on at least an occasional basis. In larger operations, the manager may delegate this task to the chef or kitchen manager. These managers may do the receiving, or they may delegate it to one or more employees. Regardless of the organizational structure, the manager has some responsibilities that cannot be delegated. Managers must do the following:

Exhibit 8.3

- Develop and implement a policy requiring the consistent use of effective receiving procedures at all times and for all products, and take corrective actions when procedures are not used.

- Determine those employees who will be responsible for receiving and ensure that they are properly trained (*Exhibit 8.3*). These employees must know and consistently use the proper receiving procedures.

- Ensure that employees are able to identify the quality standards in product specifications. Develop and enforce policies that indicate what should be done if products do not meet the specifications.

- Provide the proper receiving equipment and ensure that it is properly maintained. For example, a receiving scale must be available in the receiving area. It may need to be routinely verified and adjusted to ensure its accuracy. Thermometers that are routinely calibrated are also very important.

- Inform vendors that their delivery persons must allow the time needed for the receiving process to be properly implemented. Alternatively, some managers arrange with vendors for receiving steps to be undertaken after delivery persons leave with the understanding that delivery invoices will be adjusted if problems are identified.

Receiving Staff

Purchasers can spend 25 to 35 percent or more of the total revenue generated by their establishment to purchase the food and beverage products needed to generate the revenue. This easily justifies the need for trained and qualified employees to perform the activities required as the operation takes ownership of and assumes responsibility for products purchased. Unfortunately, some managers believe that whoever is closest to the back door when the delivery person arrives should sign the invoice and put the items in storage. This procedure has no place in restaurant and foodservice operations, where quality is critical and profits are difficult to earn.

Some receiving procedures are physical; others are clerical and can be easily learned. However, the most important tasks, including the ability to recognize the quality of incoming items and confirm that they meet standards, require extensive training and experience.

This is especially important when receiving products such as fresh produce, meat, and seafood. These products are not typically purchased by brand name, so receiving employees cannot just read the product labels to confirm quality. Instead, employees must compare the products that are received to the standards identified in product specifications. Employees assuming receiving positions should work with experienced food production or purchasing employees. Then they can learn about and observe the features found in proper quality products.

Successful receiving staff share several characteristics:

- They maintain food safety standards. Food safety concerns are addressed in the establishment's product specifications, and they are critical aspects of quality. These concerns also apply to the receiving area, the tools and equipment used, and the procedures used to handle products being received.

- They can use technology required by the establishment. There are numerous technological advances that can make the receiving process more effective by providing better information and reports. Examples of these applications will be reviewed later in this chapter.

- They are able to lift and carry products, if necessary. Some cases of products can weigh 30 pounds or more. Flour and sugar are routinely packaged in 50-pound or even 100-pound bags, which may be purchased because of lower purchase unit prices. However, the Americans with Disabilities Act (ADA) prohibits discrimination against persons with disabilities who are seeking employment. The ability of receiving staff to lift heavy packages may or may not be a **bona fide occupational qualification (BFOQ)**. BFOQs are job qualifications legally judged reasonably necessary to safely or adequately perform a job. Managers must be aware of these issues and may need to consider ways to modify the work to accommodate persons who are otherwise qualified.

- They resolve problems. What should be done if incoming products do not meet the operation's quality requirements? If incorrect quantities are delivered? If delivery staff attempt to rush the receiving clerk to catch up on their schedule? These and other challenges can make the receiving clerk's job anything but routine.

OPEN FOR BUSINESS

KEEPING IT SAFE

Serious accidents can happen in receiving and storing areas. Managers must train employees to use safe work practices and must provide the tools and equipment necessary to work safely.

One major concern involves accidents while lifting heavy objects. Employees should be trained to lift with their leg muscles, not their back muscles. Carts or dollies should be used to transport heavy objects from receiving to storage.

Wet floors in receiving and storing areas can cause slips or falls. This is especially likely when fresh products are packed in ice and must be taken from ice cartons to preparation areas.

Most products in storage areas should be stored at shoulder height or below. If higher shelving units are used, lighter-weight packages should be stored on the highest shelves. Heavier products should be stored on lower shelves. Sturdy stepstools should be available so employees do not stand on cases or shelves.

• They maintain an attitude of concern. The best employees in all departments want to be part of the team and help the establishment meet its goals. They are informed about and recognize their important role in helping the operation serve customers, and they are contributing members of their team.

Receiving Space, Tools, and Equipment

The receiving area should have been carefully considered when the property was planned, but this does not always occur. Typically, receiving areas in a small operation are close to a back door. However, in large organizations such as hotels or educational facilities, they are often centered around a loading dock, which can be a long distance from storage areas. In small establishments, the receiving area may be little more than a space near a back entrance where no other equipment is located. However, adequate space is needed to perform the receiving activities explained in this chapter.

Space needs can be much greater if pallet loads of products are received. A **pallet** is a portable platform, or rack, typically made of wooden slats, that is used to store and move cases of products stacked on it.

Receiving areas may require space for a desk and file cabinet. This can be useful to store product specifications needed to review the quality of incoming products. It can also be used to retain copies of purchase orders, delivery invoices, approved vendor lists, order lists, typical vendor delivery times, and other documents until they are routed according to the operation's policy.

Equipment frequently used by receiving staff includes plastic tote boxes or other containers to hold ice into which products such as fresh poultry or seafood may be placed. Tools and equipment used to keep the area clean and in proper condition are also important.

Increasingly, notebook or laptop computers and other wireless devices are also required to access purchasing and inventory records when products are received. The receiving area may also include a telephone, fax/copy machine, and ample office supplies such as pens, pencils, and a stapler.

Receiving scales should be of two types. One should be accurate to a fraction of a pound for large items (*Exhibit 8.4*). Another should be accurate to a fraction of an ounce for smaller items including pre-portioned meat. Scales should be checked for accuracy on a regular basis and adjusted as needed.

Wheeled equipment such as hand trucks, carts, or dollies should be available to move incoming products quickly and efficiently to their storage areas. Box cutters must be properly maintained and used safely as receiving staff remove packaging to verify quality.

Exhibit 8.4

Thermometers are used to ensure that food products are delivered at their proper storage temperatures. *Exhibit 8.5* shows the correct temperatures for refrigerated and frozen items.

Exhibit 8.5	
TEMPERATURE RANGES FOR FROZEN AND REFRIGERATED FOOD	
Item	**Acceptable Temperature Range**
Frozen food	The proper frozen-storage temperature varies from product to product. A temperature that is good for one product may affect the quality of another product. Frozen storage is for items such as frozen meat, seafood, French fries, and vegetables purchased in this market form.
Refrigerated food	41°F (5°C) or lower

A calculator or adding machine may be needed to check calculations on delivery invoices, especially if prepared manually. A printing calculator is best. It will be useful when the original delivery invoice is changed because of incorrect pricing or because items listed were not delivered. In addition, invoice totals will change when some or all of a delivery is rejected for substandard quality. These tasks may be done by receiving staff in some operations and by accounting employees in other operations.

Basic Receiving Procedures

Several procedures should always be used when receiving incoming products and supplies. Coaching and observation will be helpful to confirm that the correct procedures are always used. If a supervisor notices deviations from the proper procedures, corrective actions should be taken. Hopefully, problems will be minimized and no additional approved vendors will need to be selected. The procedures apply to all types of operations regardless of business volume, and to almost any type of product or supply. *Exhibit 8.6* provides an overview of the steps required for effective receiving.

Notice that the first step involves the vendor's delivery invoice that will accompany incoming products. The delivery invoice should be compared with a copy of the purchase order, routed from the purchaser, that specifies what is being purchased. A close comparison of the delivery invoice and the purchase order is very important.

Exhibit 8.6

STEPS IN AN EFFECTIVE RECEIVING PROCESS

Step 1: Compare Delivery Invoice and Purchase Order
— Product Quantity (Weight or Count)
— Product Unit Price

Step 2: Confirm Product Quality

Step 3: Sign Delivery Invoice
— Issue Credit Memo (if necessary)
— Move Product to Storage

Step 4: Complete Receiving Report

It will help ensure that the quantity, pack size (or purchase unit), and price of each product agreed on at time of purchase are correct when delivered and summarized on the delivery invoice.

Some items, such as cases of canned goods, can be counted. Other items, such as fresh meat ordered by the pound, must be weighed to confirm that the required weight or quantity was received. Lettuce purchased in cases can be counted on a routine and random basis. Many vendors will allow this count to be done after the delivery person leaves with the understanding that any shortages will be credited on the delivery invoice. *Exhibit 8.7* shows a sample delivery invoice.

Exhibit 8.7

SAMPLE DELIVERY INVOICE

Delivery Invoice

Invoice No. 236668   Invoice Date: 6/14/12

Sold by:
XYZ Meat Company
200 Ironwood
Lakeland, NV 00000
Telephone: 000-000-0000
Fax: 000-000-0000

Sold to:
Henry G's Grill
700 10th Ave.
Anyville, NV 11111
Account No. 556678

Ship to:
Henry G's Grill
700 10th Ave.
Anyville, NV 11111

Purchaser's Purchase Order No. 397885

Delivery No. E 556656

Delivery Date: 6/15/12

Item	Product No.	Quantity	Purchase Unit	Price per Unit	Total Price
Bulk ground beef	23	3	10# poly bag	$44.80	$134.40
Pork patties	32	4	Case (10#)	44.67	178.68

Terms: Net 7   Total Amount Due: $477.97

Received by: _____   Date: _____

Distribution: Retain original copy; second copy to purchaser.

When reviewing *Exhibit 8.7*, note that the sample delivery invoice summarizes a delivery made by XYZ Meat Company to Henry G's Grill on 6/15/12. The invoice number and date, the purchaser's account number and purchase order number, and the vendor's delivery number and purchase terms are noted.

The delivery invoice lists each item ordered and delivered. The operation's employee who receives the products must sign and date the delivery invoice. There are typically several copies of the delivery invoice. This sample provides one copy for the establishment and another for the vendor.

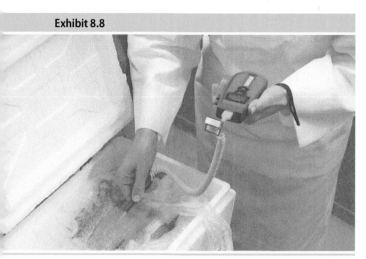

Exhibit 8.8

Exhibit 8.6 indicates that the second step in the receiving process is to confirm that the quality, including temperatures, of the products being received meets the property's product specifications that have previously been sent to approved vendors (*Exhibit 8.8*). This step is very important and probably the most challenging if standards have not been established. The standards incorporated into product specifications should be relatively easy to observe or determine. If they are, a trained receiver will not have difficulty ensuring the specification requirements are met.

It does little good to develop product specifications describing product quality requirements unless these specifications are used during the receiving process to confirm quality. Experienced purchasers understand that their establishment will pay for the quality of products identified in the product specification even if the proper quality is not received. Therefore, receiving staff must be able to recognize the desired and actual quality of all products coming into the operation. This is especially so for **A items**: those relatively few products that cost the most.

Some products are difficult to check for quality even when product specifications are carefully written. For example, there is no easy way to verify the fat content of ground beef, such as 93 percent lean, or the butter fat content of premium ice creams. Large-volume purchasers may hire the services of a quality laboratory for periodic analysis of these types of products.

It is easy to confirm weights of portion-controlled products. For example, individual portions of 4-ounce AP hamburger patties can be randomly weighed. Results of spot checks should be recorded. The establishment may use a spot-check log for recording this information on a computer or manually. The purchaser and manager should regularly review this information to determine whether there are trends that need to be addressed. At the least, the vendor should be notified every time a quality defect is observed. If the problem continues, supplier sourcing decisions may be in order.

When problems are identified, one reason for contacting the vendor is to receive credit for unacceptable products. Another important reason is to relay a message: "We check our incoming products. We have procedures in place to consistently ensure that the quality of products being ordered and paid for is, in fact, the quality delivered."

Ongoing spot-checks on a routine but random basis are an important activity in the receiving process. Purchasers and those receiving products must do their jobs effectively so production staff will have products of the required quality to prepare food for customers. Purchasers look to vendors for assistance and cooperation as a value-added element in the purchaser–vendor relationship.

Product specifications may include a description of basic receiving procedures to help confirm that quality requirements are addressed. If there are concerns, the employee receiving the products should ask the chef or manager to determine whether quality requirements are met. As this occurs, the receiver will learn more about quality standards. This will be helpful during future deliveries.

If no problems are observed, the delivery invoice can be signed. However, if there are product shortages or other problems, a credit memo should be signed by both the receiving employee and the vendor's delivery person. A credit memo is used to adjust information about product quantities or costs recorded on a delivery invoice. Delivery invoices with credit memos will require special handling during payment processing.

Careful checking of the purchase order against the delivery invoice should identify item shortages, and completion of a credit memo will ensure that the operation does not pay for the shortage. This action may be all that is needed if the establishment seldom has problems with the vendor and the product is not needed immediately. However, if the product is required for current production needs, additional actions are required. Procedures for expediting the delivery of products were addressed in chapter 6.

Product shortages can occur even if vendors deliver the quantity ordered. This type of problem relates to inventory management, which are the procedures to determine the quantities of product available and needed for order periods. Shortages can also occur if problems arise when order quantities are relayed to purchasers, when purchase orders are sent to vendors, and when ordering decisions are made. Each of these possible causes must be considered every time there are item shortages, and corrective actions are required to eliminate the problems.

The manager, purchaser, and inventory and production employees should be included on the problem-solving team to address item shortages. These challenges are sometimes difficult to resolve because they can involve several departments. Communication problems can arise, and there is often a need to involve the vendor to resolve problems.

After the delivery invoice has been signed, the employee receiving the products must quickly move them to their storage areas for two reasons:

- To help prevent lowered product quality or food safety for items that should be stored at refrigerated or frozen temperatures
- To reduce the possibility of product theft by employees

Manager's Memo

Effective receiving staff are able to determine whether incoming products meet quality requirements. This task is among their most important responsibilities. For example, sometimes they must recognize slack-out seafood. Slack-out seafood is seafood that has been frozen and is then thawed and represented as fresh so it can be sold at a higher price.

At other times, receivers must confirm that the lengthy and sometimes confusing names of imported wines match those on the purchase order. They also know to check expiration dates on applicable items and understand that produce in the center of a container may not be of the same quality as that on more visible levels. Both intentional fraud and accidental error have the same impact on the establishment: products will be paid for that cannot be used and will not, therefore, generate revenues.

Exhibit 8.6 suggests a final step in product receiving: complete a receiving report, also sometimes called receiving log. This document may be used in operations that calculate food costs on a daily basis. It helps separate information on delivery invoices into the components required for daily food costing. A receiving report can also be used by establishments that want to separate the costs of products by category for other control purposes. *Exhibit 8.9* shows a sample receiving report.

Exhibit 8.9

SAMPLE RECEIVING REPORT

Date: 11/30/12

Vendor	Invoice #	Meat	Poultry	Seafood	Produce	Dairy	Eggs	Groceries	Alcoholic Beverages
A	10762	$479.89	$310.15						
B	68088			$784.15					
C	65554				$615.07				
TOTAL		**$479.89**	**$310.15**	**$784.15**	**$615.07**	**0**	**0**	**0**	**0**

Technology and Receiving

Many procedures at every step in the receiving process increasingly are computerized. The purposes are to provide more accurate data and reports useful for decision making and to free managers' time.

How has technology impacted receiving tasks? First of all, paperwork can be eliminated and many communication problems that occur as hard-copy documents are circulated can be reduced. For example, purchase orders can be electronically routed to receiving staff for use when products are received (step 1 in *Exhibit 8.6*).

Wireless technology allows receiving employees to check incoming products without the need to print a copy of the purchase order. Those who purchase in large volumes can specify that bar code labels be used on containers of incoming products. **Bar codes** have numerous machine-readable rectangular bars and spaces arranged in a specific way to identify a product (see *Exhibit 8.10*). After products are received, quantity and cost information can be scanned by receiving staff and automatically entered into the inventory management system. Products being removed from inventory can be scanned to automatically adjust inventory quantities and costs.

Many case products are now shipped with bar codes. Operations with bar code readers and required software can use bar code technology to assist with purchasing and inventory management.

Radio frequency identification (RFID) technology uses wireless transponders affixed to the products in inventory. This creates a tracking system that provides noncontact, automatic location of stock throughout the operation. These systems expand applications beyond just identifying inventory information in locations where bar codes are read. They also enable wireless tracking of inventory in real time throughout the property.

Technology enables electronic product specifications, schedules of expected deliveries on specified dates, and communication between production, purchasing, accounting, and receiving staff. Also, information from invoices can be summarized on daily receiving reports to generate information for daily food costing or other control purposes.

Security and Receiving

Security issues can affect the establishment's ability to receive all of the products it has ordered and agreed to pay for. Procedures must be in place to guard against common problems:

- **Short weights:** A carton containing, for example, 35 pounds of fresh steaks should be weighed. Ideally, steaks will be removed from the shipping carton to determine their exact weight. The problem of container weight becomes more important when fresh seafood or poultry is packed in heavy, waxed cardboard containers in shaved ice. Then the weight of the container and its packing can be significant, and product removal is needed to determine the weight on which charges will be based.

- **Assorted contents:** A carton containing 30 pounds of ground beef and 20 pounds of pre-portioned steaks will weigh the same as a carton containing 40 pounds of ground beef and 10 pounds of fresh-cut steaks (50 pounds). However, the value of the first carton is much more than that of the second. Different items must be weighed separately because of their different costs.

Exhibit 8.10

Manager's Memo

Vendors are sometimes asked for advice about receiving, and their responses can be insightful. Managers asking this question may obtain information that can be helpful as procedures are developed and revised.

Typical responses from vendors often make several points. For example, they are likely to suggest that it is important to ensure that effective receiving practices are consistently used. They are also likely to mention the value-added services that reputable vendors can provide. Managers can simply ask vendors about both general receiving practices and specific factors to look for as products are being received.

Vendors may also point out that their reputable peers want to provide products meeting a purchaser's specifications at a reasonable price. It is to the vendor's benefit to educate purchasers about how less-reputable vendors can offer lower prices, provide still lower quality products, and benefit themselves while doing a disservice to other vendors and the purchaser.

- **Missing items:** Use of proper receiving procedures should identify short-weight or short-count problems. However, following a delivery person's suggestion to sign the invoice and expect additional products with the next delivery is not a good idea. The same receiving employee may not be working or may not remember the missing items. Also, a delivery person will not likely have the authority to request that products not listed on delivery invoices be placed on the truck.

Another security-related problem during receiving can occur when delivery persons have access to any area of the operation except those designated as delivery areas. Theft can occur, for example, from storage areas, especially where alcoholic beverages or expensive meat or seafood are stored.

PAYMENT FOR PURCHASES

The task of paying the bills for products purchased involves much more than writing a check. Much of the revenue generated by an operation is spent on products and services required to generate the revenue. Managers must reduce costs without sacrificing quality, and an effectively operated purchasing function is one way to do this.

All vendors must be paid what they are owed in a timely manner according to the terms of the contract. However, it is equally important to ensure that they are not paid more than they are owed. The responsibility for making correct payments begins when initial product purchase decisions are made, continues as products are received, and ends when payments are made.

Documentation Is Important

How does the person paying vendors actually know that the products were ordered and received? How does he or she know the agreed-upon price? These questions are answered in the documents needed to process vendor invoices or statements for payment.

INTERNAL FLOW OF DOCUMENTS

The task of paying vendors' bills requires communication, information, and coordination between purchasing, receiving, and accounting staff. The process is basically the same regardless of whether a manual or electronic system is used. However, there are fewer specialized positions in a small-volume operation, so one or a very few persons must perform all purchasing and accounting tasks.

Exhibit 8.11 shows the basic types of documents that contain information useful for verifying the amounts owed vendors. Each becomes increasingly important as the dollar value of purchases increases.

Exhibit 8.11

PURCHASING-RELATED DOCUMENTS

Document	Purpose
Product specifications	Indicate the quality of the products for which price quotations should be made.
Purchase requisition (Req)	Used by storeroom or production employees to alert purchasers that additional quantities of products are required to rebuild inventory levels.
Request for proposal (RFP)	Used by purchasing staff to request prices from approved vendors for products of specified quality.
Purchase order	Used by purchasing staff to formally order products from vendors.
Delivery invoice	Used by vendors to indicate products, including quantities and prices, that are delivered to the operation. Purchasers pay the amount specified on the delivery invoice after it is signed by the person receiving products for the establishment.
Vendor statement	Used by vendors to summarize delivery invoice charges during a specific time period. For example, agreements with managers may allow payment of all invoices for two weeks according to a statement that reviews delivery invoice numbers, dates, and amounts owed.

Common methods used to route purchasing documents depend on the size of the operation:

- **Small-volume establishment with owner-manager present:** Products are ordered by the manager and may be received by him or her. A copy of the purchase order or the vendor's order form along with the applicable delivery invoice are used by the owner-manager for payment purposes. The owner may pay the bills or transfer documentation to a bookkeeper for payment.

- **Small-volume establishment with absentee owner:** In this situation, a manager is employed by the owner. Purchasing and receiving activities may be undertaken by the manager and his or her staff with documentation routed to the bookkeeper for payment. However, the vendor may be requested to send a separate copy of each delivery invoice directly to the absentee owner or bookkeeper. This permits comparison of both copies of delivery invoices.

- **Mid-volume establishment:** Department heads may be responsible for purchasing the products that will be needed for their departments. Purchase orders may be held until products are delivered and received because they will be needed at that time. Alternatively, another copy of the purchase order may be routed to the person with accounting responsibilities. If there is an absentee owner, copies of purchase orders and matching delivery invoices may be sent to the owner.

- **Large operation with separate purchasing and accounting departments:** A copy of the purchase order is sent from purchasing to receiving and storage staff. Incoming orders are checked against the purchase order. The purchase order and signed delivery invoice are then routed to the purchasing department to be matched up before being routed to the accounting department as authorization for payment. In some large establishments, purchase orders and applicable delivery invoices move from receiving staff to the chef or manager, who forwards them to purchasing staff. These staff members have significant knowledge about the needs of the organization. As they review this documentation, they ask: "Do we normally purchase all of these items in these quantities?", "Do prices seem reasonable and in line with other recent purchases?", and "Is the delivery invoice from one of our approved vendors?"

After documentation from the purchaser is received, an employee with accounting responsibilities must process the documents for payment. Careful analysis of purchase and delivery documents will often identify and resolve most potential problems and enable bills to be paid when due. Concerns identified can then be corrected as the bill payer communicates with the purchaser and receiving employees.

MANAGING CREDIT PROCEDURES

Accounting employees have less need to interact with vendors about pricing and related concerns if proper documentation is available. However, one potential problem that arises as bills are prepared for payment relates to credit memos issued during receiving.

Well-trained and knowledgeable receiving staff may sometimes identify problems during delivery that must be corrected with a credit memo:

Exhibit 8.12

- **Incorrect price charged:** For example, purchase order price is $3.17 per pound; delivery invoice states $3.27 per pound.

- **Backorder:** Product is not available and cannot be delivered, but it is included on the delivery invoice.

- **Short weight or count:** For example, 30 cases were ordered per purchase order and delivery invoice, but only 25 cases were received.

- **Items rejected as unacceptable:** For example, items do not meet product specification requirements and are rejected on attempted delivery (*Exhibit 8.12*).

It is critical that any product delivery problems be noted. Then a credit memo can be issued to reduce the amount that the operation owes the vendor for the order. *Exhibit 8.13* shows a sample credit memo.

Exhibit 8.13

SAMPLE CREDIT MEMO

Date: _____   Credit memo no.: _____

Vendor: _____
           _____
           _____
           _____
           _____
           _____

Issued to: _____
           _____
           _____
           _____

Account no.: _____
For invoice no.: _____

Item	Purchase Unit	Number Purchase Units	Price per Purchase Unit	Total Price
			Total	$

Reason for credit (check):

☐ Backorder   ☐ Incorrect quality   ☐ Incorrect item
☐ Short count/weight   ☐ Incorrect price   ☐ Not ordered

Other:

_____

_____

Authorized signatures:

_____   _____
   Vendor's representative   Purchaser's representative

The vendor's representative, typically the delivery person, issues the credit memo to the establishment. The memo applies to a specific invoice. Items to be deducted from the amount owed are listed along with the reason the credit is being granted. The signature of the vendor's representative confirms that the products noted in the credit memo were not received or accepted and that their value should be deducted from the amount owed. The receiving employee should also sign the credit memo to confirm that a copy was received.

Manager's Memo

An operation's relationship with vendors is based on the interactions of all affected employees including accounting staff. The need for frequent credit memos typically suggests that the purchaser should evaluate the benefits of continuing to do business with the vendor. Differences between agreed-upon and delivery prices, as well as quality and quantity concerns, should be investigated. If problems are found to be caused by employees of the operation, the reasons should be studied and procedures revised. If problems are caused by vendors, they should be directed to take corrective action.

Purchasers, not accounting staff, typically make vendor selection decisions. As they do so, input from all affected employees, including accounting staff, should be considered. Excessive credit memos increase the likelihood that the operation will not have products when needed, increase the amount of effort required to process bills, and increase the likelihood that vendors may be paid for products never accepted.

THINK ABOUT IT ...

The best purchasers know that extensions must be verified on electronically generated delivery invoices. Some purchasers, however, do not confirm the accuracy of machine-generated data.

What do you think of this practice?

Duplicate copies of credit memos are required so that one copy may be given to the vendor, and one copy to the operation. Some vendors or purchasers may require more than one copy.

Credit memos are typically issued at the time of delivery. Prepared purchasers have blank copies that can be used if the delivery person does not have one available.

Credit memos should be treated like cash because they represent a credit, or a reduction of the amount otherwise owed, based on the delivery invoice. They must be routed to the accounting department in a way that best ensures they will not be lost, discarded, or ignored. Most frequently, they are attached to the applicable delivery invoice for routing to purchasing and then on to accounting staff for their use in adjusting invoice amounts and subsequent payments.

Special procedures are sometimes used to process credit memos:

- Accounting staff may contact the vendor from whom a credit memo has been issued to confirm that it was received, that no processing problems exist, and that credit will be reflected on the next statement.
- When the purchase order and delivery invoice are received in the accounting department and filed for payment, the credit memo is included with that documentation.

An internal record-keeping system is also necessary to ensure that the operation does not pay bills until they have been adjusted by any applicable credit memos.

Payment Procedures

Delivery invoices indicate the products and quantities for which vendors make a payment request. They must be carefully studied for accuracy before a payment is made:

- Ensure that there are no quantity or price differences between the purchase order and the items received as listed on the delivery invoice.
- Ensure that all extensions on the delivery invoice are correct. Extensions are arithmetic calculations made on delivery invoices. For example, the item quantity and the unit price must be multiplied to determine the total cost for each product. This total cost must be added for all products to confirm that the total amount of the invoice is correct.
- File the invoice with the applicable purchase documentation for future payment.
- Pay the invoice at the appropriate time.

Two basic methods can be used to pay vendors for purchased products and services:

- **By invoice:** After their review, purchase orders and delivery invoices are manually or electronically filed for payment by a specific due date and paid when due. For example, if an approved invoice must be paid by July 16, it may be "pulled" on July 10 for final review, signature, and mailing on July 11 to allow time for mail delivery.

- **By statement:** Processed documentation is filed by name of vendor while accounting staff await receipt of a statement of account. For example, a produce vendor may request payment every two weeks by submitting a statement listing delivery invoices for the two-week period. When the vendor's statement is received, applicable invoices are retrieved. Then all invoices covered by the statement, less any adjustments required by credit memos, are paid at the same time.

Exhibit 8.14 shows a sample vendor's statement.

Exhibit 8.14

SAMPLE VENDOR'S STATEMENT

Statement 96773

Shoreside Produce
122 Ocean Blvd.
Shoreside, FL 00000
Telephone: 000-000-0000
Fax: 000-000-0000

Account no.: 166634
Delivered to: Deep Sands Bistro
342 Batters Ave.
Deep Sands, FL 00000
Attention: Jordan, Director of Purchasing
Telephone: 000-000-0000

Invoice No.	Delivery Date	Amount Due	Adjustment	Net Amount Due
162	3/11/12	$163.59		$163.59
10428	3/13/12	210.80	($23.44)	187.36
1214	3/17/12	143.51	Credit memo	143.51
13099	3/22/12	209.18	#2479	209.18

Payment due upon receipt. Please send payment to the above address.

Duplicate: Please return top copy with payment, and retain second copy for your records.

Thank you.

Some purchasers and their vendors are using electronic funds transfer (EFT) to simplify the payment process and reduce associated payment costs. For example, purchasers can authorize automatic payments to be charged to a business credit card or withdrawn from a business checking or savings account. The payments that are collected are then directly deposited into the vendor's business account. Vendors can communicate with purchasers about the amount of the charge by email.

One advantage to vendors offering EFT options is the faster receipt of payments due to them. The loss of several days required for checks to reach vendors and clear the establishment's account is a disadvantage to the purchaser. However, this may be offset by reduced costs for check processing.

When invoices are to be paid either individually or as part of a statement, a check covering the correct amount should be prepared for signing. If a manual system is used, each invoice or statement paid should be marked to indicate the date, the amount of payment, and the check number. Marking and processing should be done in a way that enables verification that payment has been made and reduces the chance that an invoice could be paid twice.

Petty Cash Purchases

Operations should normally minimize the use of cash payments for purchases. Checks allow better control of expenses. They are easier to classify for accounting purposes because audit trails can be developed and traced. An **audit trail** is a step-by-step record that traces financial data to its source. Consider, for example, a food purchase. It begins with a purchase order, continues with a delivery invoice, and ends with a check written to pay for the products delivered.

Minor expenses, however, are best paid in cash because it is more practical and less expensive. Examples may include a small number of light bulbs, some office supplies, and even "emergency" purchases from grocery stores. These and related expenses are often paid for with a **petty cash fund**, a small amount of cash on hand that is used to make relatively low-cost purchases (*Exhibit 8.15*).

These petty cash banks can be misused. Therefore, procedures governing their use for purchasing should be established and consistently used.

Petty cash funds must be secured in safe locations such as the manager's office and controlled by a manager who is held responsible for them. Policies and procedures governing the use of petty cash banks and the frequency with which their current balances are verified should be developed and consistently used for all cash purchases.

Petty cash funds should be established on a cash advance system:

- The amount of money in the petty cash fund should be based on the normal amount of cash purchases for a specific time frame, such as three weeks.

- A check to "petty cash fund" should be written and its proceeds used to establish the petty cash fund.

- As cash purchases are made, cash is removed from the petty cash bank as needed. The change from the transaction and the receipt for the purchase are returned to the responsible manager. He or she verifies that the amount of the change plus the receipt equals the amount removed from the petty cash fund. Then the change and receipt are placed in the petty cash bank. In many establishments, the original petty cash voucher is attached to the receipt.

Exhibit 8.15

- When the petty cash fund must be replenished, a check is again written to "petty cash." This time it is for the value of paid receipts in the fund. This check, converted to cash, will replenish the fund to its original value.

- At any point in time, the actual amount of money and paid receipts in the petty cash fund should equal the original amount of money allocated to petty cash.

Exhibit 8.16 shows a sample petty cash voucher, which is deposited in the petty cash bank when cash is withdrawn for a purchase. This voucher, along with the receipt and change, should be deposited in the cash bank at the completion of the transaction.

Exhibit 8.16

PETTY CASH VOUCHER

Deep Sands Bistro
Petty Cash Voucher

Date: _____   Voucher no.: _____

Description of purchase: _____

_____

Amount of cash issued: _____

Signatures:

_____   _____
       Funds issued by   Funds received by

Instructions:
This petty cash voucher along with the purchase receipt and change equal to the voucher amount must be returned to the person responsible for the cash bank.

Policies should be established about items that can be purchased, frequency of purchases, and the dollar value of cash purchases that can be made with petty cash. Certain procedures typically apply to the management of a petty cash fund:

- All purchases must be supported with receipts. If necessary, a note should be written on the receipt to identify the item purchased.

- The petty cash fund must be kept secure at all times; money should not remain in unlocked and easily accessible areas.

- Petty cash funds should not be mixed with cash register or other cash bank funds.

- Unless the person responsible for the petty cash fund is the establishment's owner or manager, the person should not be allowed to write a check to replenish the fund. Also, the check should be made out to "petty cash" rather than to "cash" or to the employee.

- There should be no long-term, unauthorized "borrowing" of money from the petty cash fund. Cash advances for employees, if any, should not come from this fund.

- When the petty cash fund is reimbursed to its approved level, all receipts should be examined to ensure that they comply with requirements for using the fund.

- The petty cash fund should be spot-checked on a routine but random basis to ensure that it remains intact. The amount available (cash plus paid receipts) should always equal the authorized amount.

PURCHASING EVALUATION

Purchasing activities are very important to the success of a restaurant or foodservice operation. As with all other management and operating activities, evaluation is important for understanding the extent to which purchasing goals have been attained. Concerns about how purchasing can be improved are a natural outcome of the evaluation process.

Unfortunately, some managers and purchasers do not take the time to properly evaluate purchasing. Some may not be aware that it is necessary, and others may do it without careful thought about the best evaluation process. Still others might not think evaluation is important because they do not believe procedures can be improved.

In contrast, the best managers and purchasers recognize that purchasing does not automatically evolve from simply buying things to becoming an important component of the organization's success. Instead, an ongoing program of improvement activities must be in place.

Reasons to Evaluate Purchasing

There are several reasons purchasing activities should be evaluated:

- **To recognize the importance of purchasing:** Busy managers are concerned that they spend their limited time doing the things that are most important. What happens if managers do not take the time to evaluate the overall performance of purchasing? This suggests that purchasing is unimportant in comparison to other activities, which is clearly a mistake.

- **To determine improvement benchmarks:** Measurable factors should be used to evaluate purchasing. This provides the standards against which to assess improvement. For example, if the number of inventory stockouts is known for a previous period, a goal to reduce them can be established. Process improvement plans can then be implemented and their results can be measured to determine if stockouts have been reduced.

- **To control costs:** Money saved through effective purchasing increases profitability. Purchasers and product users should be challenged to determine how costs can be reduced without sacrificing quality.

- **To establish procedures for measuring and rewarding purchaser performance:** The performance of full-time purchasers should be evaluated in the same way as the work of all others in the operation. Employees who purchase as one of many job tasks must be held responsible for all of their activities, including purchasing.

- **To improve the purchasing function:** Purchasing evaluation can help purchasers and managers learn how the process can be improved. As this occurs, new goals might be established to make the purchasing function better help the establishment attain its mission.

Evaluation Improves Purchasing

Exhibit 8.17 provides an overview of how purchasing performance can be determined and improved.

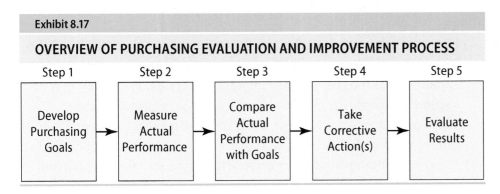

Exhibit 8.17

OVERVIEW OF PURCHASING EVALUATION AND IMPROVEMENT PROCESS

Step 1	Step 2	Step 3	Step 4	Step 5
Develop Purchasing Goals	Measure Actual Performance	Compare Actual Performance with Goals	Take Corrective Action(s)	Evaluate Results

Consider that one goal of purchasing is to reduce product costs without lowering the quality of products required. *Exhibit 8.17* suggests a process to evaluate and, if possible, to improve on this goal:

- **Step 1: Develop purchasing goals.** Efforts to reduce product costs without sacrificing quality should always be a primary concern. However, it is often difficult to determine causes. If cost evaluations are based on total dollar purchases, high costs could be due to ineffective purchasing. However, they could also be caused, at least in part, by ineffective handling and control procedures that waste products. Higher costs can also be caused by higher sales; more products must be purchased to serve more customers.

However, if product costs are based on purchase unit costs, they might be better linked to the efforts of the purchasers. Unfortunately, purchasers have no control over the marketplace, which significantly influences purchase unit costs. One compromise is expressed in the following goal: "Purchasing staff shall maintain per-unit purchase costs for A items to no more than 2 percent above the adjusted market costs for the time period covered by the evaluation." This goal compares the actual costs to the market prices for the products during the time period. Recall that A items are the most expensive items. Market prices for these products are publicly available, and purchasers can ask their vendors for the best sources for this information. They can then be used as a benchmark against which to compare purchase prices.

- **Step 2: Measure actual performance.** Delivery invoices available for steaks, for instance, can be analyzed to determine their average cost per pound. The average cost per pound might be calculated by determining the average cost for the first several and last several weeks in the evaluation period:

$$\left(\begin{array}{c} \textbf{Average beginning} \\ \textbf{purchase unit cost} \end{array} + \begin{array}{c} \textbf{Average ending} \\ \textbf{purchase unit cost} \end{array} \right) \div 2$$

- **Step 3: Compare actual performance with goals.** The actual purchase unit cost for the steaks is known from step 2, and it can be compared to the average purchase unit cost for the steaks purchased in the previous evaluation period. If the actual purchase unit cost is not more than 103 percent of the previous purchase unit cost, the goal was attained. However, if the actual purchase unit cost was greater than the planned cost, a questioning and analysis process may help assess reasons for the variation. Was the goal attained in previous periods? If so, there may be a special problem that must be identified and investigated. If the purchase unit goal was not previously met, the manager and purchaser can reconsider whether the goal is reasonable. If it is, it might be used in future evaluation periods after corrective actions are taken to plan how purchase unit costs can be better controlled.

- **Step 4: Take corrective action(s).** When the comparison between expected and actual performance in step 3 suggests a problem, corrective action is required. If multiple problems are observed, purchasers typically address the most significant one first unless "quick and easy" successes with minor problems are possible. Consider, for example, that the purchase unit costs were higher than they reasonably should have been. Purchasing in unnecessarily small volumes in small package sizes might be a cause. Other suggestions from vendors and employees should be requested and considered. The strategies judged most likely to reduce purchase unit cost should be carefully analyzed and implemented.

- **Step 5: Evaluate results.** Did the corrective action in step 4 adequately address problems discovered during the evaluation? Purchasers should also confirm that no "spin-off" problems were created. They may determine, for example, that high costs can be reduced by using different vendors. However, while costs might decrease, other problems such as late deliveries might occur. If purchasers determine that corrective actions were successful, the evaluation process was effective: problems were identified and corrected as a result. However, if a problem is not satisfactorily addressed or if new problems occur, it is necessary to plan additional corrective actions to further improve the purchasing process.

Purchasing Goals and Evaluation Concerns

Purchasing goals should be developed based on the desired results of purchasing in the operation. For example, if low product costs and per-unit prices are of greatest concern, the emphasis of the evaluation will likely be on purchasing products at the lowest possible price. If price and quality are both important, there will be an increasing emphasis on value: the relationship between price and quality. *Exhibit 8.18* shows how the focus of evaluation changes as the role of purchasing in the establishment changes.

Exhibit 8.18

EVALUATION OF PURCHASING BASED ON ITS ROLE

Role of Purchasing	Focus of Evaluation
Price-conscious purchasing	• Cost per purchase unit • Total purchase costs • Maintain budget
Price and quality purchasing	• Development of specifications • Vendor performance (selection) • Make-or-buy analyses • Vendors' assistance
Purchaser–vendor "partnership"	• Methods by which vendors provide value • Vendors' assistance in solving problems • Purchaser's role as member of top-level management team

Notice in *Exhibit 8.18* that when price-conscious purchasing is most important, the tasks are essentially reactive and mostly clerical. The priority purchasing goal is to get products at a low cost when they are needed.

The importance of purchasing increases as value concerns become important. Price will still be important, but it will be evaluated along with other factors

Manager's Memo

This book has emphasized the importance of obtaining information from approved suppliers as purchase decisions are made and as product usage challenges arise.

There are several ways that vendors can help with the purchase evaluation process. Consider the example of cost per purchase unit. First, the vendor may have some knowledge about the expected market price for steaks during the period for which purchasing is being evaluated. Second, he or she may have information about purchase unit costs during the previous period that may help explain the reasons for higher-than-expected costs. Third, the vendor may be able to suggest ways to reduce product cost without sacrificing quality.

These examples show the types of information that vendors can supply if asked. This information should be of great value to managers and purchasers as they work to improve their purchasing activities.

including the number of specifications developed, the number of vendor problems, the number of make-or-buy analyses completed, and instances of vendor assistance.

When the function of purchasing is seen to include the relationship between the purchaser and vendor, other concerns may be evaluated. These include the methods by which vendors provide value, such as scheduled and unscheduled meetings and information shared about future market prices. Other examples include the quantity and types of assistance vendors provide to help purchasers with purchasing- and operation-related problems. Finally, the purchaser's role as a member of the top-level management team can be evaluated. For example, are projects completed on time and with high-quality responses? What types of contributions are purchasing asked to make in long-range planning strategies, and are the results as expected?

Purchasing evaluation factors can also consider operational concerns, financial issues, and other concerns.

OPERATIONAL CONCERNS AND EVALUATION

Basic operational concerns relate to identifying who will be responsible for purchasing. This topic was discussed earlier in the chapter when alternative ways to organize the purchasing tasks were discussed. Other operating concerns relate to product or service quality, quantity, timing, and price. In other words, they consider the evaluation of the orders placed to meet the ongoing product needs of the operation. Examples of how some of these factors can be measured are shown in *Exhibit 8.19*.

Exhibit 8.19

OPERATIONAL CONCERNS AND EVALUATION FACTORS

Operational Concern	Evaluation Factor
Quality	Percentage of shipment rejects Number of production problems related to product quality
Quantity	Number of stockouts Inventory turnover rates compared to goals Number of expedited orders
Timing	Vendors' delivery performance Time for requisition processing Time required for corrective action
Price	Prices paid against expected prices Prices paid for A items compared with market indexes Prices paid against budget

Note that some of the evaluation factors in *Exhibit 8.19* are relatively easy to measure because the information necessary is often collected and used for other purposes. For example, purchasers may record and monitor the number of reject shipments, a measure of quality, as part of vendor performance rating systems. Inventory turnover rates, a measure of quantity, may be assessed for accounting purposes. Timing factors are also important for vendor performance evaluations, and prices paid for products impact budgets developed by almost every operation.

Other evaluation factors may be more difficult to assess because information must be collected specifically for the evaluation process. Examples include the number of production problems related to product quality, the number of orders that must be expedited, the time vendors take to correct delivery problems, and the prices paid for A items compared with market indexes.

Managers and purchasers cannot resolve problems until they are aware of them. A purchasing evaluation process that focuses on goals and the extent to which they are attained can help identify problems, which can then be corrected. Any problems related to the factors in *Exhibit 8.19* can be of concern every time orders are placed. They also affect the day-to-day operation of the establishment. Therefore, these concerns should be of priority importance.

After ordering problems are identified and resolved, ongoing review is needed. For example, ordering sheets and lists of approved vendors can be analyzed to determine if any changes can be helpful. This will help ensure that problems are corrected, that no additional problems arise, and that the purchasing process is done as well as it can be.

OTHER EVALUATION CONCERNS

Purchasing activities can be evaluated relative to other concerns in addition to ordering procedures and results. These concerns apply to small-volume operations with purchasers who perform many other duties, to full-time purchasers in larger establishments, and to midsized operations using other purchasing procedures.

- **Relationships with other departments:** How many purchasing-related complaints were identified by staff in other departments? Are complaints made by purchasing staff regarding other department staff? How many purchase orders must be expedited?

- **Creative assistance:** Have purchasing staff discovered more than one useful vendor for difficult-to-locate products? Have purchasers helped resolve product-related problems?

- **Effective purchasing policies:** Purchasing staff can advise about policies for specification development, make-or-buy analysis, and single or multiple supply sources. What policies are needed? Are existing policies clearly stated? Are they understood and applied fairly?

• **Vendor performance:** Many challenges in the purchasing function concern the failure of vendors to meet expectations. Are expectations reasonable? Why do purchasers continue to interact with "problem" vendors?

Evaluation of purchasing activities should also address the employees with these responsibilities. Are they qualified and able to perform effectively in their positions? Do purchasing staff in large-volume operations participate in organizational activities?

Purchasing evaluation should be an ongoing process. It should not be undertaken only when there is a problem. Effective purchasers and managers know that the most successful establishments emphasize continuous improvement. This concern relates to all departments and functions, including purchasing.

SUMMARY

1. **Explain the basic procedures to monitor vendor compliance with quality standards at the time of receiving.**

   Receiving is a series of activities that ends with the transfer of product ownership from a vendor to an operation. Receiving is important because the delivery invoice will be the basis for the amount owed to the vendor. Incoming products should be checked against the purchase order and product specifications. The quality of incoming products must be verified, and the delivery invoice must be signed before products are moved to storage. A receiving report may be used to categorize invoice information.

2. **Summarize the basic requirements for effective product receiving.**

   Receiving staff must be identified and properly trained, especially so they can recognize proper quality. Receiving areas must be large enough to do receiving tasks, and basic tools and equipment will be required including scales and thermometers. Receiving data including vendor lists, product specifications, delivery times, and order lists should always be available. Deviations from receiving procedures must be noticed and corrected by managers.

   Receiving staff must guard against security problems. They must ensure that product weights are correct and that there are no missing items.

3. **Explain the necessary documentation and procedures that should be followed to pay vendors for product purchases.**

   Purchase requisitions can be used to alert purchasers that quantities of products are needed. This information can be included in an RFP to approved vendors. The selected vendor is issued a purchase order, and the items delivered are listed on a delivery invoice. Some establishments pay individual delivery invoices; others pay on the basis of statements that include products from several invoices.

Credit memos address product shortages and products that were not accepted. Staff must ensure that these amounts are subtracted from the payment. They must also check the extensions, or calculations, on the delivery invoice.

Petty cash funds can be used to make small cash purchases. Cash is removed from the fund as needed. The receipt and change are returned to the fund. The fund always retains its original balance in the form of cash plus paid receipts.

4. **Describe the importance of and basic methods that can be used to evaluate the purchasing process.**

   Purchasing should be evaluated to recognize its importance, to determine improvement benchmarks, to control costs, to measure and reward performance of purchasers, and to make improvements.

   The process of evaluation involves determining goals, measuring actual performance, and comparing goals and performance. Then any corrective actions can be taken and the results evaluated.

   Factors used to evaluate purchasing should relate to product quality and quantity, timing of deliveries, and prices paid. Other factors include relationships among departments, creative assistance by vendors, effectiveness of policies, and performance of vendors.

APPLICATION EXERCISE

At the end of the day, a manager noticed a credit memo on a clipboard hanging on the wall in the receiving area. It was for that day's meat delivery earlier and was for approximately $75. It was signed by someone from the vendor's company and by the operation's dish washer.

The next day the dish washer explained to the manager that he was the only one not busy when the delivery was made. The delivery person said that the credit memo was generated because several cartons of ground beef were not delivered.

The manager also spoke to the chef, who indicated that the delivery came during the lunch rush, and that he asked the dish washer to sign the invoice and put the products in the refrigerator.

The manager talked to the bookkeeper and learned that credit memos are rarely received. When they are, they are brought to the bookkeeper whenever time permits, often after the affected invoice has been paid. The bookkeeper says, "We've been dealing with the same vendors for years, and they always tell us about shortages. Then credits show up on the statements before we pay them."

What is the problem with managing credit memos at the establishment? Make a list of procedures for each function:

A. Product receiving

B. Managing credit memos

REVIEW YOUR LEARNING

Select the best answer for each question.

1. **When does transfer of product ownership from a vendor to an operation occur?**

   A. When a purchase order is issued

   B. When a check is written to the vendor

   C. When the delivery invoice is signed

   D. When products are placed in storage

2. **Which receiving task is not clerical or physical and thus requires extensive training and experience?**

   A. Signing the delivery invoice

   B. Recognizing product quality

   C. Counting product cases

   D. Moving products to storage

3. **How many types of scales are normally required in a receiving area?**

   A. 1

   B. 2

   C. 3

   D. 4

4. **When should a delivery invoice be signed?**

   A. Before opening any containers of product

   B. Before removing products from the delivery vehicle

   C. After verifying information against the purchase order

   D. After placing products in the proper storage areas

5. **What is the purpose of a credit memo?**

   A. To correct information on delivery invoices

   B. To indicate a price reduction for timely payment

   C. To verify the operation's ability to pay for products

   D. To balance the amount of money added to petty cash

6. **What is a vendor statement?**

   A. A contract including payment terms

   B. A document that replaces credit memos

   C. A summary of delivery invoice charges

   D. An agreement regarding receiving procedures

7. **What is a backorder?**

   A. A product that has been substituted for another product

   B. An unavailable product on a vendor's delivery invoice

   C. An item not meeting product specification requirements

   D. The dollar value of purchases that have not been paid for

8. **What is the purpose of a petty cash fund?**

   A. To make relatively low-cost purchases

   B. To buy products when bank balances are low

   C. To use for approved employee cash advances

   D. To pay for backorder items delivered separately

9. **What is the first step in the process of purchasing evaluation and improvement?**

   A. Measure actual performance.

   B. Take necessary corrective action.

   C. Develop a mission statement.

   D. Develop purchasing goals.

10. **Which is most likely to be an important evaluation factor for price-conscious purchasers?**

    A. Number of product specifications developed

    B. Number of make-or-buy analyses performed

    C. Methods by which vendors provide value

    D. Cost of products per purchase unit

FIELD PROJECT

Wise managers know that their ability to pay delivery invoices or statements on a timely basis will affect the prices that vendors will charge them for the products that are ordered. They are also aware that effective purchasing follow-up procedures must be in place to ensure that payments are made in the correct amounts for only those products that are received.

Summarize the information you learned from the restaurant or foodservice operation questionnaire and the vendor questionnaire from chapter 1.

Part A: Basic Receiving Procedures for Food and Beverage Products Use the information for product receiving that you learned from the questionnaire responses for question 8 from the restaurant or foodservice operation, and from chapter 8 in the text, to develop a list of basic receiving procedures.	
Part B: Responses from restaurant or foodservice operation questionnaire for invoice/statement processing procedures (questions 11 and 12)	Summary of Responses
Part C: Responses from vendor questionnaire for invoice/statement processing procedures (question 7)	Summary of Responses
Part D: Additional invoice/statement processing recommendations from the text (chapter 8)	

FIELD PROJECT

PRINCIPLES OF PURCHASING MANAGEMENT

The Pineville Steakhouse is an independently owned establishment in the suburbs of a large city. The owner is a son of the operation's founder, and he has been active in the business for more than 60 years! This long track record began when the owner was 10 years old, when he began doing odd jobs at the establishment. It has continued ever since with time away just for college. The owner has been managing the operation for the past 30 years since his father retired. A new general manager was recently hired, and she has been on the job for about two months.

The Pineville Steakhouse is an institution in the community. Its menu has changed very little over the years. The same can be said of many of the operating procedures, including those for the purchase of food and beverage products.

The operation generates about $1,200,000 during the year, or $100,000 per month. There is little seasonal business fluctuation. The establishment seats about 100 persons, and there is a bar or lounge area that seats an additional 30 to 40 persons.

The present owner knows that changes could be made to reduce costs. However, he has indicated numerous times that cost-cutting could not come at the sake of quality because the reputation of his family is tied to the property. The owner wants to generate profits at a pace that, combined with his savings, will be sufficient to enable his family and him to live comfortably.

The new manager has been cautious about making too many changes too quickly. First, she wanted to know how things were currently done and why they are done that way. Second, she was concerned that long-time employees would become upset if too many changes were made too quickly.

Her analysis to this point indicates that numerous changes in purchasing procedures could yield cost savings without sacrificing quality. As evidence, the food cost is currently about 43 percent. This figure is high compared to a food cost of about 37 percent in a similar operation that she managed in a nearby community. A quick calculation shows that the operation could save more than $70,000 if the food cost could be reduced to approximately that percentage rate:

$$\underset{\text{Revenue}}{\$1,200,000} \quad \times \quad [\underset{\substack{\text{Current food} \\ \text{cost percentage}}}{43} \quad - \quad \underset{\substack{\text{Target food} \\ \text{cost percentage}}}{37\%}] \quad = \quad \underset{\substack{\text{Variance in} \\ \text{revenue}}}{\$72,000}$$

PART I: Quality Requirements

In chapter 2 you completed a make-or-buy field project exercise to learn how to evaluate the quality of two different salad dressings. You may wish to review that exercise.

When buyers conduct a make-or-buy analysis, they first confirm that the quality of each alternative is acceptable. Then they must determine the cost of each alternative.

For this activity, assume your evaluation of the two dressings in the field project exercise for chapter 2 indicated that both dressings were of acceptable quality, and could be used at the Pineville Steakhouse. Assume also that one of the salad dressings is currently made by the operation staff and that the other is available from the vendor that you interviewed for the chapter 1 field project.

The purpose of this activity is to analyze the cost of each dressing. This is important because, since the quality of both dressings is acceptable, the dressing that is the least expensive can be served to the customers.

1. What is the food cost per quart for the dressing currently made by the Pineville Steakhouse cooks?
   Here is the recipe:

Recipe Ingredients	Quantity	Purchase Unit	Cost per Purchase Unit*	Ingredient Cost
Blue cheese crumbled	4 oz	Pound		
Mayonnaise	1 pt	Quart		
Sour cream	8 fl oz	Pint		
Buttermilk	4 fl oz	Quart		
Milk	2 fl oz	Quart		

Note: *Minimal amounts of Worcestershire sauce, garlic paste, pureed onions, lemon juice, and ground black pepper are also used in the recipe on an as-needed basis, and their costs will not be considered in this exercise.*

*Obtain the cost per purchase unit for the ingredients from a local grocery store or ask the manager or chef at your school's foodservice operation for the current costs.

2. What is the labor cost to prepare the salad dressing on-site?

   Assume:

   - One-half hour of labor is needed
   - The cook is paid $14.50 per hour
   - The cook's rate of fringe benefits is 28.5 percent
   - One gallon of dressing is prepared at the same time

   Labor cost per quart: _____

3. What is the total cost to prepare one quart of the salad dressing at the Pineville Steakhouse?

   Food cost: _____

   Labor cost: _____

   Total cost: _____

4. What is the cost per quart based on the response to question 3 on the vendor questionnaire you used in chapter 1?

   Cost per quart: _____

5. Should the manager of the Pineville Steakhouse continue to make blue cheese salad dressing, or should she purchase pre-made dressing? When developing your response address quality, cost, and the feedback about the make-or-buy analysis. Include also the results from your interviews with the restaurant or foodservice operation and the vendor in the chapter 1 questionnaires.

PART II: Vendor Selection

In chapter 4 you completed a field project to develop a list of factors used to determine the approved vendors for a restaurant or foodservice operation. In this exercise, you will use that information to help develop vendor approval recommendations for the new manager of the Pineville Steakhouse.

A. List the vendor approval factors from the restaurant or foodservice operation, the vendor, and Exhibit 4.3 that you developed in chapter 4.

_____

_____

_____

_____

_____

_____

B. Make recommendations to the Pineville Steakhouse manager about how the vendor approval process should be implemented:

- How should information about the factors in part A be obtained?

- Who should obtain the information?

- Who should be involved in evaluating each of the factors for each supplier to make supplier approval decisions?

- How long should vendors be approved before the approval process should be repeated?

- What should the Pineville Steakhouse manager say or do if she is approached by a new vendor that desires to do business with the establishment?

PART III: Product Ordering Procedures

The product ordering system currently in use at the Pineville Steakhouse allows each department head (chef, dining-room manager, and bar manager) to order the products they need, in any quantity up to a specified dollar limit. When the limit is reached, prior approval by the owner or manager is required.

The new manager does not like this system for several reasons:

- It increases the opportunity for improper relationships between the departmental buyers and the vendors.

- It does not encourage effective pricing because, for example, some of the same products might be ordered by more than one buyer.

- There are few existing procedures and, in effect, each departmental buyer can do it the way he or she desires.

- Incoming products are received, and the delivery invoice is signed, by whomever is available to do so when the delivery is made.

The purpose of this activity is for you to develop a list of standard operating procedures for how the product ordering process should be done at the Pineville Steakhouse. As sources for your recommendations, use the input from the restaurant and foodservice operation questionnaire (questions 5 to 7). Also, review the basic steps in the ordering process for small-volume operations discussed in chapter 6. You may decide that a centralized purchasing system should be used. If so, support this recommendation.

When developing your recommendations, be sure to address each of the concerns identified in the questionnaire for the operation:

A. Who (what position) should order food products?

B. Who (what position) should order beverage products?

C. Who (what position) should order dining-room and other items?

D. Should there be a dollar limit above which the manager's approval is needed?

E. How should price quotations be obtained?

F. How should purchase orders be awarded?

PART IV: Purchasing Ethics and Vendor Relations

The new manager of the Pineville Steakhouse recognizes the need for an ongoing professional relationship between the establishment's management team and the approved vendors. In addition to developing procedures for purchasing (see the field project for chapter 6), the manager also wants to ensure that the best procedures for interacting with vendors are used.

A. Review and document here the list of recommendations to maintain an ongoing relationship between the restaurant or foodservice manager and its vendors that you developed in the chapter 7 field project.

_____

_____

_____

_____

_____

B. Add additional suggestions from the text (chapter 7).

_____

_____

_____

_____

_____

C. Assume that the manager of the Pineville Steakhouse will present the list of procedures identified previously during a department head meeting. Indicate concepts that she should use:

• Explain why the list of operating procedures is needed (how it will be helpful).

• Tell how the procedures will drive the purchasing decisions made at the Pineville Steakhouse.

PART V: Purchasing Follow-Up

The manager of the Pineville Steakhouse must ensure that procedures are in place to effectively process delivery invoices or statements of accounts from vendors. Use the recommendations from the restaurant or foodservice manager, the vendor, and the text that you developed in the field project for chapter 8 to complete the following:

A.   Document the recommendations for standard operating procedures for processing delivery invoices and vendors' statements of account for payment.

_____

_____

_____

_____

_____

B.   Assume that the owner (the past manager of the Pineville Steakhouse) wants to be involved in the bill payment process of the establishment. What are your suggestions to the owner and the manager about the best ways to do this?

_____

_____

_____

_____

_____

C.   What are some suggestions to the establishment manager about how to evaluate the effectiveness of the purchasing function?

_____

_____

_____

_____

_____

GLOSSARY

Acceptance (contract) An agreement to the exact details of an offer.

Account An organization to which a vendor sells products.

A item The more expensive items that an establishment purchases.

As purchased (AP) The weight of a product before it is processed, prepared, or cooked.

Audit trail A step-by-step record that traces financial data to their source.

Backorder A situation that occurs when a vendor does not have the products required to fill a purchaser's order.

Bar code A label that has numerous machine-readable rectangular bars and spaces arranged in a specific way to identify a product.

Benchmarking The search for best practices and an understanding of how they are achieved, used to determine how well an organization is doing and how it can improve.

Bid A price quotation from a vendor.

Boilerplate (contract language) Contract clauses that do not change even though the contracts are developed for use with different vendors selling different products.

Bona fide occupational qualification (BFOQ) A job qualification legally judged reasonably necessary to safely or adequately perform a job.

Broad-line vendor A vendor that offers a wide variety of products.

Buyer's club A retail organization in which, after payment of a member fee, persons can purchase food and other products in large-volume package sizes.

Cash on delivery (COD) A requirement that a buyer pay the full amount owed in cash or other acceptable payment form at the time products are delivered.

Centralized purchasing system A system in which most or all purchases are made by a purchasing director for the entire organization.

Cherry picker A buyer who requests bids from several vendors and then buys only those items each vendor has on sale or for the lowest price.

Close-out A strategy used by vendors or manufacturers to quickly sell unwanted inventory by reducing prices.

Code of purchasing ethics Guidelines that should be followed as purchasers implement purchasing procedures and make purchasing decisions.

Competitive advantage A benefit an operation has that allows it to generate greater revenues or retain more customers than its competition.

Competitive bidding A strategy for comparing vendors' prices for products of acceptable quality to determine the lowest price.

Consideration (contract) The payment to be made in exchange for the promise(s) contained in the contract.

Contract A legally enforceable agreement or promise.

Convenience food A food item in which some or all of the labor required to prepare the item is "built in."

Cost per servable pound The cost of one pound of product that can be served to customers.

Counteroffer An offer made in response to another offer that was not acceptable.

Credit memo A document used to adjust information about product quantities or costs recorded on a delivery invoice.

Decentralized purchasing system A system in which all or most purchases are made by department heads or a designated employee in the department.

Delivery invoice A document signed by a representative of the operation to transfer product ownership to the property.

Demand The total amount of a product or service that buyers want to purchase at a specific price.

Differential pricing Charging different customers different prices for the same product such as, for example, giving a discount for purchasing larger quantities.

Discount A deduction from the normal price that is paid for something.

Distribution channel An organization or individual involved in the process of making a product or service available to an organization.

Distributor sales representative (DSR) The purchaser's most immediate contact with the vendor, also referred to as a *salesperson* or *account executive*.

E-commerce Activities related to buying and selling products and services through online sources.

Edible portion (EP) The weight of a product after it is processed, prepared, and cooked.

Edible yield The amount of a product that can be consumed.

Enforceable (contract) A contract that is recognized as valid by the courts and is, therefore, subject to the court's ability to require compliance with its terms.

Ethical Behavior that society in general or the culture of the establishment or the industry considers "the right thing to do."

Expedite To perform activities that hasten the delivery of products that have been ordered but not yet received.

Express contract A contract in which the components of the agreement are clearly understood and are stated orally or in writing.

Extension (calculations) An arithmetic calculation made on a delivery invoice; for example, the item quantity and the unit price are multiplied to determine the total cost for each product.

Fall-back position (negotiation) An alternative position that is not the buyer's first choice in negotiations, but one that is acceptable.

Family-service (establishment) An establishment that features a wide variety of lower-priced meals where convenience food products are frequently used.

Franchisee A party in a franchising agreement that uses the logo, name, systems, and resources of a business for a fee.

Franchisor A company that owns and manages a brand and sells the rights to use its name, trademarks, and operating systems.

Free market A situation in which the prices paid for products and services are determined by the vendor and the buyer who voluntarily enter into a contract.

Going-in position (negotiation) A position that prioritizes the desired outcomes from a negotiation session.

Grading (quality) A voluntary assessment of food items against predetermined quality standards.

Green purchasing Purchasing procedures that place a priority on a product's environmental impact.

Hazard Analysis Critical Control Point (HACCP) A system used to control risks and hazards throughout the food supply process.

High check average (establishment) An establishment that offers higher-priced meals because of the higher costs of products, service, and other features of the dining experience.

Individually quick frozen (IQF) A process that involves blast-freezing food in individual pieces before packaging; mostly used with fish or fruit.

Inspection A process that ensures that meat and poultry products are fit for human consumption.

Issuing Transferring products from storage areas to user departments so user staff can meet production needs.

Job description A description of the tasks that a person working in a specific position must perform.

Job specification A document that lists specific knowledge and skills required to perform a job.

Just-in-time (JIT) purchasing A system in which a purchaser has a long-term commitment with a vendor to make frequent product deliveries.

Kickback Money or other gifts that are received by an employee in return for purchasing from a specific vendor.

Legal Permitted by law.

Make-or-buy analysis A study that suggests whether a product should be prepared "from scratch" on-site, or purchased as a partially or fully processed item.

Market form Alternative ways that food products can be purchased.

Menu item popularity index The percentage of customers likely to order specific menu items.

Minimum–maximum inventory An inventory system that requires the buyer to determine the minimum and maximum quantity that inventory levels must fall between.

Moral A standard that is based on principles about what is right and wrong.

National account An organization with very large-volume purchase requirements that are spread across the manufacturer's sales regions.

Negotiation A process by which parties with mutual interests try to reach an agreement about something.

Net price The total or per-unit amount paid for something after all discounts have been applied to the original purchase price.

Offer (contract) A proposal to perform an act or to pay an amount that, if accepted, becomes a legally valid contract.

Ordering A process that occurs when a purchaser makes a commitment to a vendor relating to a specific purchase.

Order point The number of purchase units that should be available in inventory when an order is placed.

Pallet A portable platform, or rack, typically made of wooden slats, used to store and move cases of products stacked on it.

Par level inventory A system in which a specified quantity of products should always be in inventory.

Payment card discount A reduction in processing fees that credit and debit card issuers charge to those accepting payment cards.

Petty cash fund A small amount of cash on hand that is used to make relatively low-cost purchases.

Petty cash system A cash fund used to make infrequent and low-cost product purchases.

Point-of-sale (POS) system An electronic system that collects information about revenue, customer counts, item sales, and other operating data.

Portion-control (packets) Individual servings of an item.

Production loss The amount by weight or percentage of a product's AP weight that is not servable.

Purchase order (PO) A document used to inform vendors that their prices for products of the specified quality and quantity in the RFP have been accepted and that the shipment should be delivered.

Purchase requisition A document used to inform the purchasing staff that more products need to be ordered.

Purchase unit (PU) The weight, volume, or container size in which a food product is normally purchased.

Purchasing The entire process of selecting, buying, and evaluating the products and services needed by the restaurant or foodservice operation.

Qualified buyer A person with the authority to make purchase decisions for his or her organization.

Quality Suitability for intended use.

Quality assurance All activities that an organization uses to attain quality.

Quality standards The factors that are used to compare an actual product or service with the desired product or service.

Rebate A deduction offered *after* a purchase has been made at the normal selling price; also referred to as a "cash back" offer.

Receiving A series of activities that ends with the transfer of product ownership from a vendor to a restaurant or foodservice operation.

Reciprocity A situation that occurs when a purchaser agrees to buy something from a vendor in return for some kind of business from the vendor.

Request for proposal (RFP) A document used to request prices from approved vendors for products of a specified quality and in a specified quantity.

Revenue The amount of money received from the sale of food and beverage products.

Sales history The number of each specific menu item that is sold.

Shelf life The amount of time a product remains suitable for use.

Signature dish A menu item that customers associate with a specific operation.

Specialty-line vendor A vendor that offers a deep selection of relatively few products.

Split case A case of less-than-full purchase unit size sold by a vendor, also called a *broken case*.

Standardized recipe A recipe that provides detailed instructions, including the amount of every ingredient, to produce a food or beverage item.

Statement of business conduct A broad code of behavior that addresses many aspects of the business and its employees who have a wide variety of functional responsibilities within it.

Steward sales A situation that occurs when some companies allow their employees to buy products purchased by the establishment for their personal use.

Stockout A situation that occurs when an item is no longer available in inventory.

Supply chain A coordinated system of businesses, people, activities, information, and resources that move products from the manufacturer, processor, or grower to an operation.

Terms and conditions (contract) General provisions that apply to a vendor's responses to RFPs and a purchaser's purchase orders regardless of the specific products being sold or purchased.

Total quality management The pursuit of organization-wide quality, with emphasis placed on improving processes and procedures rather than identifying defects.

Trade-out An agreement between two businesses in which the contract's consideration is not in the form of money.

Trade show An industry-specific event that allows vendors to interact with, educate, and sell to individuals and businesses in the industry.

Value The relationship between the price paid and the quality of the products, services, and information received.

Value perception The customer's opinion of a product's value to him or her.

Vendor-managed inventory A system in which the vendor determines the quantities needed for purchase and retains ownership of products until they are issued to production.

Vendor relations The ways in which purchasers interact with their vendors.

Vendor's handbook A handbook developed by an establishment to inform vendors about the organization's purchasing policies and procedures.

Vendor sourcing Decisions that determine which vendors will be asked to quote prices for needed products.

Yield test A carefully controlled process for determining the amount (weight or percentage) of the AP (as purchased) quantity of a product remaining after production.

INDEX

NOTES

NOTES

NOTES

NOTES

NOTES